The Cobbler's Mo

A Tale of Gepetto's Frankenstein

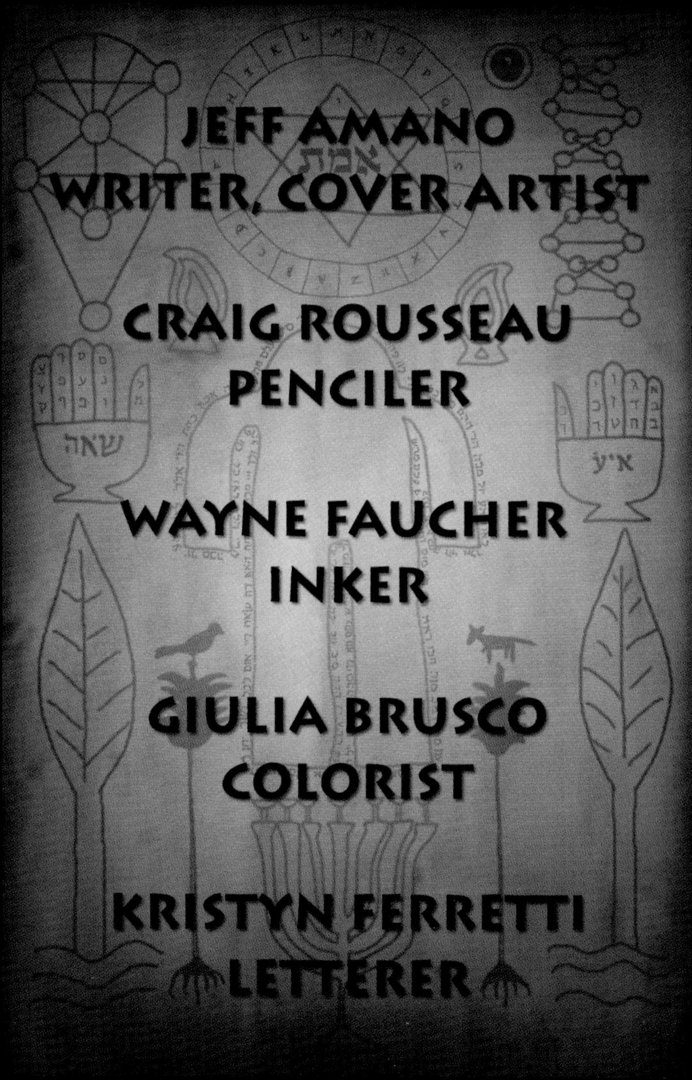

JEFF AMANO
WRITER, COVER ARTIST

CRAIG ROUSSEAU
PENCILER

WAYNE FAUCHER
INKER

GIULIA BRUSCO
COLORIST

KRISTYN FERRETTI
LETTERER

Foreword

What you have in your hands is a horror story.

But to be honest, the horror might not come from where you expect.

Don't get me wrong. There is plenty of pure terror and dread packed into the next hundred-plus pages. Included is an enraged monster, plenty of broken and flying pieces of anatomy, plenty of spilled blood, explosions, an avalanche, a battle on a sinking boat, and a very healthy body count.

But the real horror inside isn't in the violence; it's in a relationship between a father and son that goes terribly wrong. Gepetto, like all fathers, dedicates his life to making sure that his son has the best life possible.

But what do you do as a father when despite everything your own son turns against you? How do you react when your son is responsible for doing horrific and monstrous things?

Is it even possible for a father and son to come together in spite of all the pain, rage, guilt and horror?

The answer to that question is the true terror in this story.

Gabriel Benson
Writer (*The Ballad of Sleeping Beauty, Fade From Grace*)

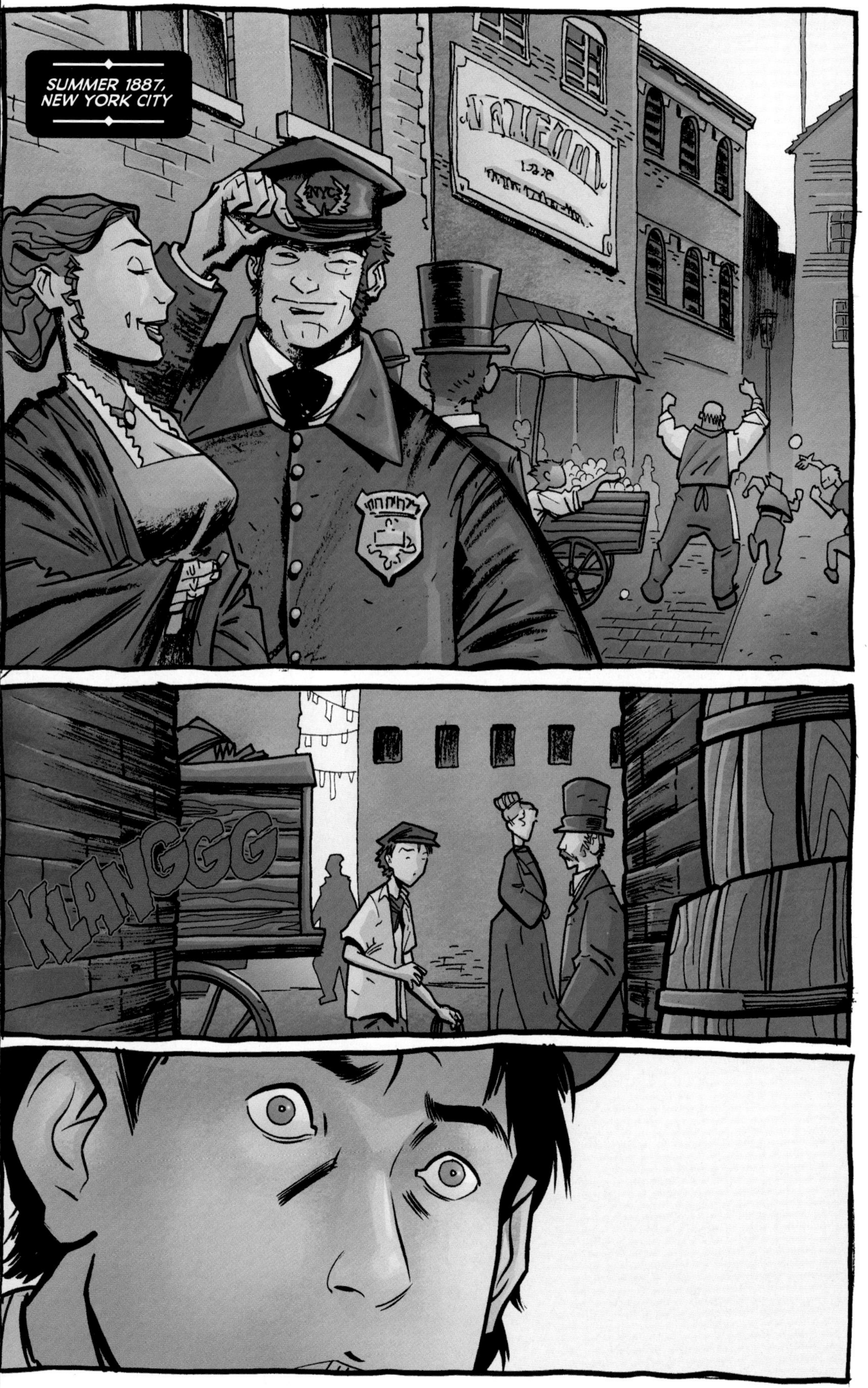
SUMMER 1887,
NEW YORK CITY
KLANGGG

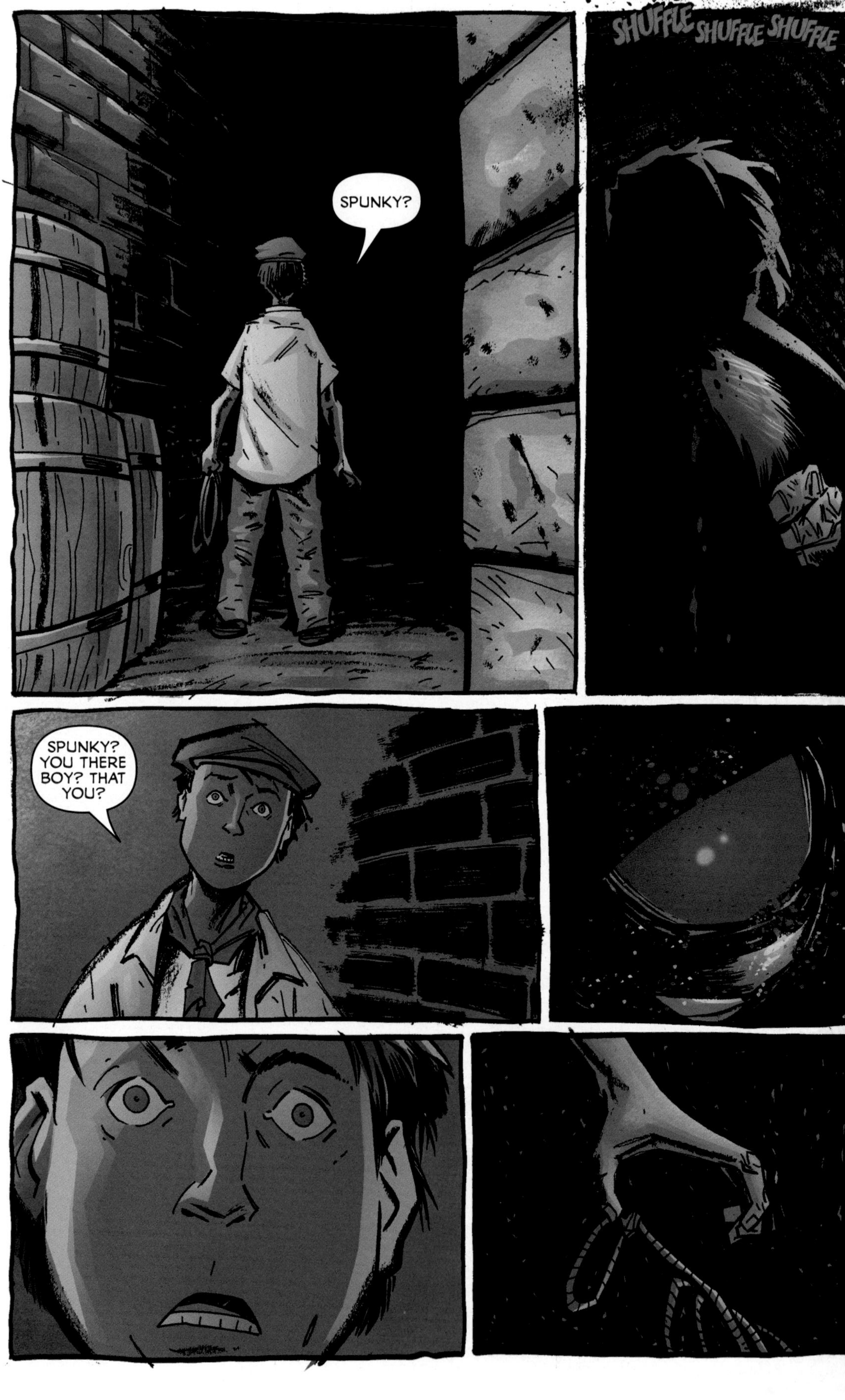
SPUNKY?
SHUFFLE SHUFFLE SHUFFLE
SPUNKY? YOU THERE BOY? THAT YOU?

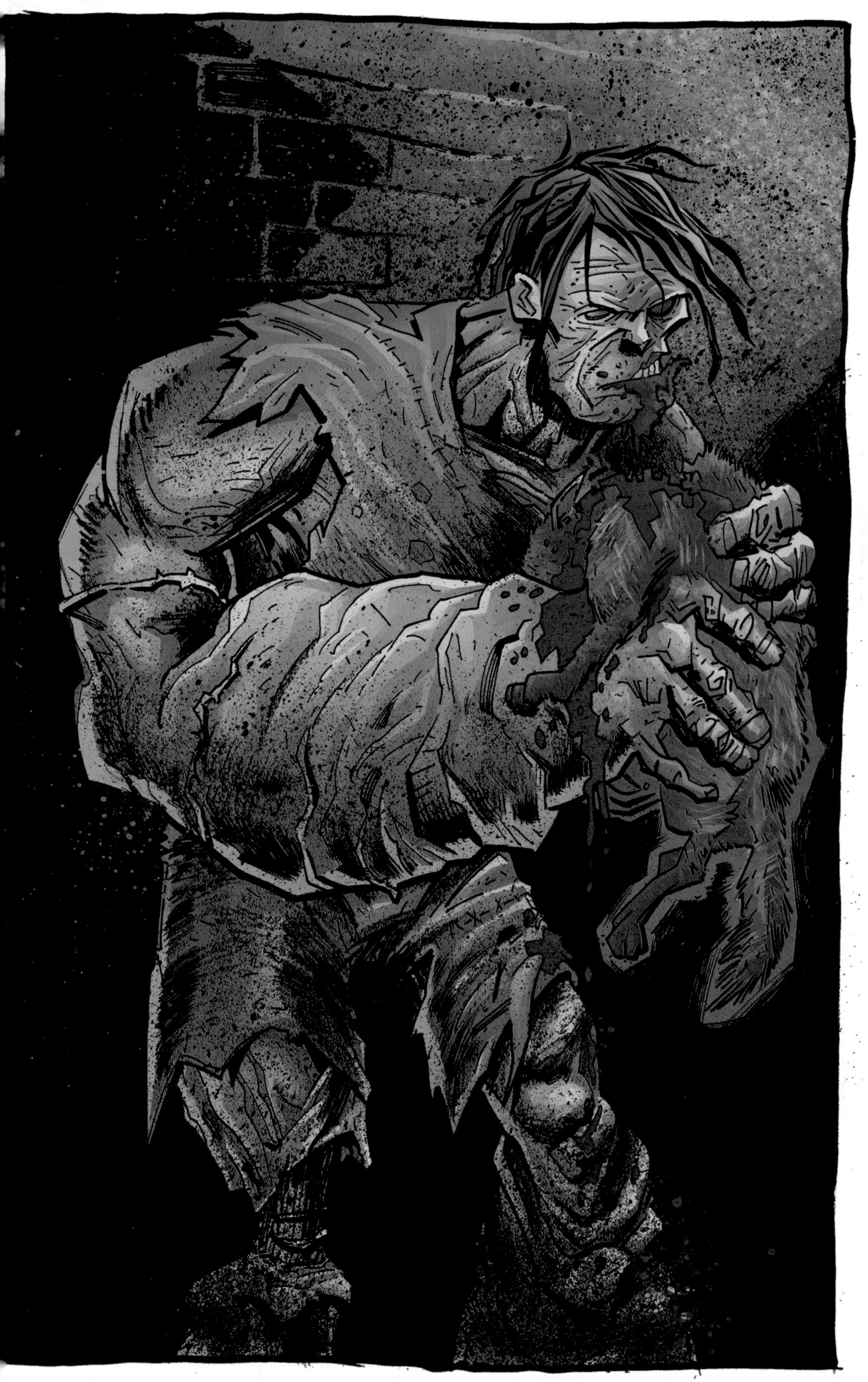

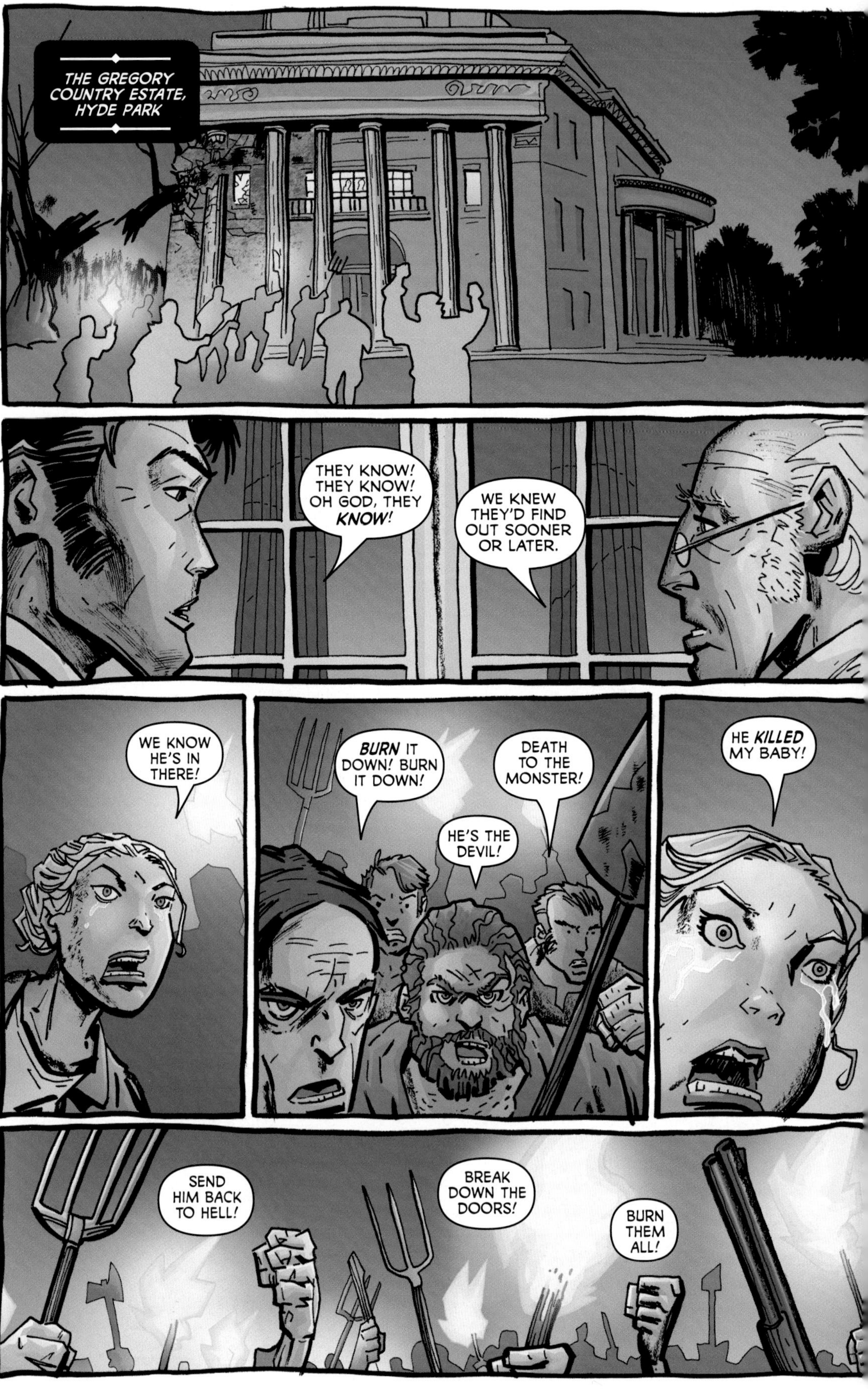
THE GREGORY COUNTRY ESTATE, HYDE PARK
THEY KNOW! THEY KNOW! OH GOD, THEY KNOW!
WE KNEW THEY'D FIND OUT SOONER OR LATER.
WE KNOW HE'S IN THERE!
BURN IT DOWN! BURN IT DOWN!
DEATH TO THE MONSTER!
HE'S THE DEVIL!
HE KILLED MY BABY!
SEND HIM BACK TO HELL!
BREAK DOWN THE DOORS!
BURN THEM ALL!

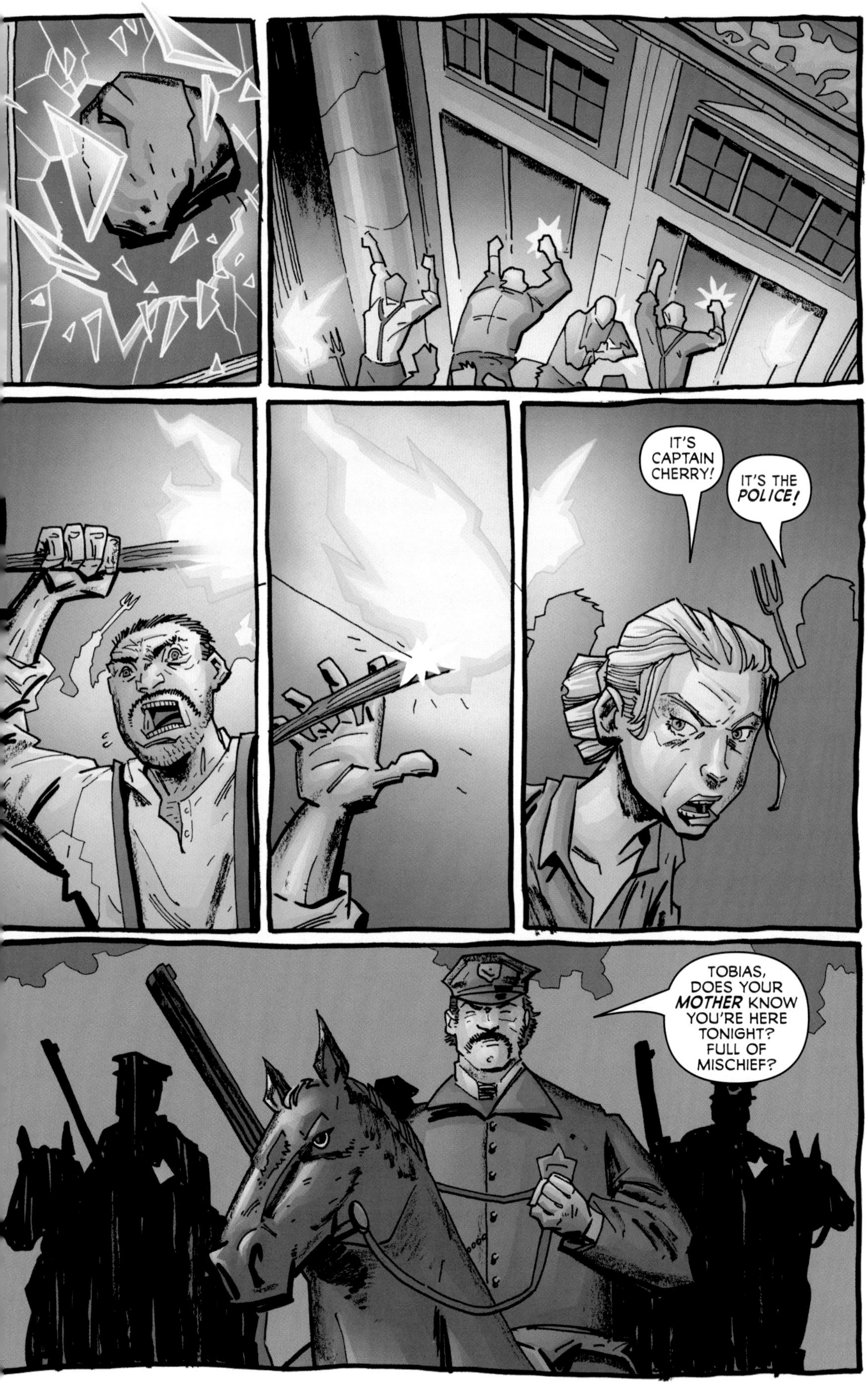
IT'S CAPTAIN CHERRY!
IT'S THE *POLICE!*
TOBIAS, DOES YOUR *MOTHER* KNOW YOU'RE HERE TONIGHT? FULL OF MISCHIEF?

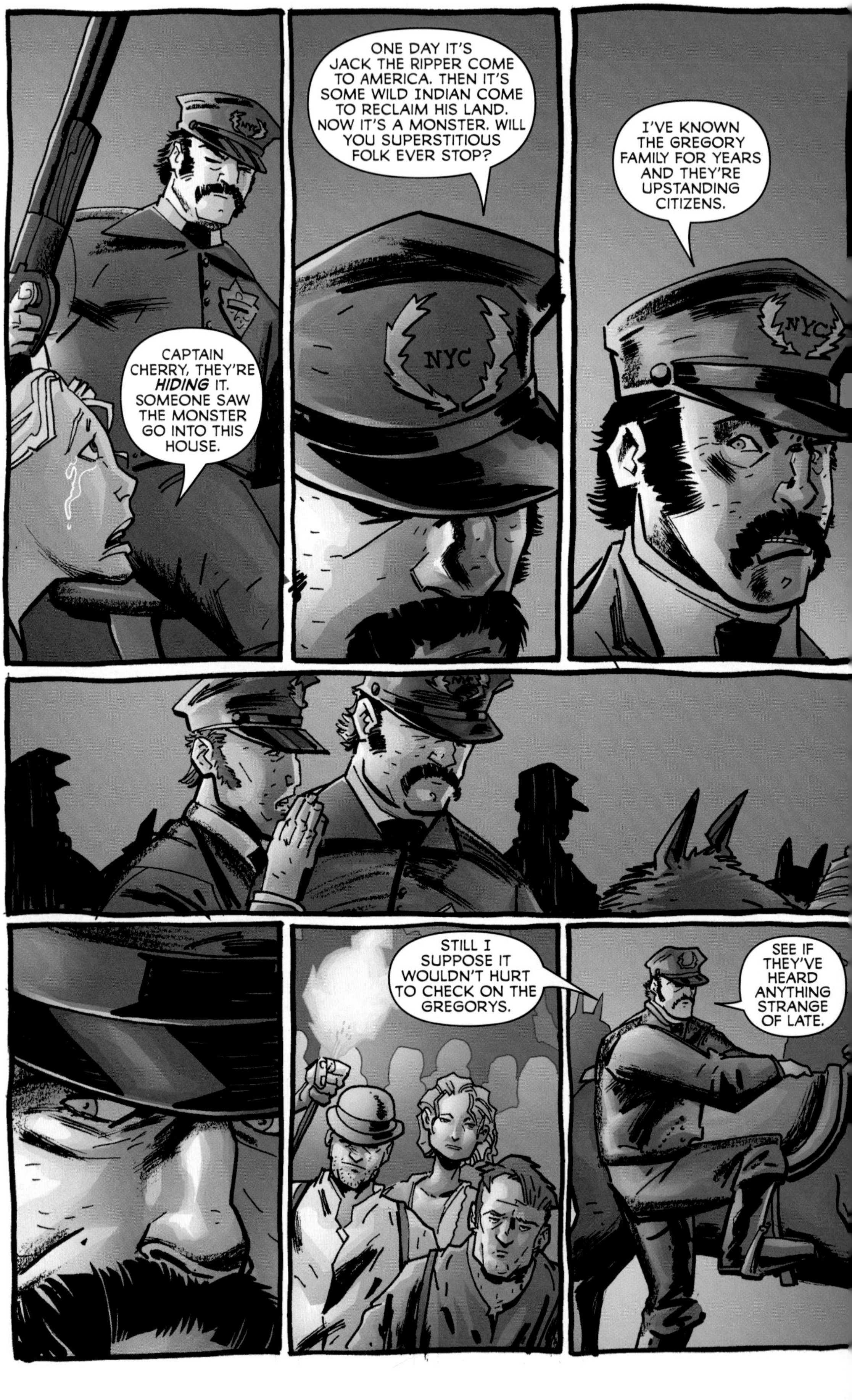
CAPTAIN CHERRY, THEY'RE *HIDING* IT. SOMEONE SAW THE MONSTER GO INTO THIS HOUSE.
ONE DAY IT'S JACK THE RIPPER COME TO AMERICA. THEN IT'S SOME WILD INDIAN COME TO RECLAIM HIS LAND. NOW IT'S A MONSTER. WILL YOU SUPERSTITIOUS FOLK EVER STOP?
I'VE KNOWN THE GREGORY FAMILY FOR YEARS AND THEY'RE UPSTANDING CITIZENS.
STILL I SUPPOSE IT WOULDN'T HURT TO CHECK ON THE GREGORYS.
SEE IF THEY'VE HEARD ANYTHING STRANGE OF LATE.

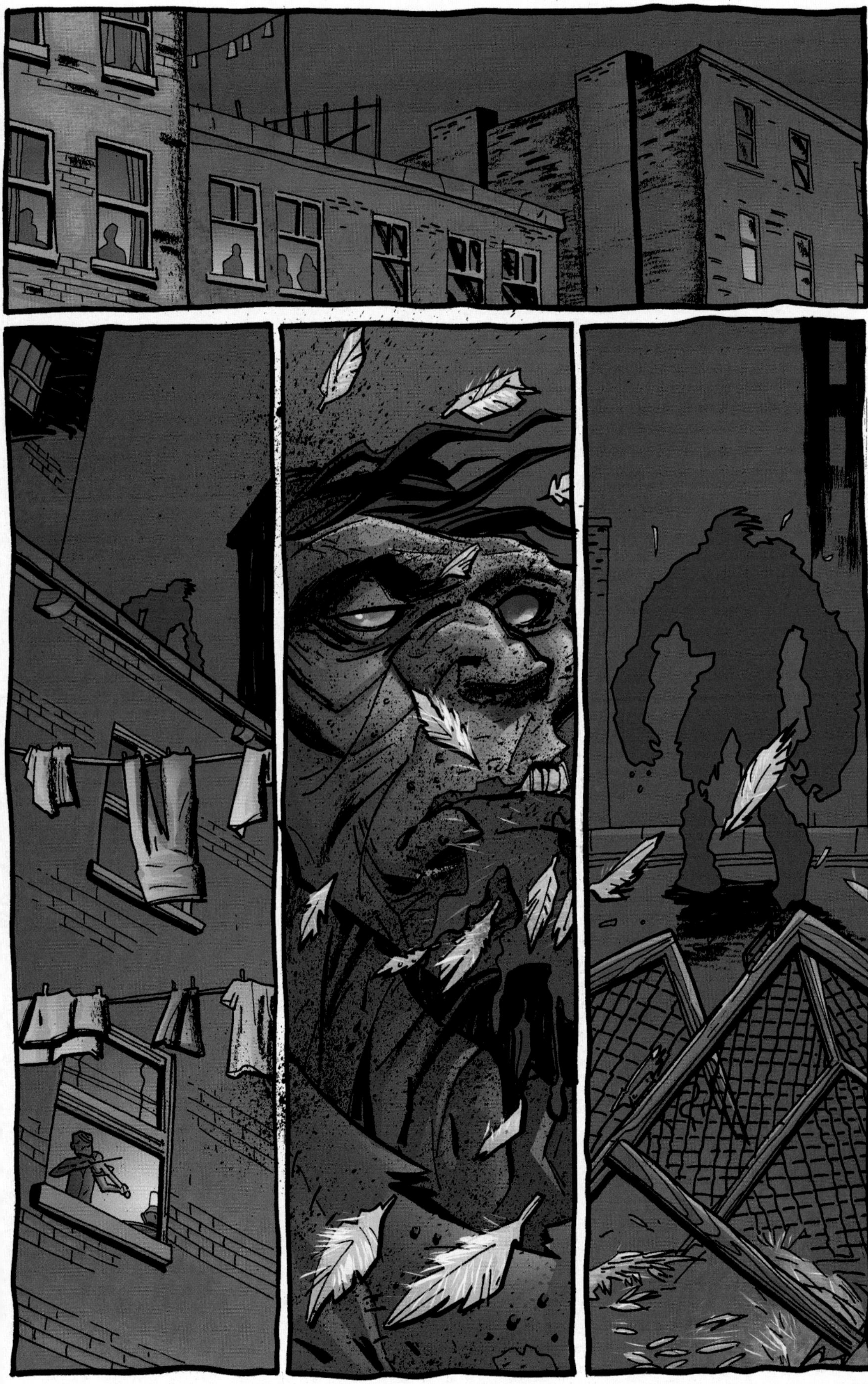

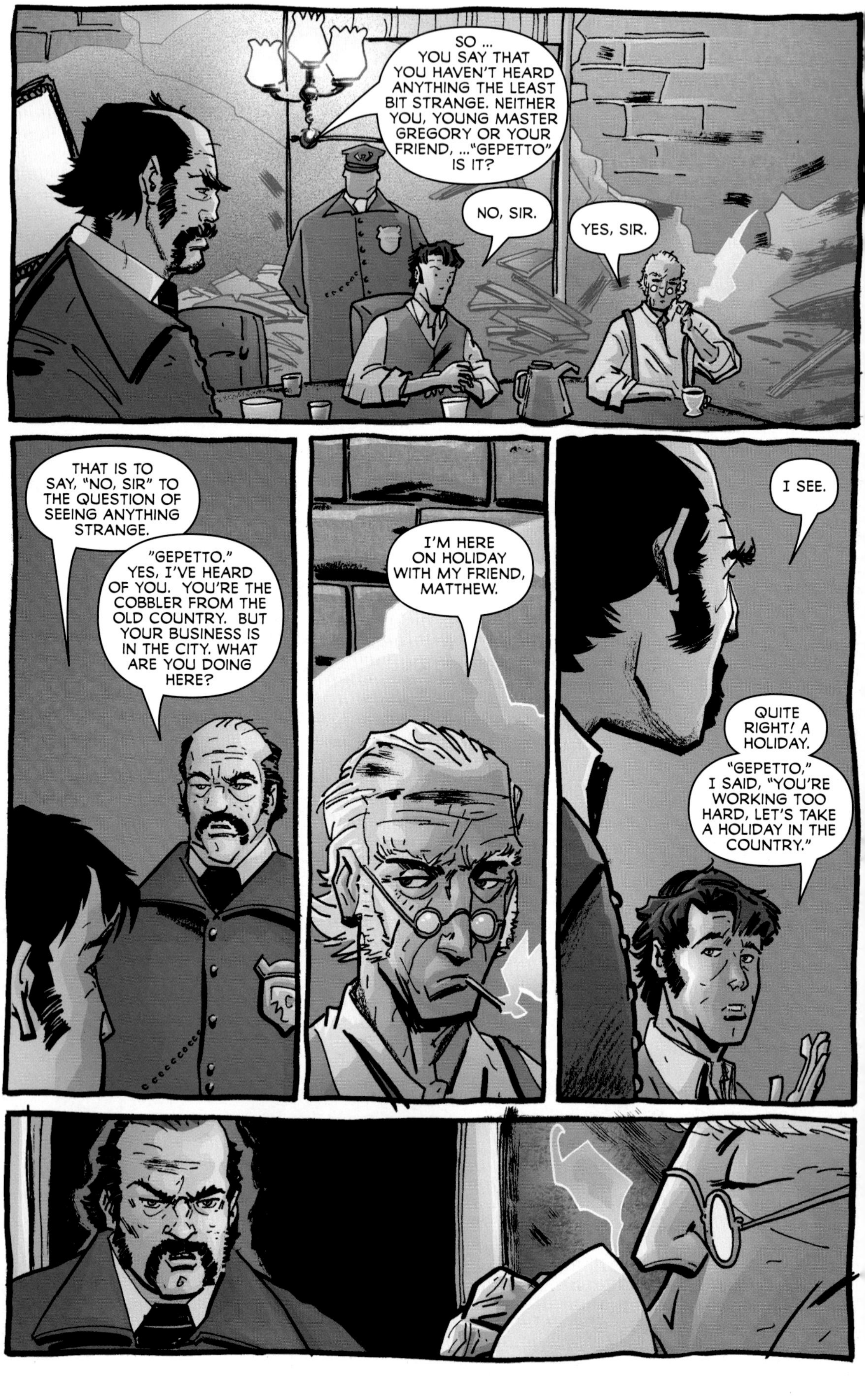
SO ...
YOU SAY THAT YOU HAVEN'T HEARD ANYTHING THE LEAST BIT STRANGE. NEITHER YOU, YOUNG MASTER GREGORY OR YOUR FRIEND, ..."GEPETTO" IS IT?
NO, SIR.
YES, SIR.
THAT IS TO SAY, "NO, SIR" TO THE QUESTION OF SEEING ANYTHING STRANGE.
"GEPETTO." YES, I'VE HEARD OF YOU. YOU'RE THE COBBLER FROM THE OLD COUNTRY. BUT YOUR BUSINESS IS IN THE CITY. WHAT ARE YOU DOING HERE?
I'M HERE ON HOLIDAY WITH MY FRIEND, MATTHEW.
I SEE.
QUITE RIGHT! A HOLIDAY.
"GEPETTO," I SAID, "YOU'RE WORKING TOO HARD, LET'S TAKE A HOLIDAY IN THE COUNTRY."

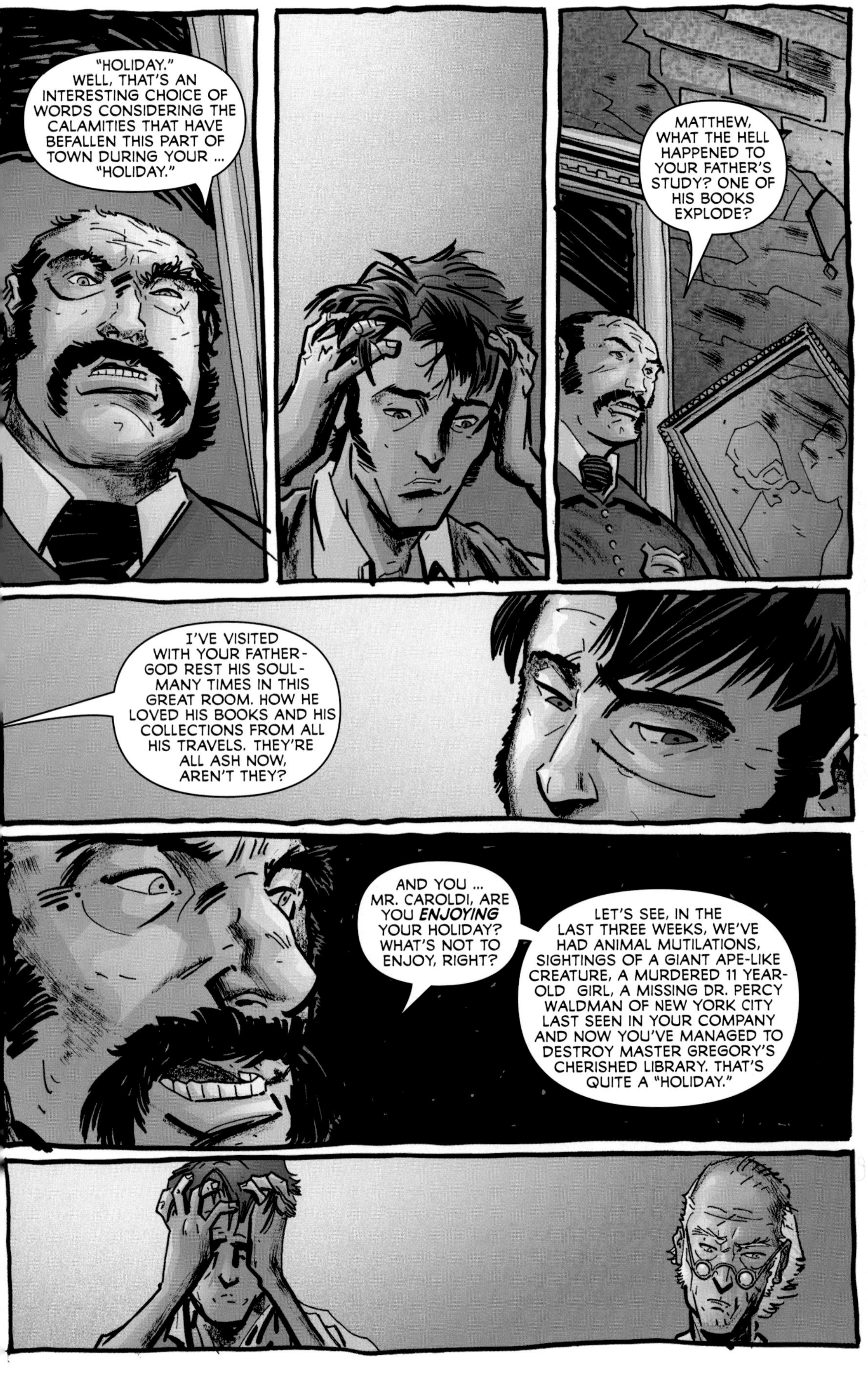
"HOLIDAY." WELL, THAT'S AN INTERESTING CHOICE OF WORDS CONSIDERING THE CALAMITIES THAT HAVE BEFALLEN THIS PART OF TOWN DURING YOUR ... "HOLIDAY."
MATTHEW, WHAT THE HELL HAPPENED TO YOUR FATHER'S STUDY? ONE OF HIS BOOKS EXPLODE?
I'VE VISITED WITH YOUR FATHER- GOD REST HIS SOUL- MANY TIMES IN THIS GREAT ROOM. HOW HE LOVED HIS BOOKS AND HIS COLLECTIONS FROM ALL HIS TRAVELS. THEY'RE ALL ASH NOW, AREN'T THEY?
AND YOU ... MR. CAROLDI, ARE YOU *ENJOYING* YOUR HOLIDAY? WHAT'S NOT TO ENJOY, RIGHT?
LET'S SEE, IN THE LAST THREE WEEKS, WE'VE HAD ANIMAL MUTILATIONS, SIGHTINGS OF A GIANT APE-LIKE CREATURE, A MURDERED 11 YEAR-OLD GIRL, A MISSING DR. PERCY WALDMAN OF NEW YORK CITY LAST SEEN IN YOUR COMPANY AND NOW YOU'VE MANAGED TO DESTROY MASTER GREGORY'S CHERISHED LIBRARY. THAT'S QUITE A "HOLIDAY."

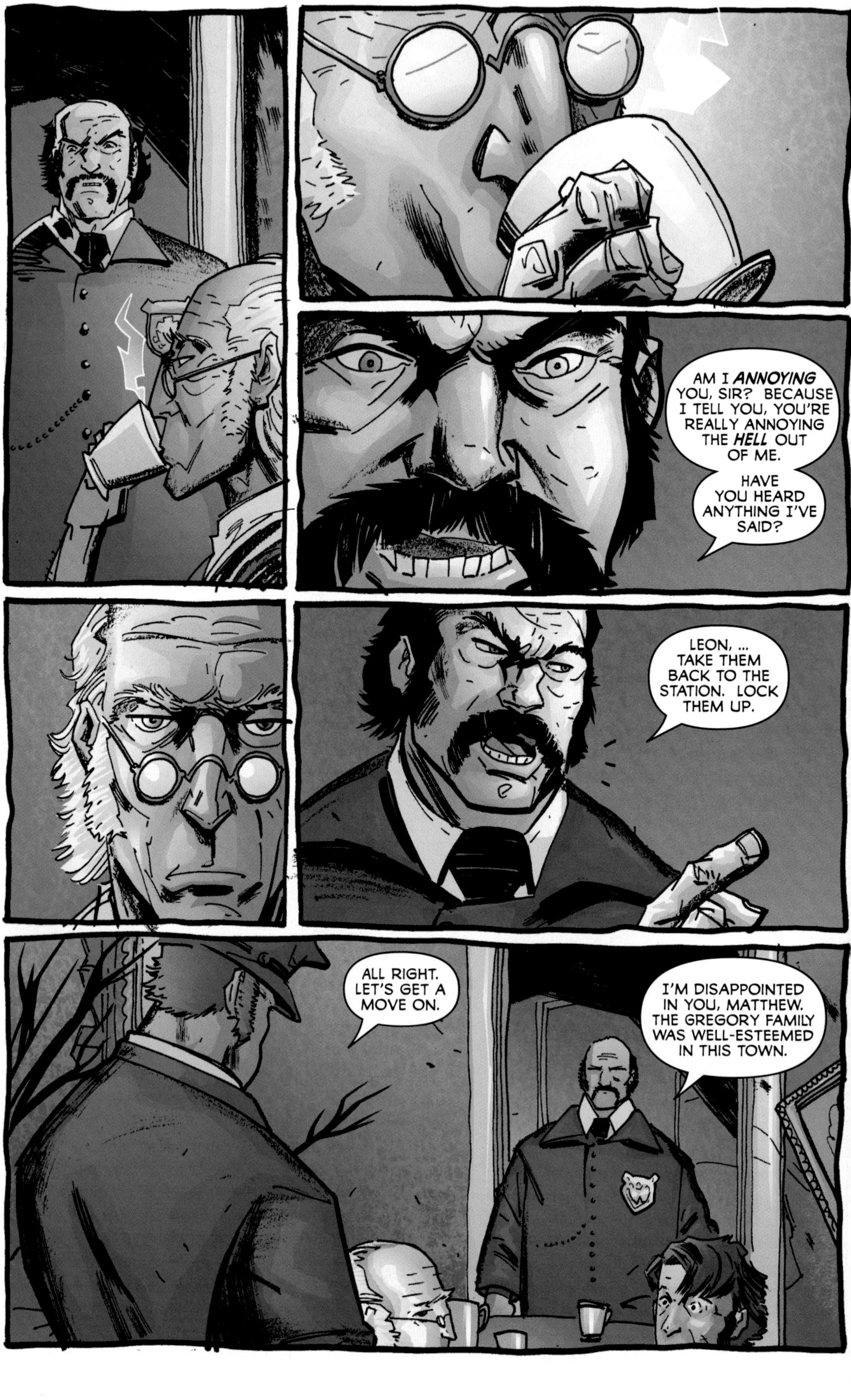
AM I *ANNOYING* YOU, SIR? BECAUSE I TELL YOU, YOU'RE REALLY ANNOYING THE *HELL* OUT OF ME.
HAVE YOU HEARD ANYTHING I'VE SAID?
LEON, ... TAKE THEM BACK TO THE STATION. LOCK THEM UP.
ALL RIGHT. LET'S GET A MOVE ON.
I'M DISAPPOINTED IN YOU, MATTHEW. THE GREGORY FAMILY WAS WELL-ESTEEMED IN THIS TOWN.

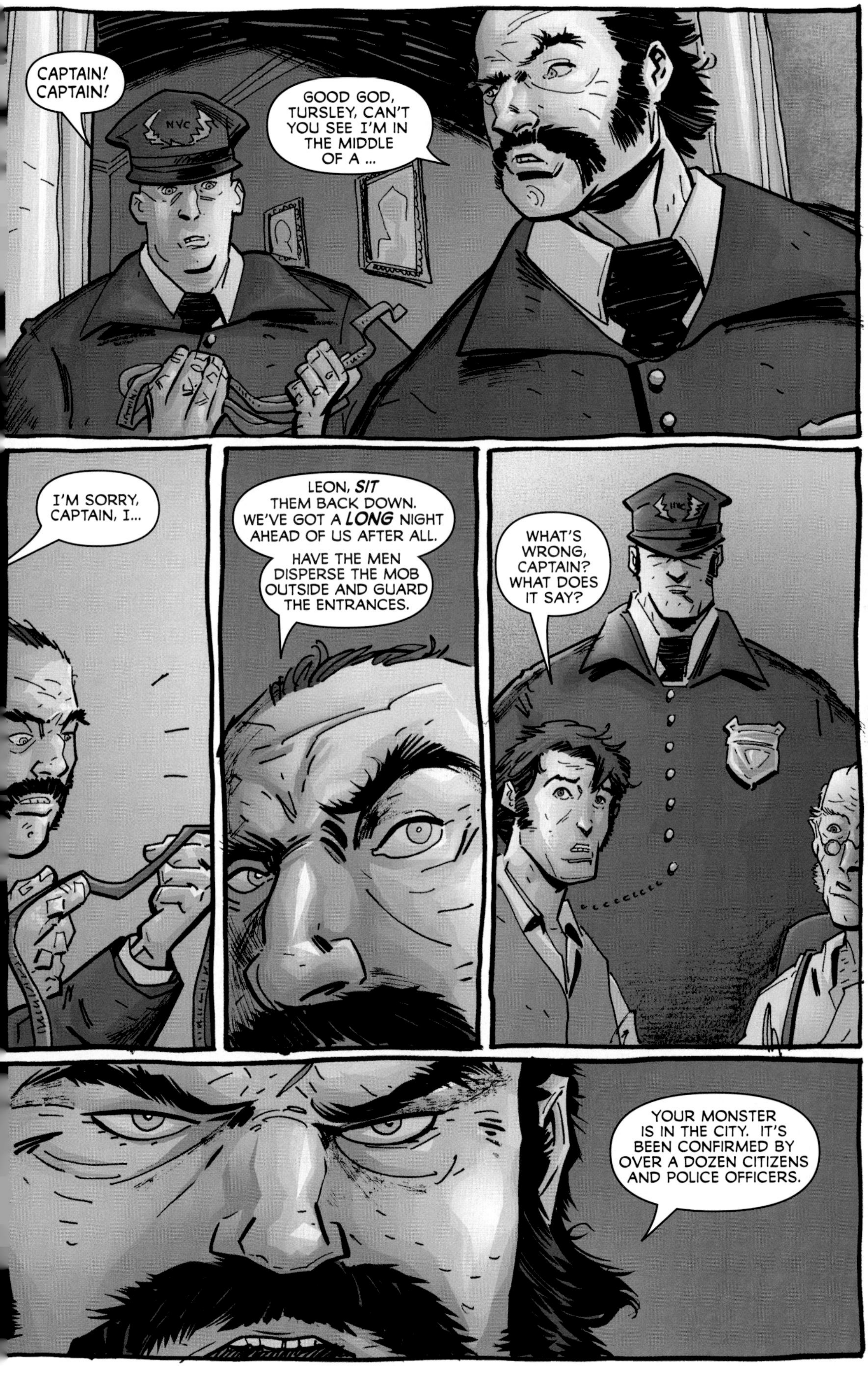
CAPTAIN! CAPTAIN!
GOOD GOD, TURSLEY, CAN'T YOU SEE I'M IN THE MIDDLE OF A ...
I'M SORRY, CAPTAIN, I...
LEON, SIT THEM BACK DOWN. WE'VE GOT A LONG NIGHT AHEAD OF US AFTER ALL.
HAVE THE MEN DISPERSE THE MOB OUTSIDE AND GUARD THE ENTRANCES.
WHAT'S WRONG, CAPTAIN? WHAT DOES IT SAY?
YOUR MONSTER IS IN THE CITY. IT'S BEEN CONFIRMED BY OVER A DOZEN CITIZENS AND POLICE OFFICERS.

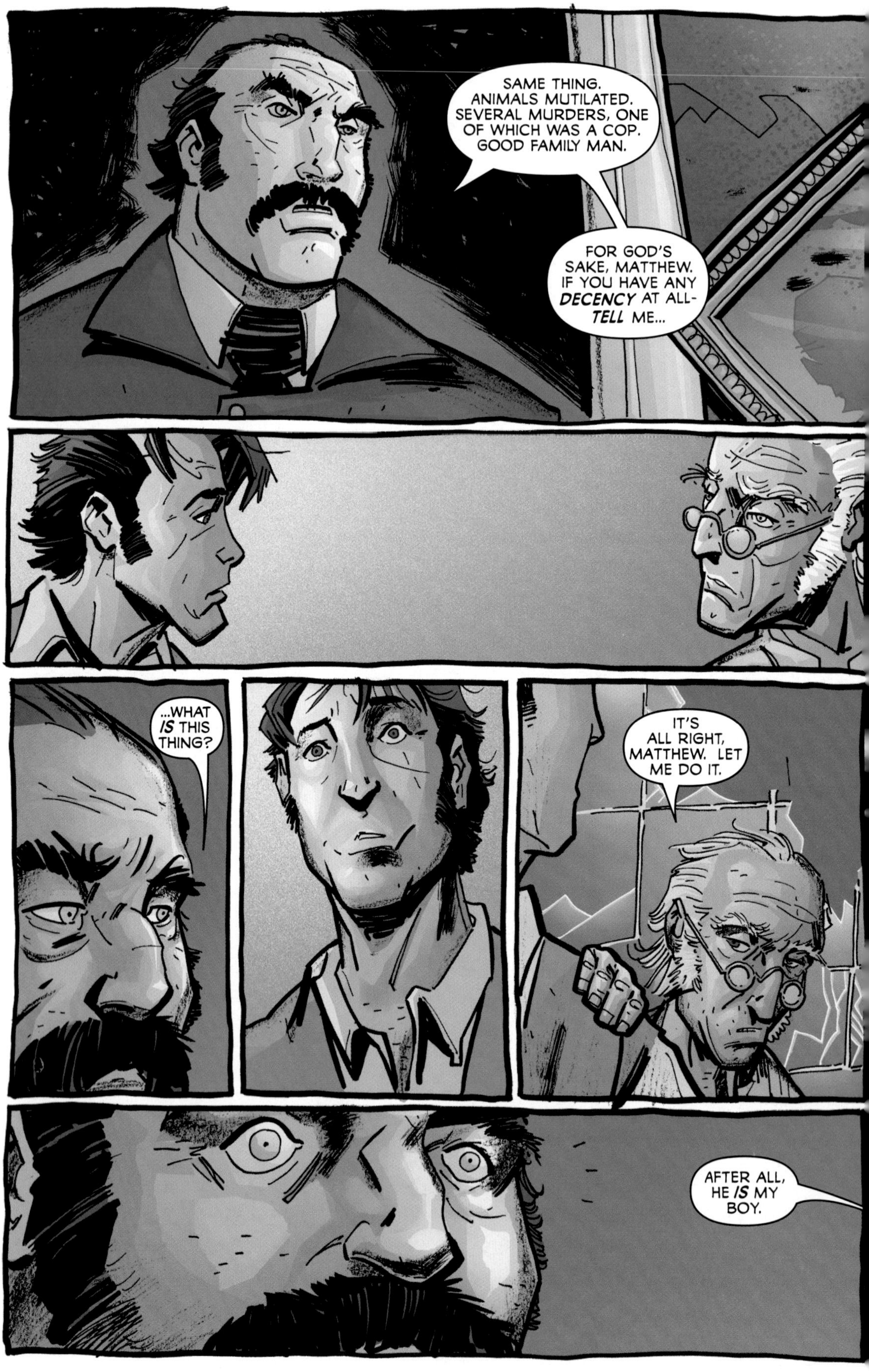
SAME THING. ANIMALS MUTILATED. SEVERAL MURDERS, ONE OF WHICH WAS A COP. GOOD FAMILY MAN.
FOR GOD'S SAKE, MATTHEW. IF YOU HAVE ANY *DECENCY* AT ALL- *TELL* ME...
...WHAT *IS* THIS THING?
IT'S ALL RIGHT, MATTHEW. LET ME DO IT.
AFTER ALL, HE *IS* MY BOY.

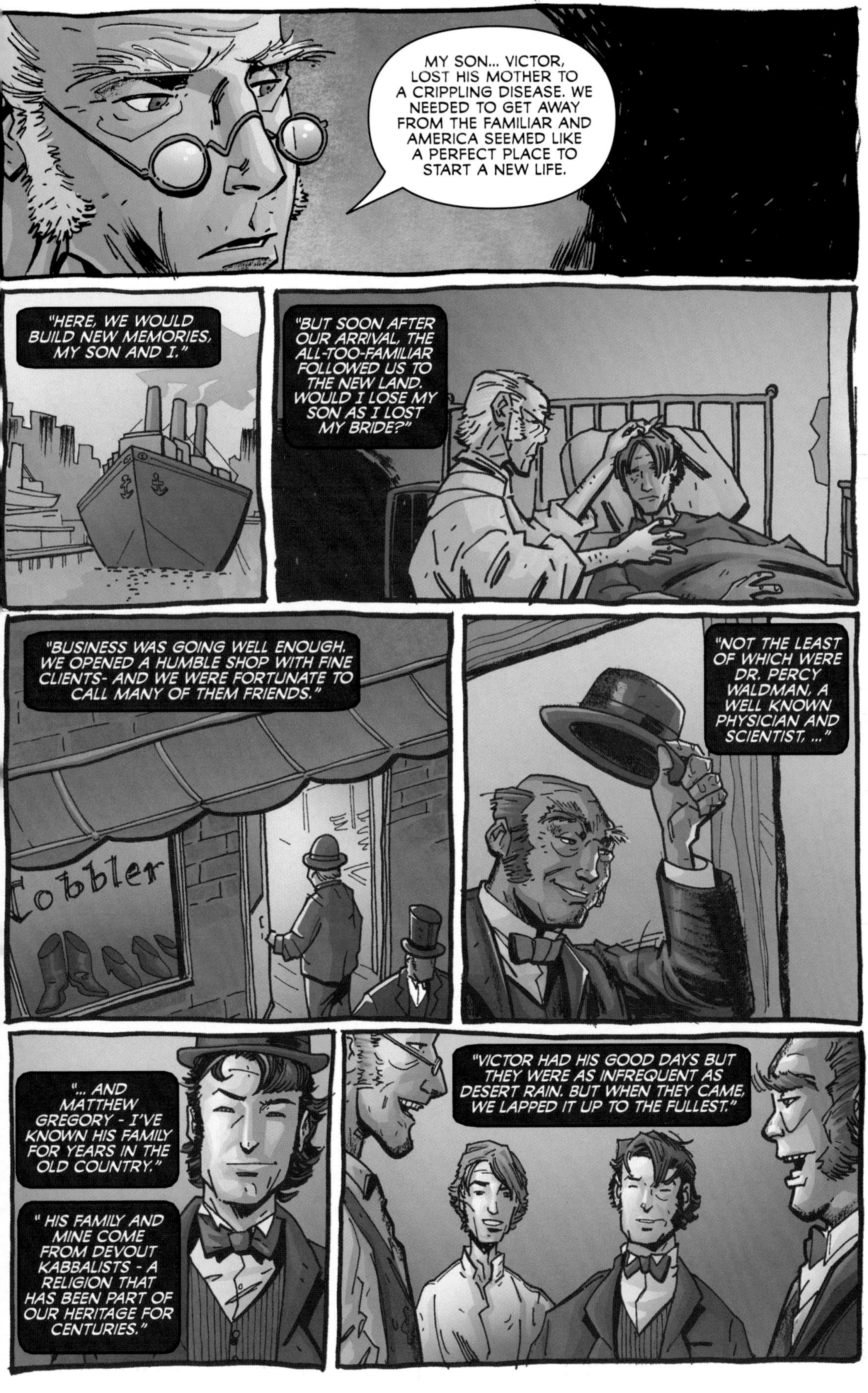
MY SON... VICTOR, LOST HIS MOTHER TO A CRIPPLING DISEASE. WE NEEDED TO GET AWAY FROM THE FAMILIAR AND AMERICA SEEMED LIKE A PERFECT PLACE TO START A NEW LIFE.
"HERE, WE WOULD BUILD NEW MEMORIES, MY SON AND I."
"BUT SOON AFTER OUR ARRIVAL, THE ALL-TOO-FAMILIAR FOLLOWED US TO THE NEW LAND. WOULD I LOSE MY SON AS I LOST MY BRIDE?"
"BUSINESS WAS GOING WELL ENOUGH. WE OPENED A HUMBLE SHOP WITH FINE CLIENTS- AND WE WERE FORTUNATE TO CALL MANY OF THEM FRIENDS."
Cobbler
"NOT THE LEAST OF WHICH WERE DR. PERCY WALDMAN, A WELL KNOWN PHYSICIAN AND SCIENTIST, ..."
"... AND MATTHEW GREGORY - I'VE KNOWN HIS FAMILY FOR YEARS IN THE OLD COUNTRY."
" HIS FAMILY AND MINE COME FROM DEVOUT KABBALISTS - A RELIGION THAT HAS BEEN PART OF OUR HERITAGE FOR CENTURIES."
"VICTOR HAD HIS GOOD DAYS BUT THEY WERE AS INFREQUENT AS DESERT RAIN. BUT WHEN THEY CAME, WE LAPPED IT UP TO THE FULLEST."

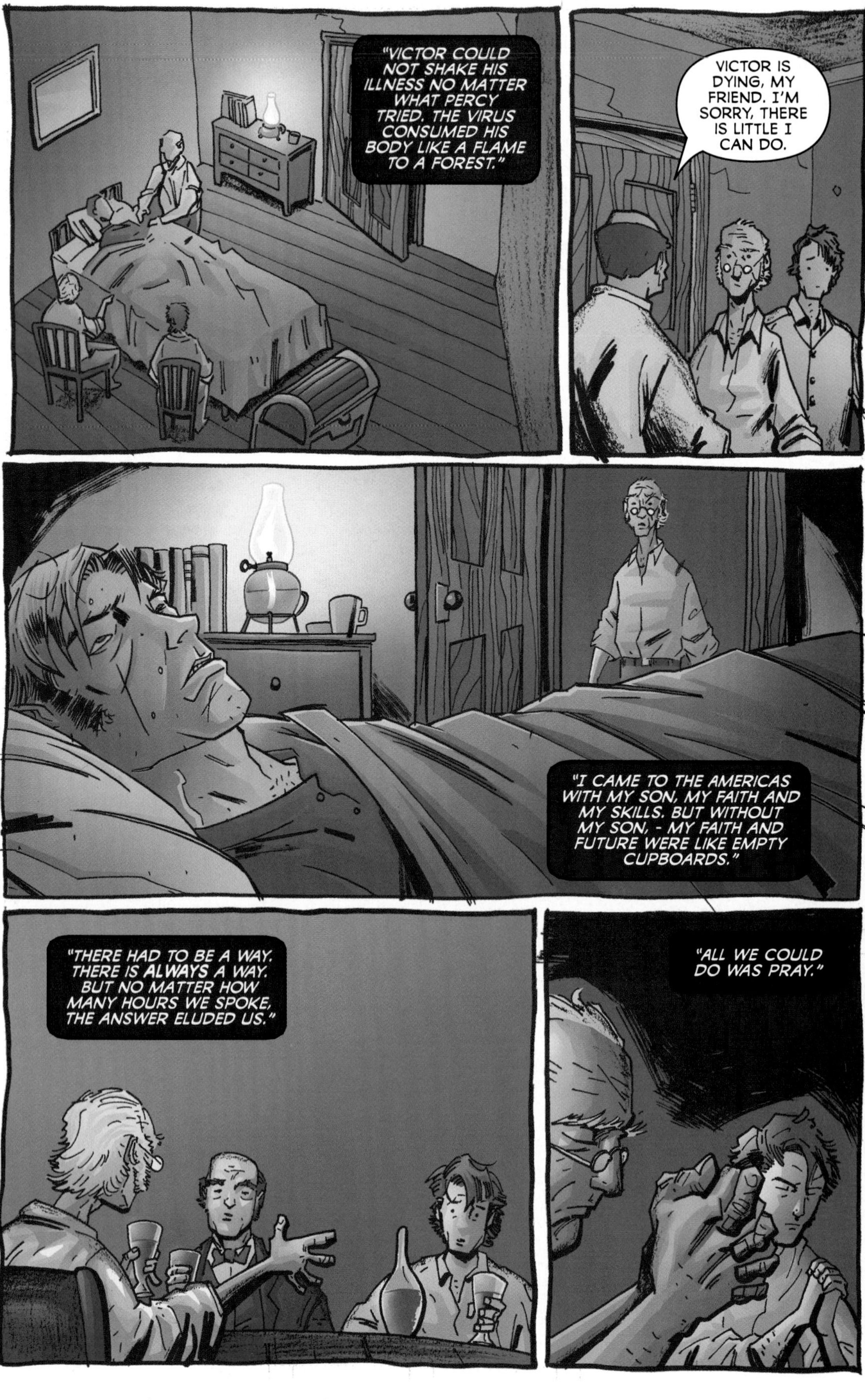
"VICTOR COULD NOT SHAKE HIS ILLNESS NO MATTER WHAT PERCY TRIED. THE VIRUS CONSUMED HIS BODY LIKE A FLAME TO A FOREST."
VICTOR IS DYING, MY FRIEND. I'M SORRY, THERE IS LITTLE I CAN DO.
"I CAME TO THE AMERICAS WITH MY SON, MY FAITH AND MY SKILLS. BUT WITHOUT MY SON, - MY FAITH AND FUTURE WERE LIKE EMPTY CUPBOARDS."
"THERE HAD TO BE A WAY. THERE IS ALWAYS A WAY. BUT NO MATTER HOW MANY HOURS WE SPOKE, THE ANSWER ELUDED US."
"ALL WE COULD DO WAS PRAY."

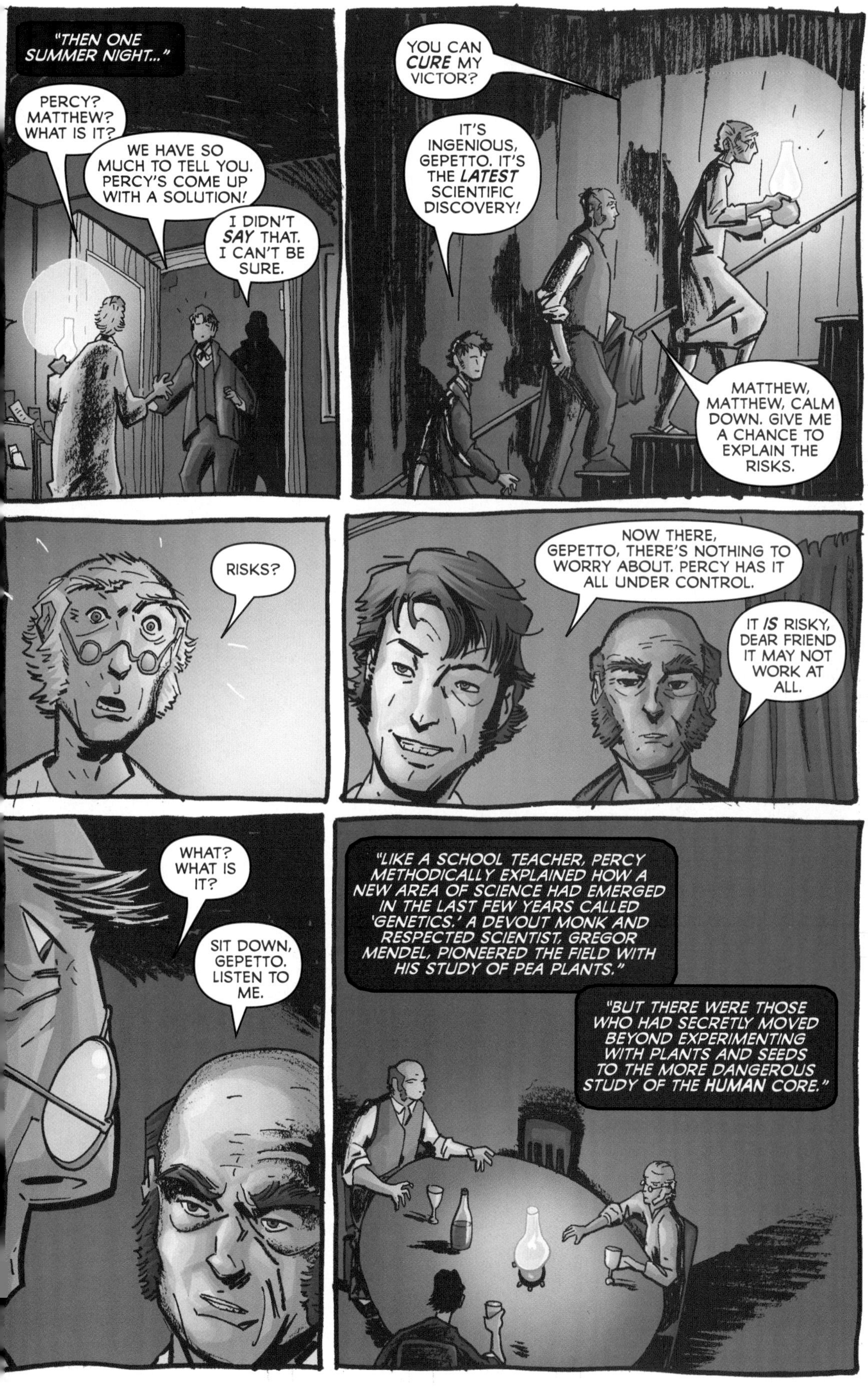
"THEN ONE SUMMER NIGHT..."
PERCY? MATTHEW? WHAT IS IT?
WE HAVE SO MUCH TO TELL YOU. PERCY'S COME UP WITH A SOLUTION!
I DIDN'T *SAY* THAT. I CAN'T BE SURE.
YOU CAN *CURE* MY VICTOR?
IT'S INGENIOUS, GEPETTO. IT'S THE *LATEST* SCIENTIFIC DISCOVERY!
MATTHEW, MATTHEW, CALM DOWN. GIVE ME A CHANCE TO EXPLAIN THE RISKS.
RISKS?
NOW THERE, GEPETTO, THERE'S NOTHING TO WORRY ABOUT. PERCY HAS IT ALL UNDER CONTROL.
IT *IS* RISKY, DEAR FRIEND IT MAY NOT WORK AT ALL.
WHAT? WHAT IS IT?
SIT DOWN, GEPETTO. LISTEN TO ME.
"LIKE A SCHOOL TEACHER, PERCY METHODICALLY EXPLAINED HOW A NEW AREA OF SCIENCE HAD EMERGED IN THE LAST FEW YEARS CALLED 'GENETICS.' A DEVOUT MONK AND RESPECTED SCIENTIST, GREGOR MENDEL, PIONEERED THE FIELD WITH HIS STUDY OF PEA PLANTS."
"BUT THERE WERE THOSE WHO HAD SECRETLY MOVED BEYOND EXPERIMENTING WITH PLANTS AND SEEDS TO THE MORE DANGEROUS STUDY OF THE **HUMAN** CORE."

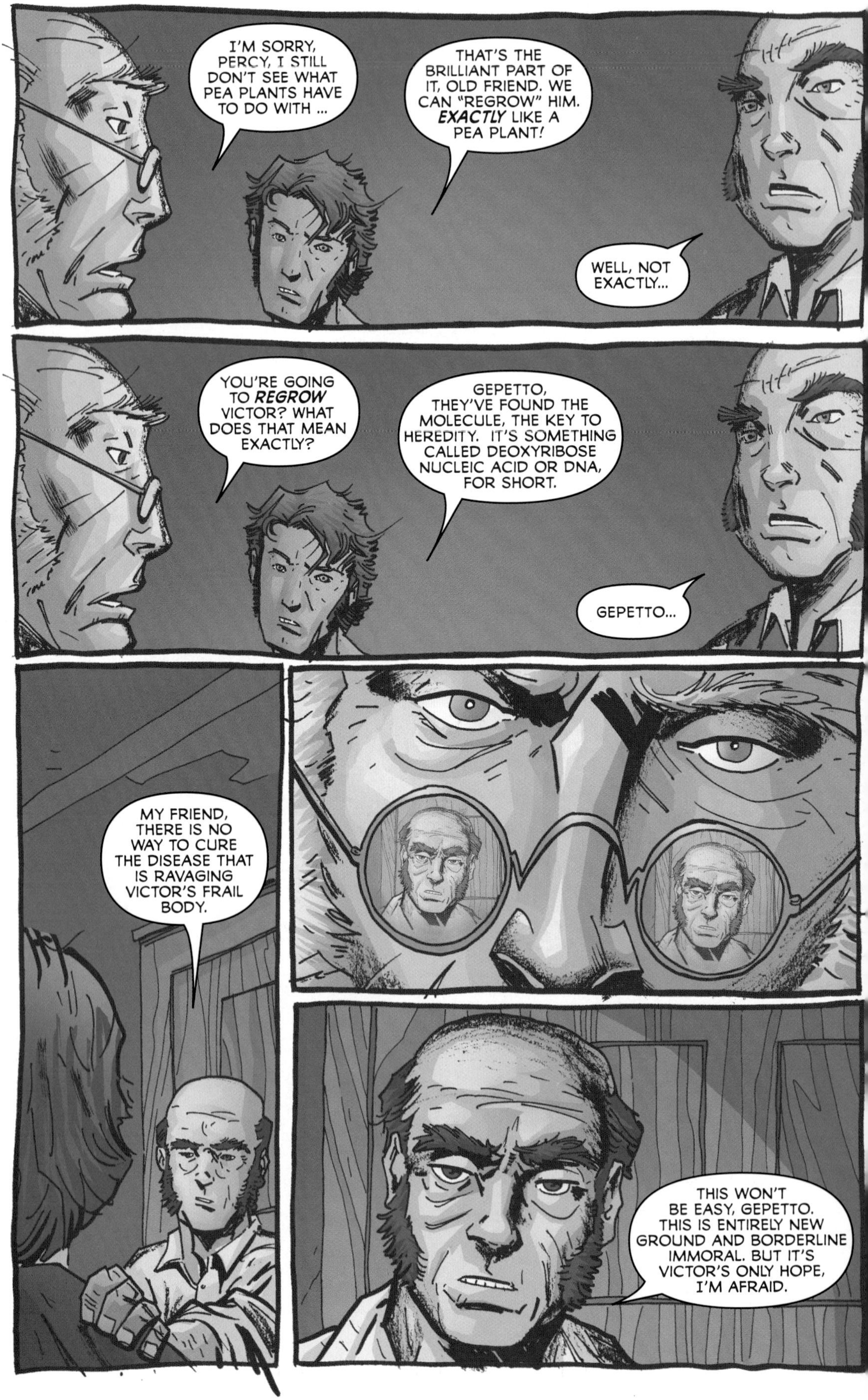
I'M SORRY, PERCY, I STILL DON'T SEE WHAT PEA PLANTS HAVE TO DO WITH ...
THAT'S THE BRILLIANT PART OF IT, OLD FRIEND. WE CAN "REGROW" HIM. *EXACTLY* LIKE A PEA PLANT!
WELL, NOT EXACTLY...
YOU'RE GOING TO *REGROW* VICTOR? WHAT DOES THAT MEAN EXACTLY?
GEPETTO, THEY'VE FOUND THE MOLECULE, THE KEY TO HEREDITY. IT'S SOMETHING CALLED DEOXYRIBOSE NUCLEIC ACID OR DNA, FOR SHORT.
GEPETTO...
MY FRIEND, THERE IS NO WAY TO CURE THE DISEASE THAT IS RAVAGING VICTOR'S FRAIL BODY.
THIS WON'T BE EASY, GEPETTO. THIS IS ENTIRELY NEW GROUND AND BORDERLINE IMMORAL. BUT IT'S VICTOR'S ONLY HOPE, I'M AFRAID.

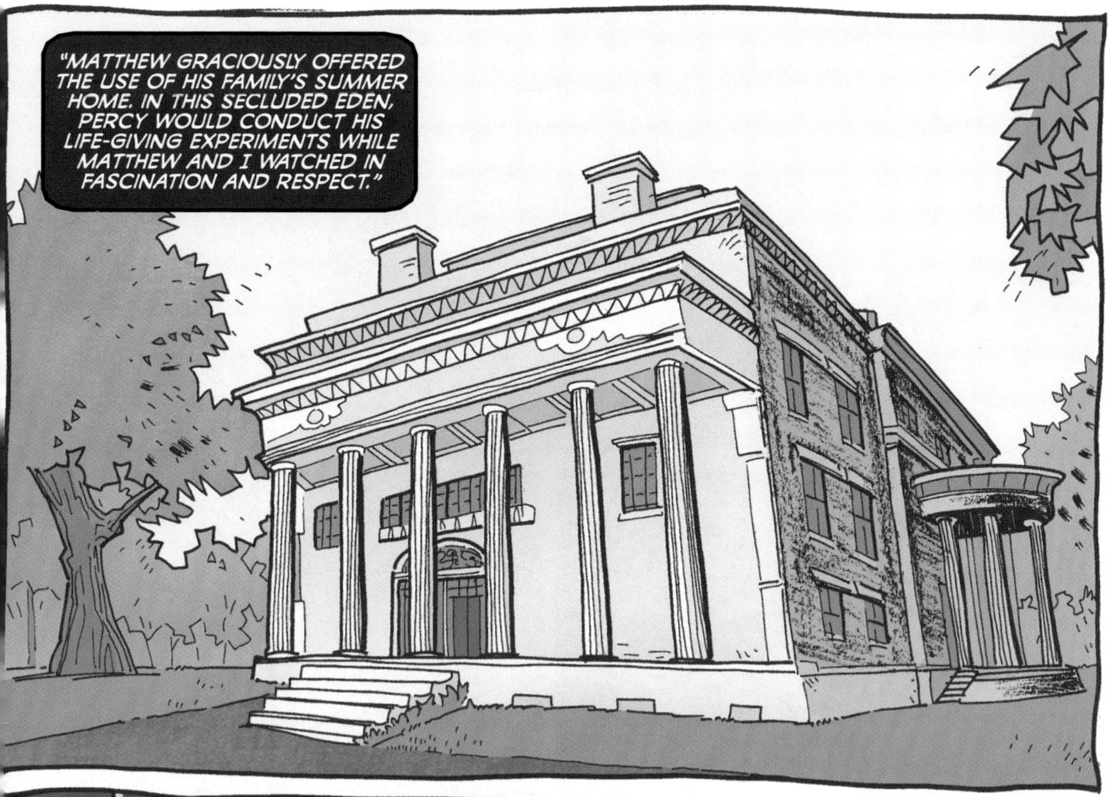
"MATTHEW GRACIOUSLY OFFERED THE USE OF HIS FAMILY'S SUMMER HOME. IN THIS SECLUDED EDEN, PERCY WOULD CONDUCT HIS LIFE-GIVING EXPERIMENTS WHILE MATTHEW AND I WATCHED IN FASCINATION AND RESPECT."

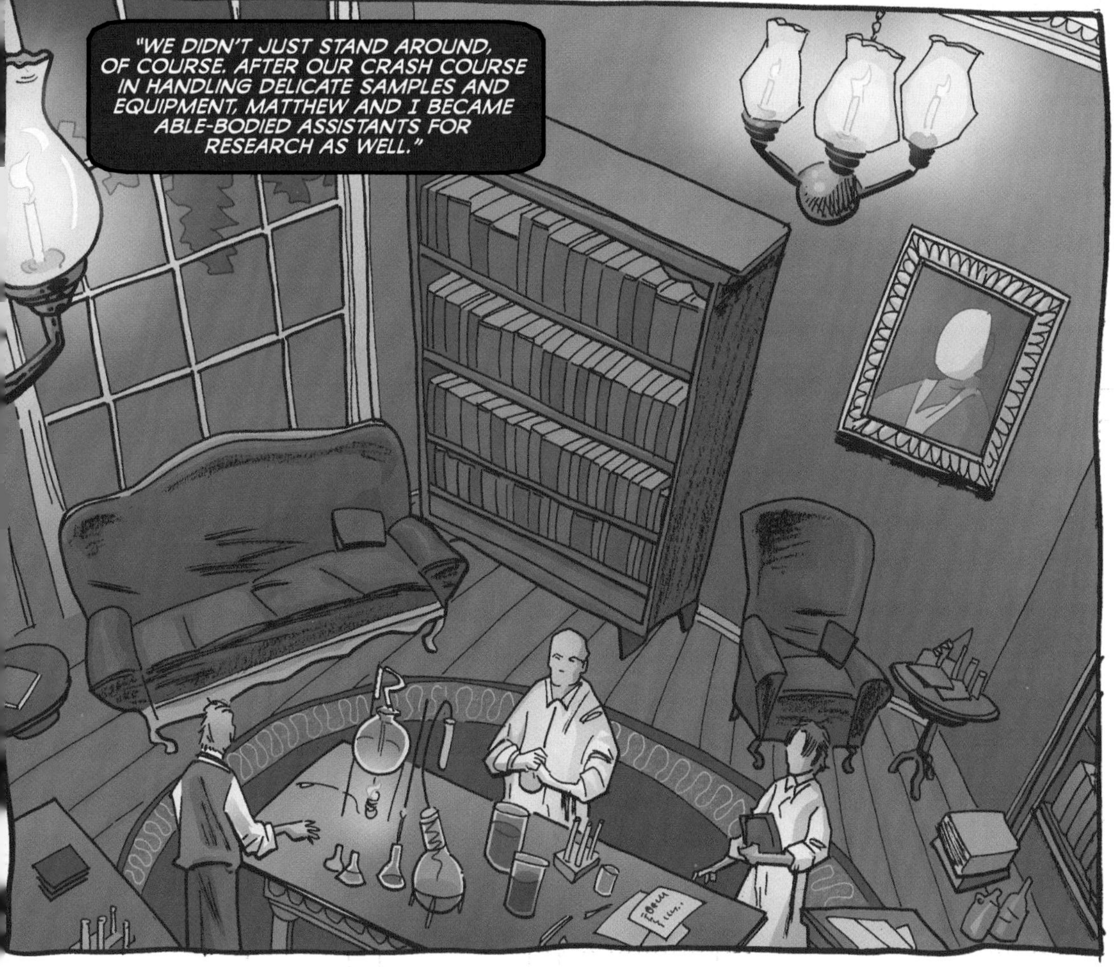
"WE DIDN'T JUST STAND AROUND, OF COURSE. AFTER OUR CRASH COURSE IN HANDLING DELICATE SAMPLES AND EQUIPMENT, MATTHEW AND I BECAME ABLE-BODIED ASSISTANTS FOR RESEARCH AS WELL."

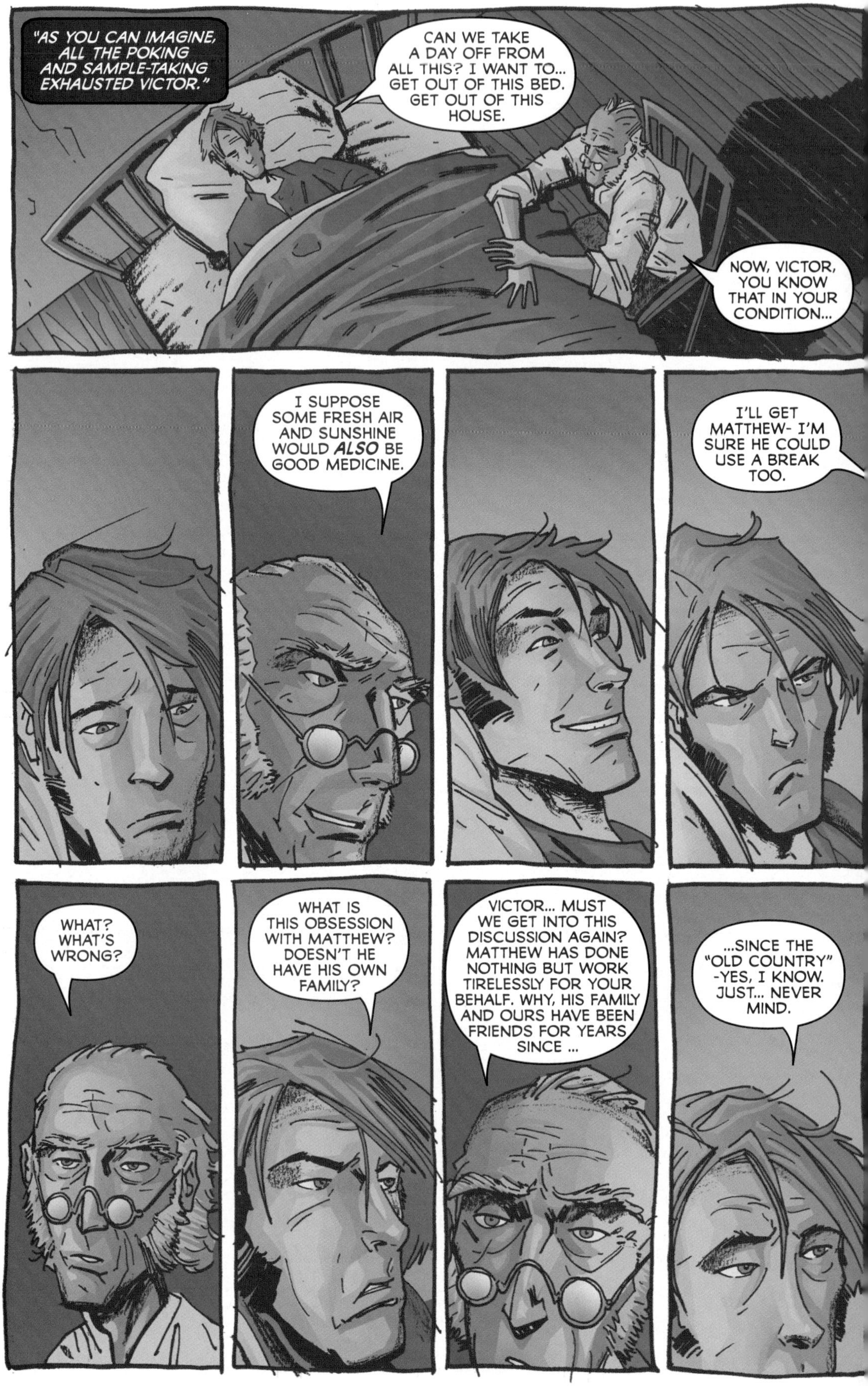
"AS YOU CAN IMAGINE, ALL THE POKING AND SAMPLE-TAKING EXHAUSTED VICTOR."
CAN WE TAKE A DAY OFF FROM ALL THIS? I WANT TO... GET OUT OF THIS BED. GET OUT OF THIS HOUSE.
NOW, VICTOR, YOU KNOW THAT IN YOUR CONDITION...
I SUPPOSE SOME FRESH AIR AND SUNSHINE WOULD ALSO BE GOOD MEDICINE.
I'LL GET MATTHEW- I'M SURE HE COULD USE A BREAK TOO.
WHAT? WHAT'S WRONG?
WHAT IS THIS OBSESSION WITH MATTHEW? DOESN'T HE HAVE HIS OWN FAMILY?
VICTOR... MUST WE GET INTO THIS DISCUSSION AGAIN? MATTHEW HAS DONE NOTHING BUT WORK TIRELESSLY FOR YOUR BEHALF. WHY, HIS FAMILY AND OURS HAVE BEEN FRIENDS FOR YEARS SINCE ...
...SINCE THE "OLD COUNTRY" -YES, I KNOW. JUST... NEVER MIND.

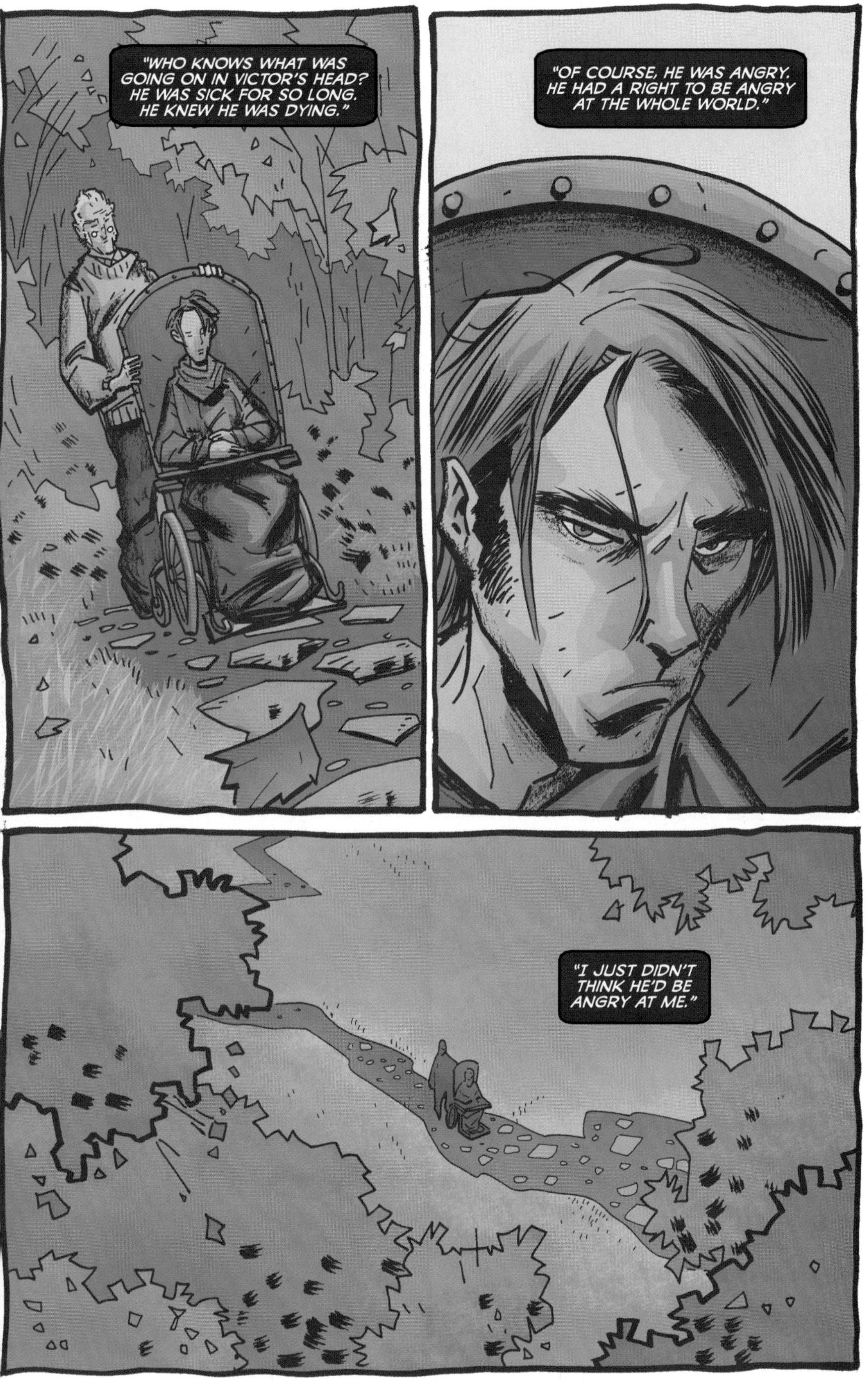
"WHO KNOWS WHAT WAS GOING ON IN VICTOR'S HEAD? HE WAS SICK FOR SO LONG. HE KNEW HE WAS DYING."
"OF COURSE, HE WAS ANGRY. HE HAD A RIGHT TO BE ANGRY AT THE WHOLE WORLD."
"I JUST DIDN'T THINK HE'D BE ANGRY AT ME."

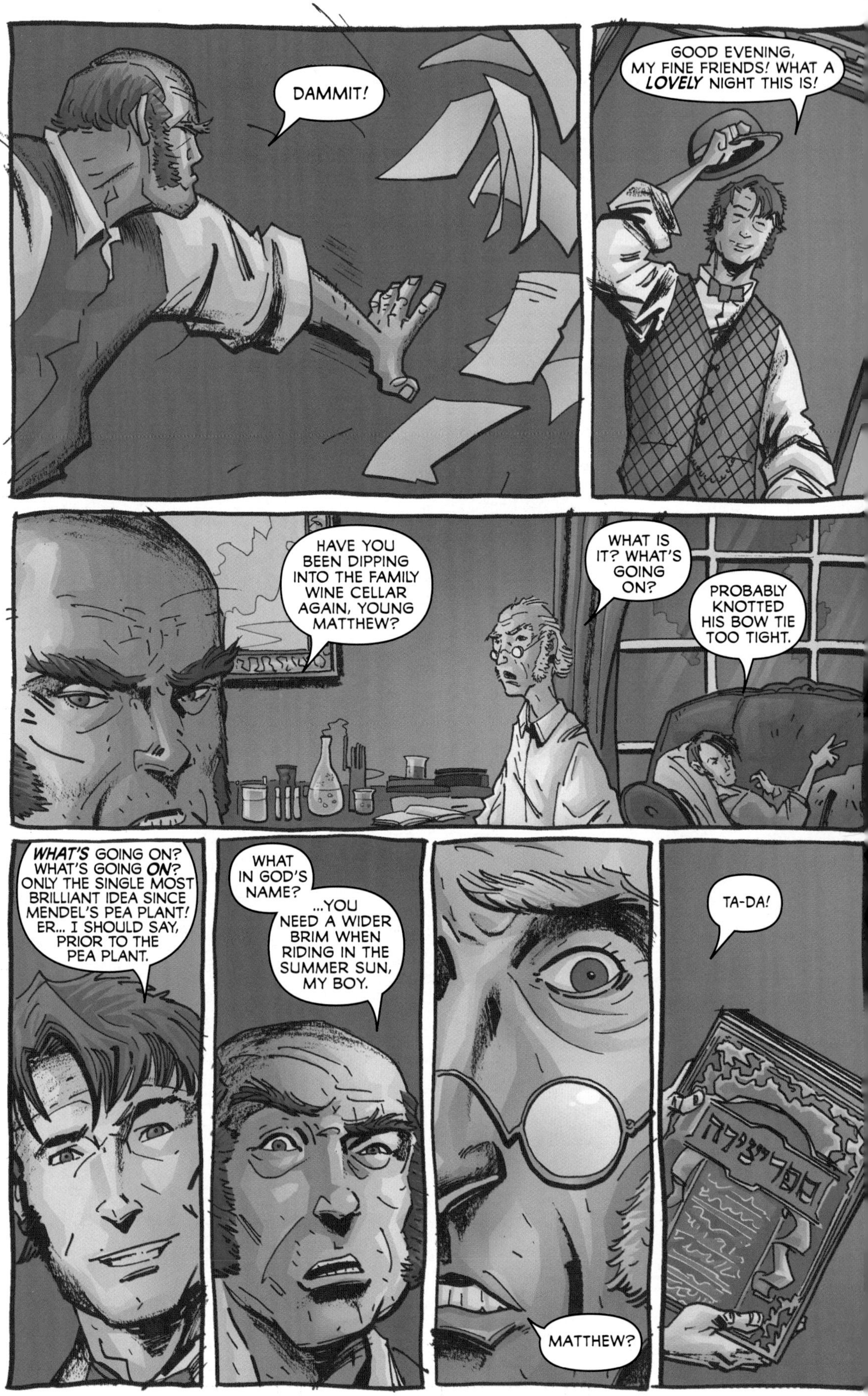
DAMMIT!
GOOD EVENING, MY FINE FRIENDS! WHAT A *LOVELY* NIGHT THIS IS!
HAVE YOU BEEN DIPPING INTO THE FAMILY WINE CELLAR AGAIN, YOUNG MATTHEW?
WHAT IS IT? WHAT'S GOING ON?
PROBABLY KNOTTED HIS BOW TIE TOO TIGHT.
WHAT'S GOING ON? WHAT'S GOING *ON*? ONLY THE SINGLE MOST BRILLIANT IDEA SINCE MENDEL'S PEA PLANT! ER... I SHOULD SAY, PRIOR TO THE PEA PLANT.
WHAT IN GOD'S NAME?
...YOU NEED A WIDER BRIM WHEN RIDING IN THE SUMMER SUN, MY BOY.
MATTHEW?
TA-DA!

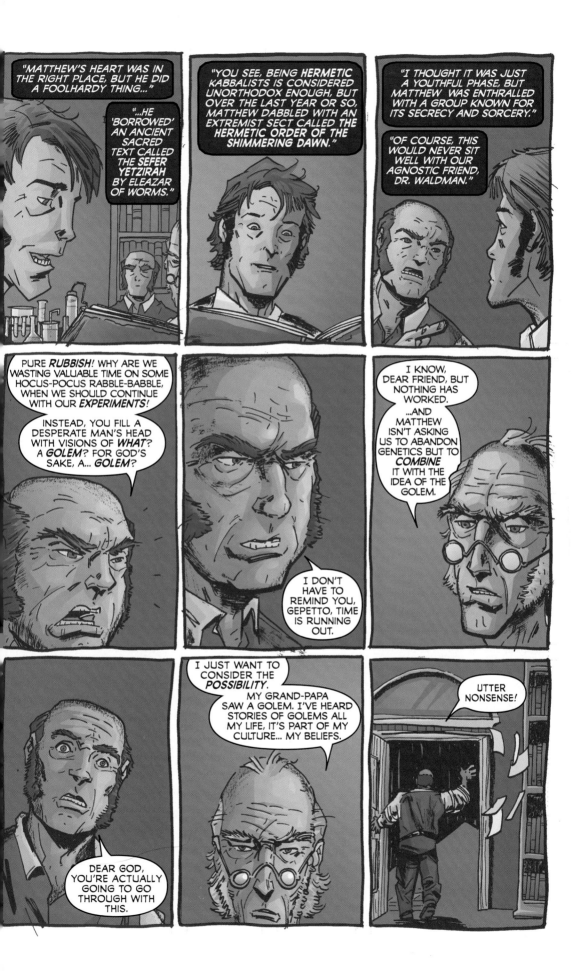

"MATTHEW'S HEART WAS IN THE RIGHT PLACE, BUT HE DID A FOOLHARDY THING..."

"...HE 'BORROWED' AN ANCIENT SACRED TEXT CALLED THE SEFER YETZIRAH BY ELEAZAR OF WORMS."

"YOU SEE, BEING HERMETIC KABBALISTS IS CONSIDERED UNORTHODOX ENOUGH, BUT OVER THE LAST YEAR OR SO, MATTHEW DABBLED WITH AN EXTREMIST SECT CALLED THE HERMETIC ORDER OF THE SHIMMERING DAWN."

"I THOUGHT IT WAS JUST A YOUTHFUL PHASE, BUT MATTHEW WAS ENTHRALLED WITH A GROUP KNOWN FOR ITS SECRECY AND SORCERY."

"OF COURSE, THIS WOULD NEVER SIT WELL WITH OUR AGNOSTIC FRIEND, DR. WALDMAN."

PURE RUBBISH! WHY ARE WE WASTING VALUABLE TIME ON SOME HOCUS-POCUS RABBLE-BABBLE, WHEN WE SHOULD CONTINUE WITH OUR EXPERIMENTS!

INSTEAD, YOU FILL A DESPERATE MAN'S HEAD WITH VISIONS OF WHAT? A GOLEM? FOR GOD'S SAKE, A... GOLEM?

I DON'T HAVE TO REMIND YOU, GEPETTO, TIME IS RUNNING OUT.

I KNOW, DEAR FRIEND, BUT NOTHING HAS WORKED.

...AND MATTHEW ISN'T ASKING US TO ABANDON GENETICS BUT TO COMBINE IT WITH THE IDEA OF THE GOLEM.

DEAR GOD, YOU'RE ACTUALLY GOING TO GO THROUGH WITH THIS.

I JUST WANT TO CONSIDER THE POSSIBILITY.

MY GRAND-PAPA SAW A GOLEM. I'VE HEARD STORIES OF GOLEMS ALL MY LIFE, IT'S PART OF MY CULTURE... MY BELIEFS.

UTTER NONSENSE!

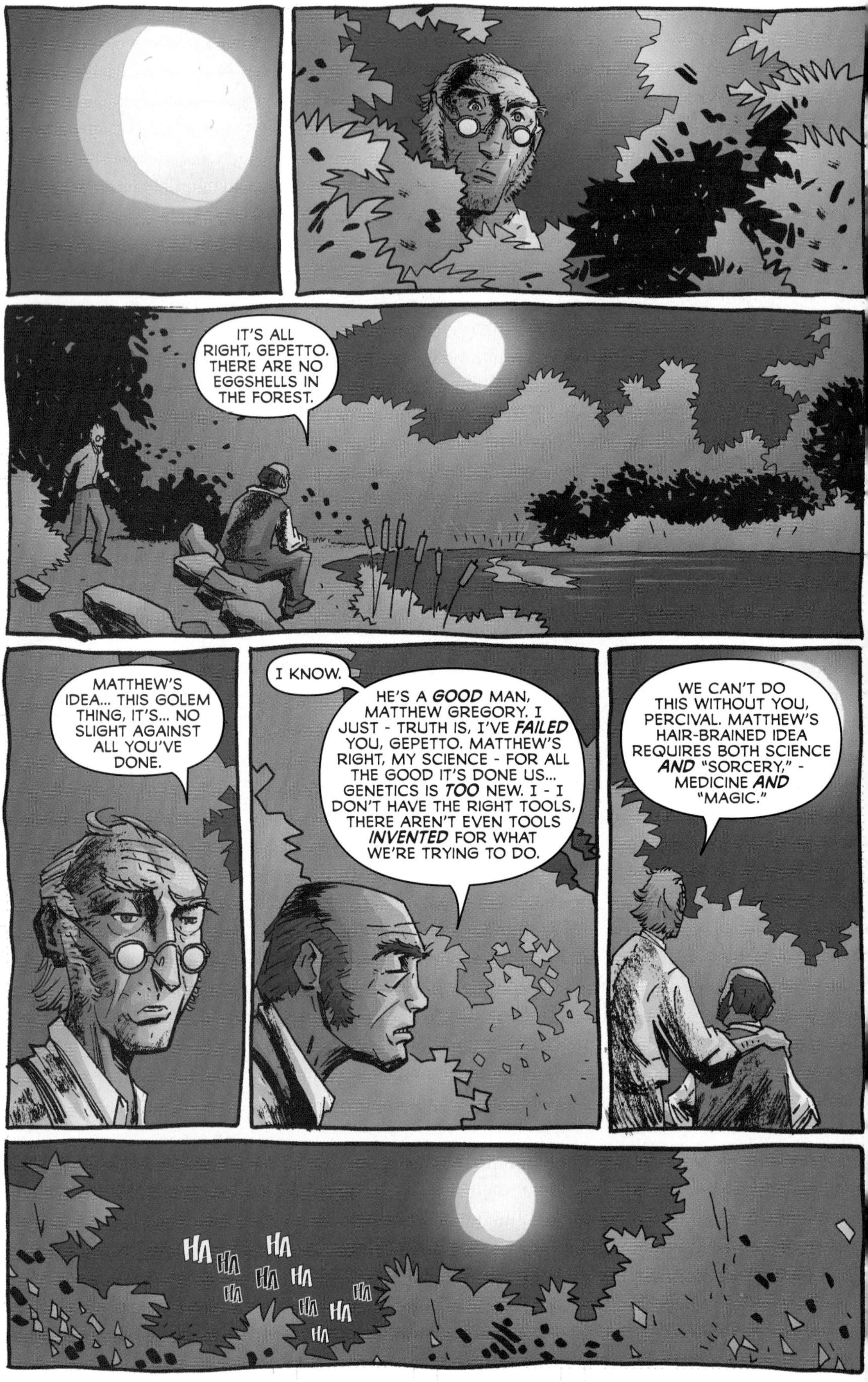
IT'S ALL RIGHT, GEPETTO. THERE ARE NO EGGSHELLS IN THE FOREST.
MATTHEW'S IDEA... THIS GOLEM THING, IT'S... NO SLIGHT AGAINST ALL YOU'VE DONE.
I KNOW.
HE'S A GOOD MAN, MATTHEW GREGORY. I JUST - TRUTH IS, I'VE FAILED YOU, GEPETTO. MATTHEW'S RIGHT, MY SCIENCE - FOR ALL THE GOOD IT'S DONE US... GENETICS IS TOO NEW. I - I DON'T HAVE THE RIGHT TOOLS, THERE AREN'T EVEN TOOLS INVENTED FOR WHAT WE'RE TRYING TO DO.
WE CAN'T DO THIS WITHOUT YOU, PERCIVAL. MATTHEW'S HAIR-BRAINED IDEA REQUIRES BOTH SCIENCE AND "SORCERY," - MEDICINE AND "MAGIC."
HA HA HA HA HA HA HA HA HA HA HA

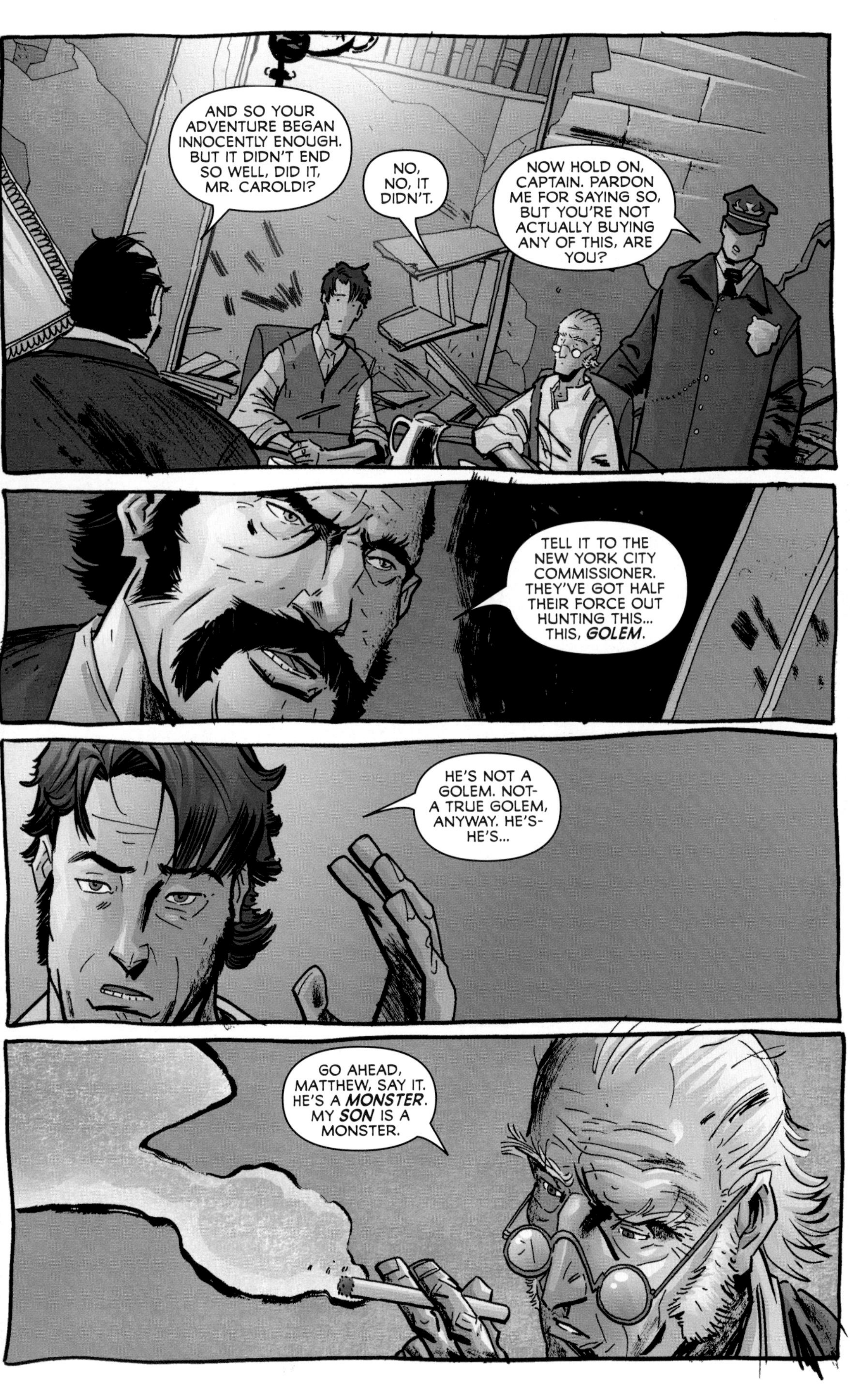
AND SO YOUR ADVENTURE BEGAN INNOCENTLY ENOUGH. BUT IT DIDN'T END SO WELL, DID IT, MR. CAROLDI?
NO, NO, IT DIDN'T.
NOW HOLD ON, CAPTAIN. PARDON ME FOR SAYING SO, BUT YOU'RE NOT ACTUALLY BUYING ANY OF THIS, ARE YOU?
TELL IT TO THE NEW YORK CITY COMMISSIONER. THEY'VE GOT HALF THEIR FORCE OUT HUNTING THIS... THIS, GOLEM.
HE'S NOT A GOLEM. NOT- A TRUE GOLEM, ANYWAY. HE'S- HE'S...
GO AHEAD, MATTHEW, SAY IT. HE'S A MONSTER. MY SON IS A MONSTER.

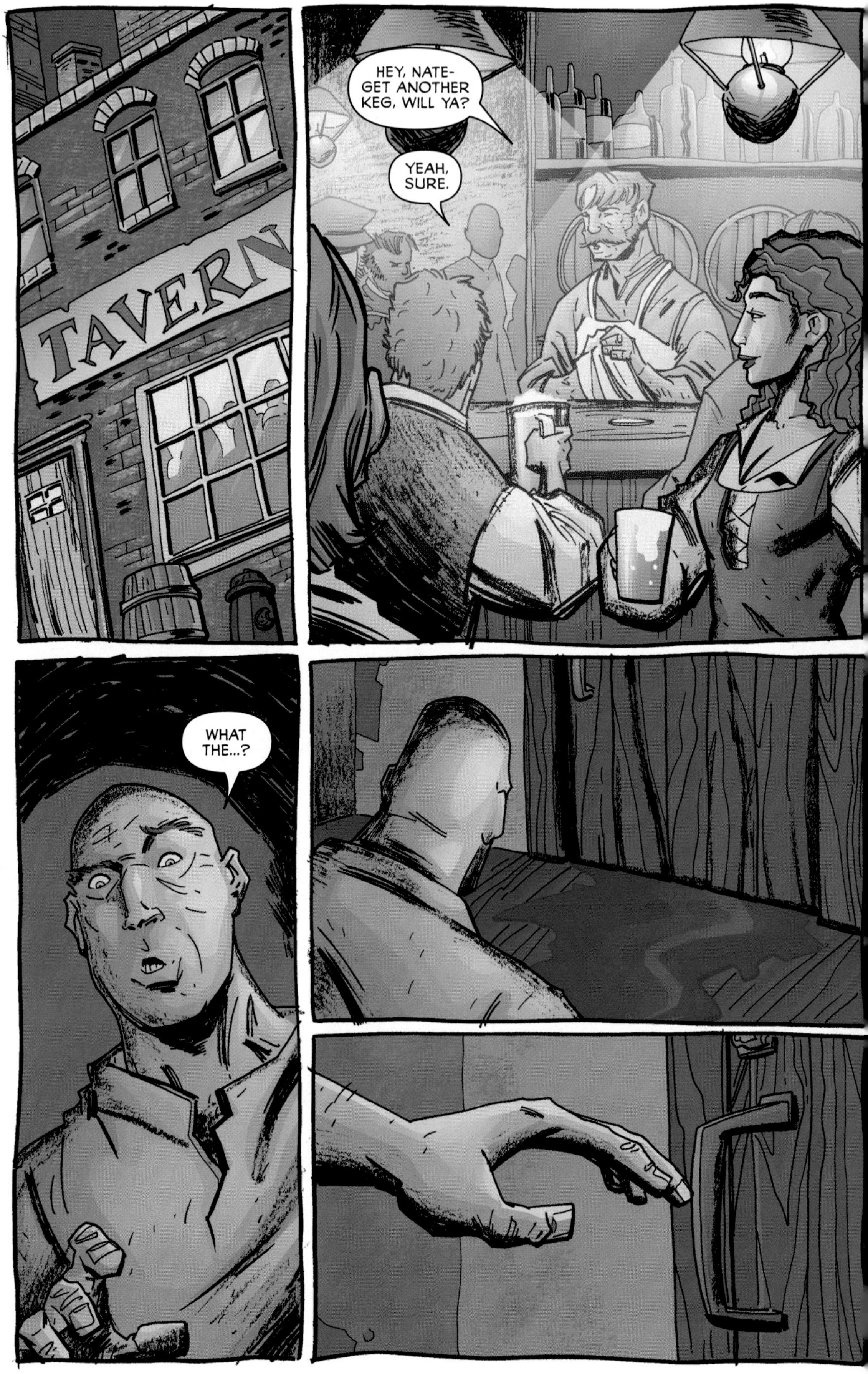
TAVERN
HEY, NATE-
GET ANOTHER
KEG, WILL YA?
YEAH,
SURE.
WHAT
THE...?

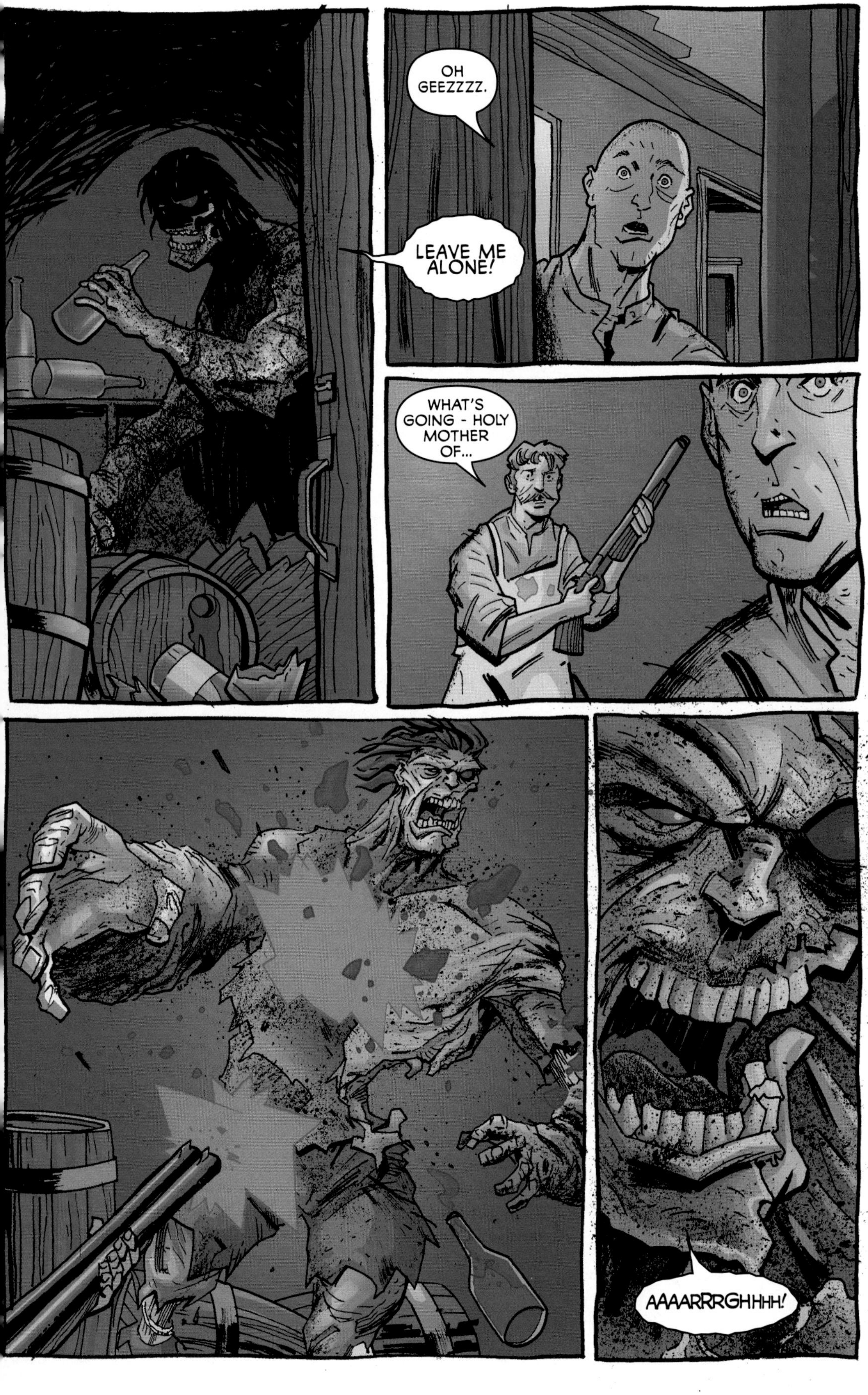
OH GEEZZZZ.
LEAVE ME ALONE!
WHAT'S GOING - HOLY MOTHER OF...
AAAARRRGHHHH!

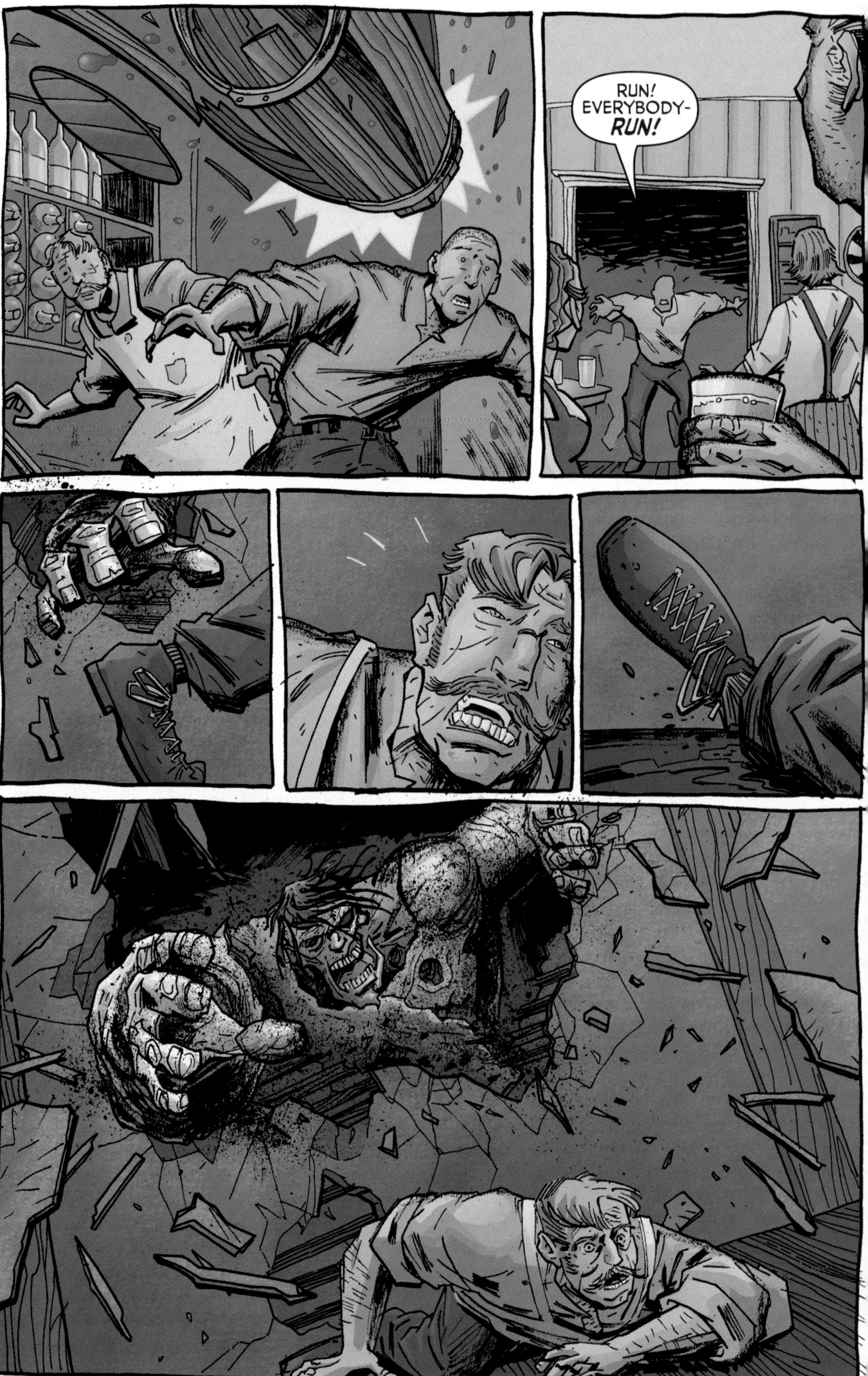
RUN! EVERYBODY- RUN!

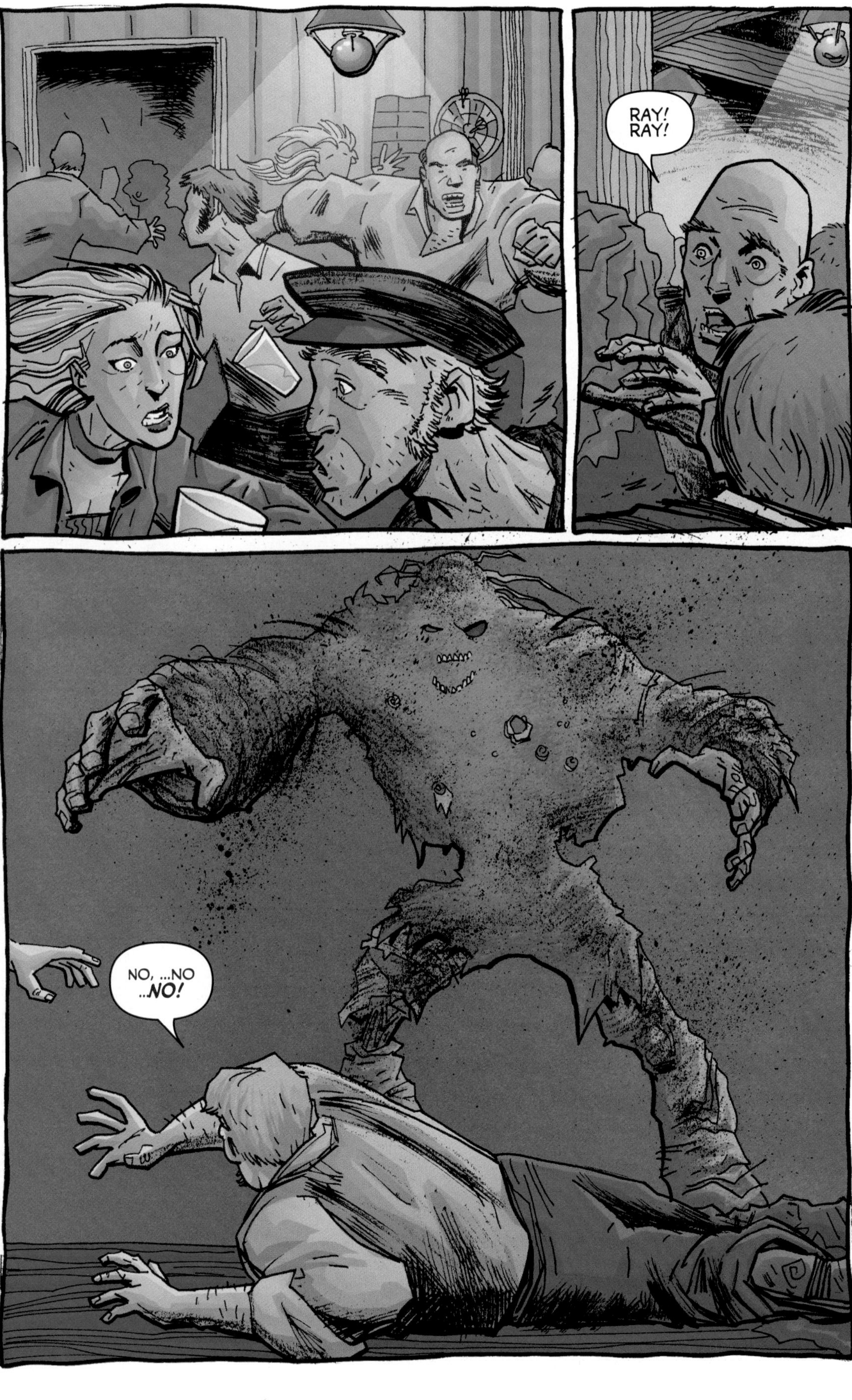
RAY! RAY!
NO, ...NO ...NO!

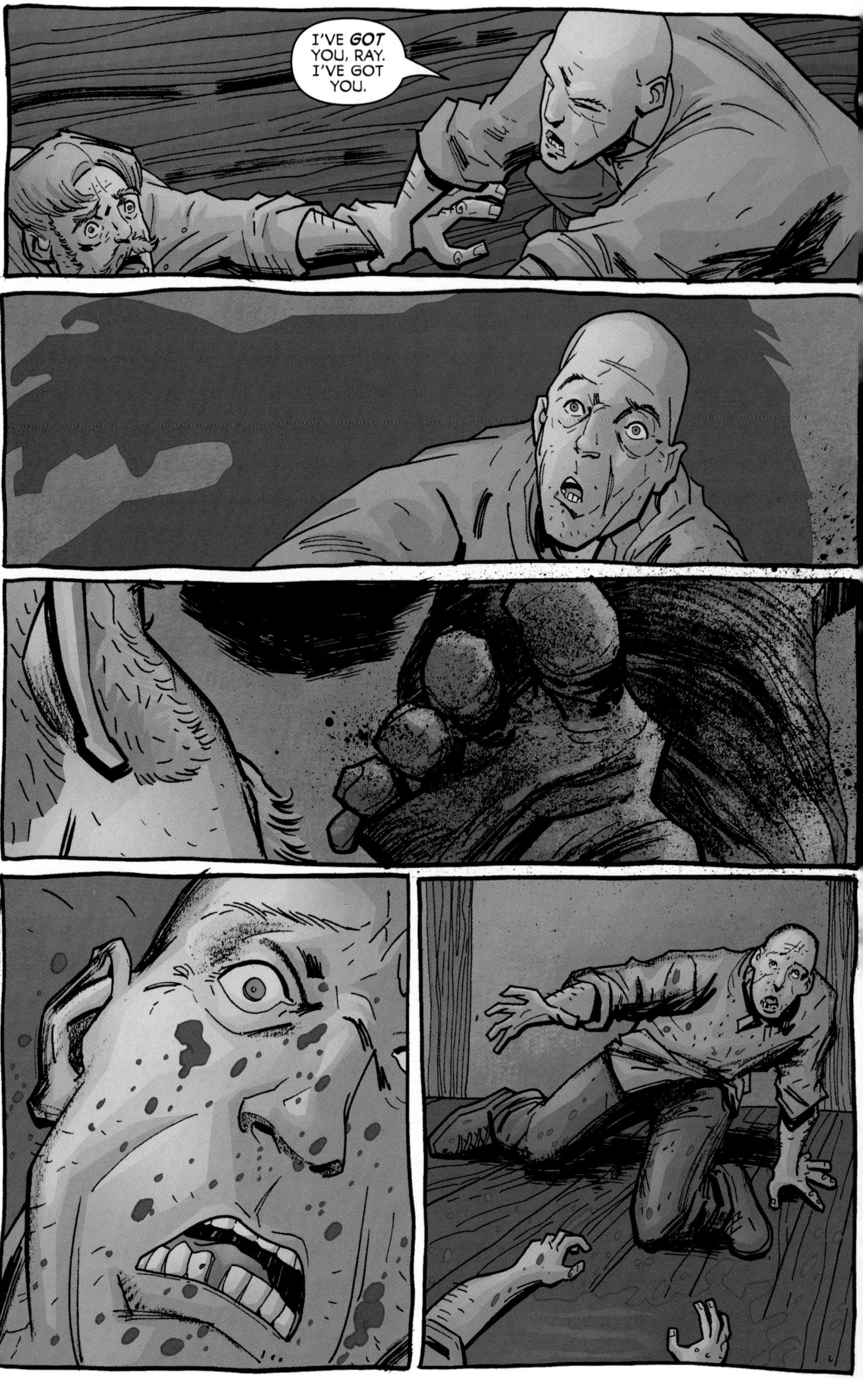
I'VE GOT YOU, RAY. I'VE GOT YOU.

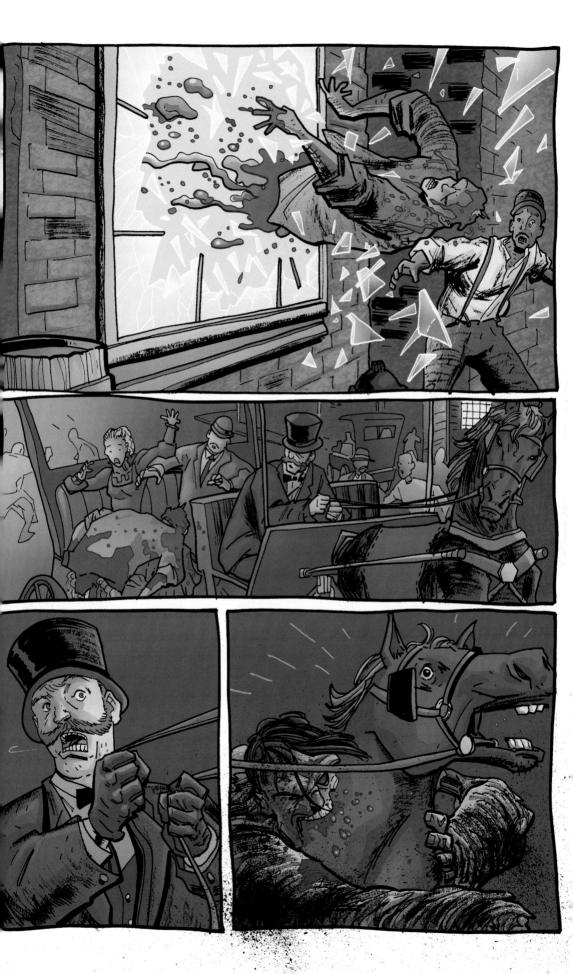

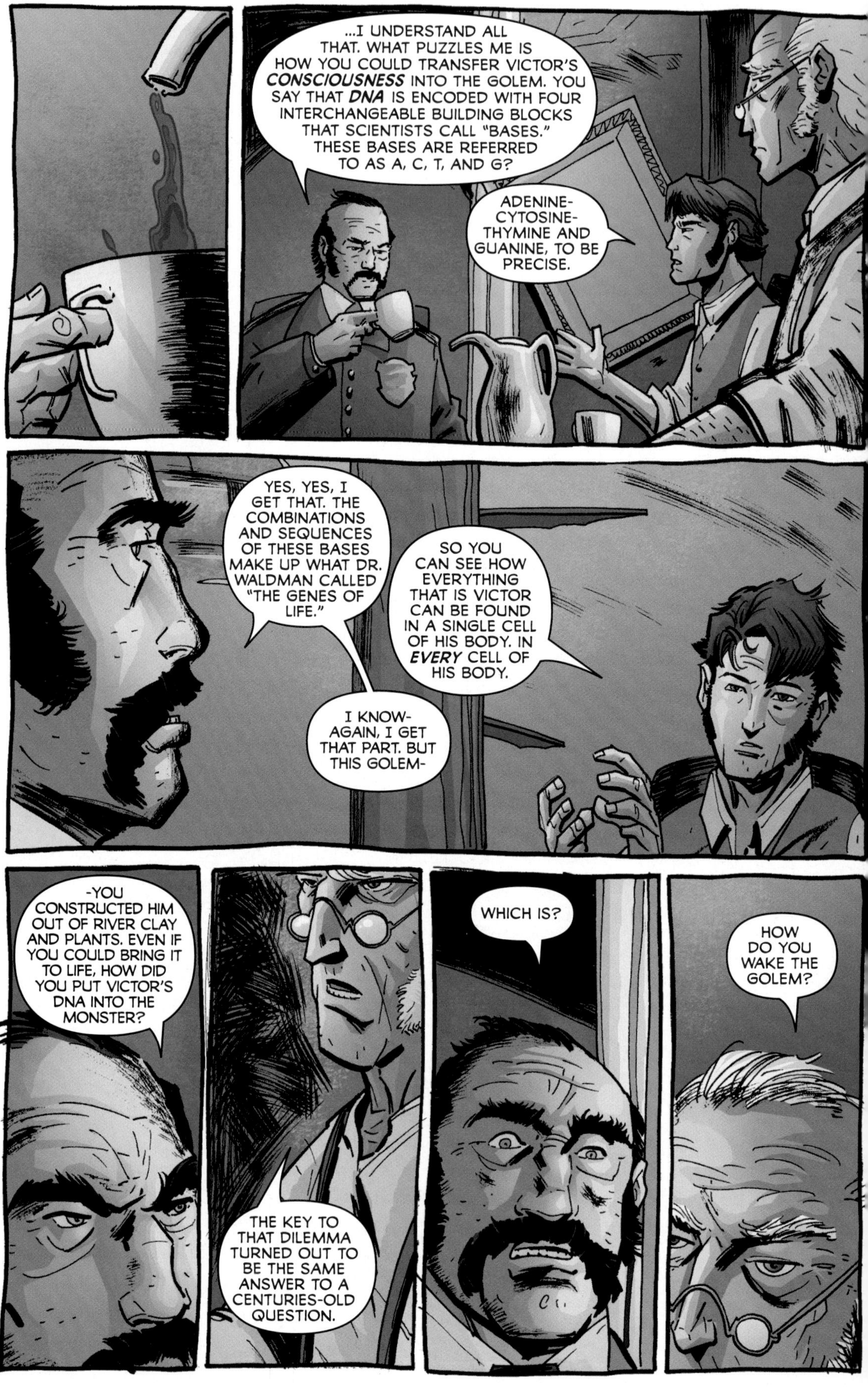

...I UNDERSTAND ALL THAT. WHAT PUZZLES ME IS HOW YOU COULD TRANSFER VICTOR'S *CONSCIOUSNESS* INTO THE GOLEM. YOU SAY THAT *DNA* IS ENCODED WITH FOUR INTERCHANGEABLE BUILDING BLOCKS THAT SCIENTISTS CALL "BASES." THESE BASES ARE REFERRED TO AS A, C, T, AND G?
ADENINE-CYTOSINE-THYMINE AND GUANINE, TO BE PRECISE.
YES, YES, I GET THAT. THE COMBINATIONS AND SEQUENCES OF THESE BASES MAKE UP WHAT DR. WALDMAN CALLED "THE GENES OF LIFE."
SO YOU CAN SEE HOW EVERYTHING THAT IS VICTOR CAN BE FOUND IN A SINGLE CELL OF HIS BODY. IN *EVERY* CELL OF HIS BODY.
I KNOW- AGAIN, I GET THAT PART. BUT THIS GOLEM-
-YOU CONSTRUCTED HIM OUT OF RIVER CLAY AND PLANTS. EVEN IF YOU COULD BRING IT TO LIFE, HOW DID YOU PUT VICTOR'S DNA INTO THE MONSTER?
THE KEY TO THAT DILEMMA TURNED OUT TO BE THE SAME ANSWER TO A CENTURIES-OLD QUESTION.
WHICH IS?
HOW DO YOU WAKE THE GOLEM?

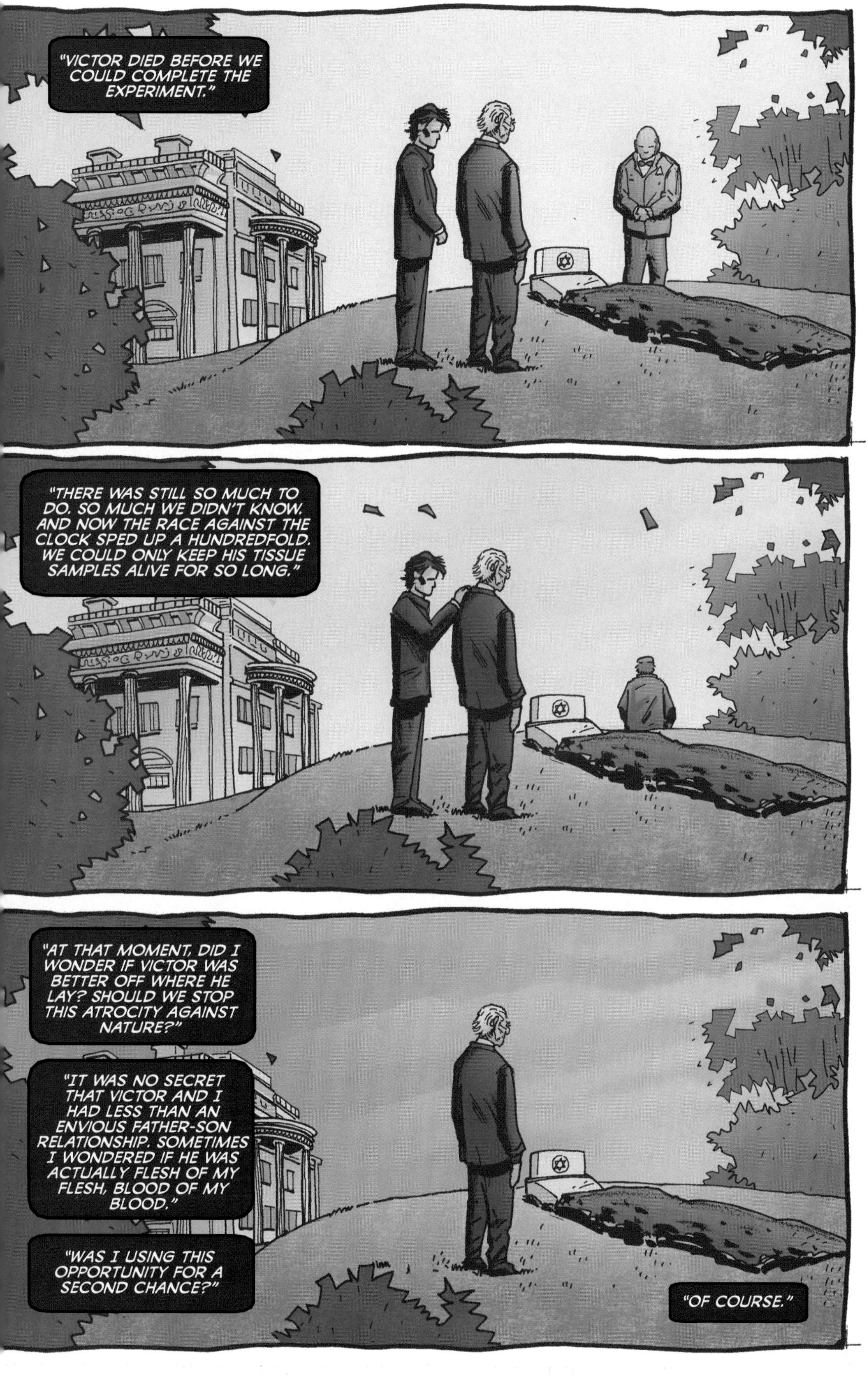
"VICTOR DIED BEFORE WE COULD COMPLETE THE EXPERIMENT."
"THERE WAS STILL SO MUCH TO DO. SO MUCH WE DIDN'T KNOW. AND NOW THE RACE AGAINST THE CLOCK SPED UP A HUNDREDFOLD. WE COULD ONLY KEEP HIS TISSUE SAMPLES ALIVE FOR SO LONG."
"AT THAT MOMENT, DID I WONDER IF VICTOR WAS BETTER OFF WHERE HE LAY? SHOULD WE STOP THIS ATROCITY AGAINST NATURE?"
"IT WAS NO SECRET THAT VICTOR AND I HAD LESS THAN AN ENVIOUS FATHER-SON RELATIONSHIP. SOMETIMES I WONDERED IF HE WAS ACTUALLY FLESH OF MY FLESH, BLOOD OF MY BLOOD."
"WAS I USING THIS OPPORTUNITY FOR A SECOND CHANCE?"
"OF COURSE."

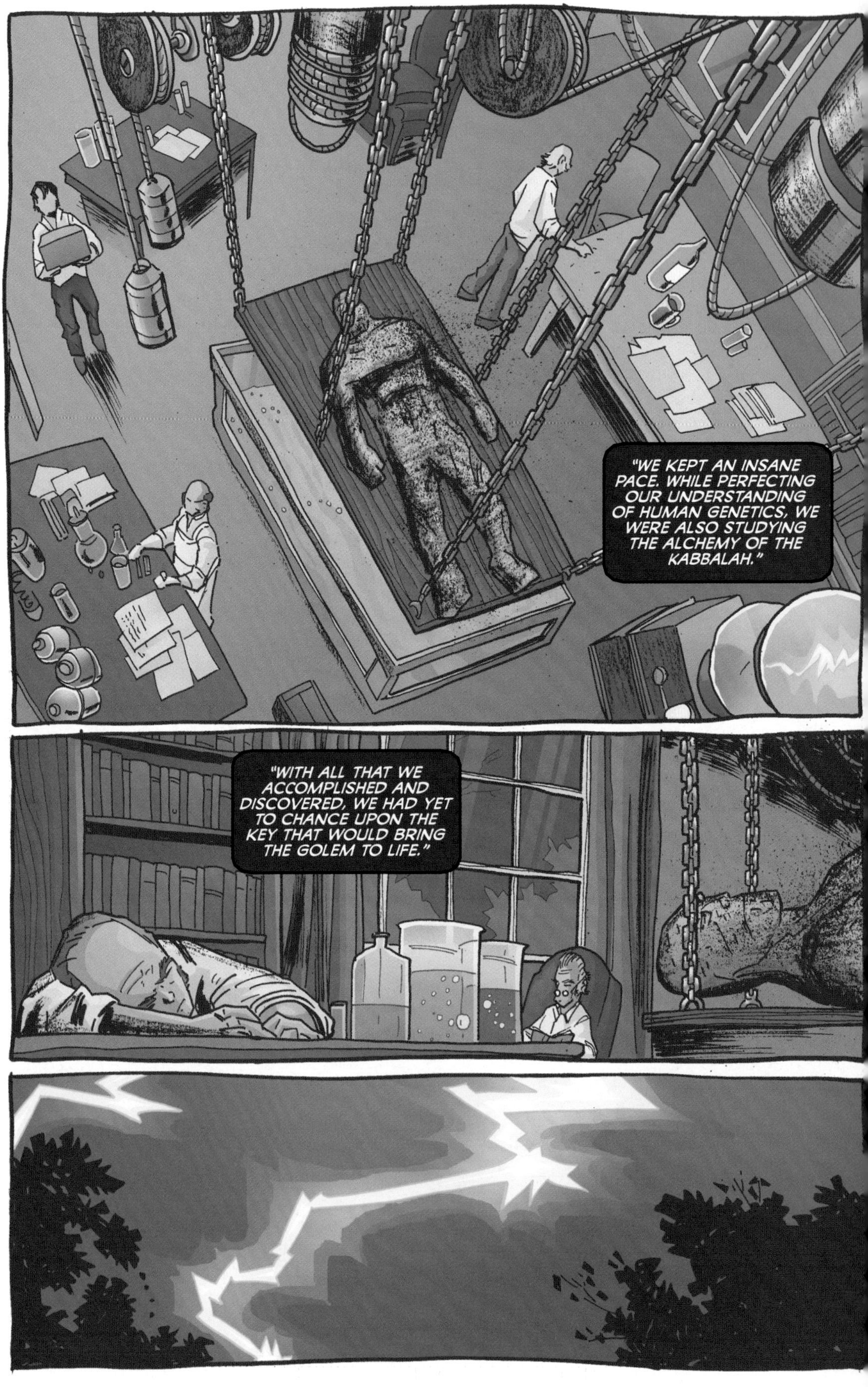
"WE KEPT AN INSANE PACE. WHILE PERFECTING OUR UNDERSTANDING OF HUMAN GENETICS, WE WERE ALSO STUDYING THE ALCHEMY OF THE KABBALAH."
"WITH ALL THAT WE ACCOMPLISHED AND DISCOVERED, WE HAD YET TO CHANCE UPON THE KEY THAT WOULD BRING THE GOLEM TO LIFE."

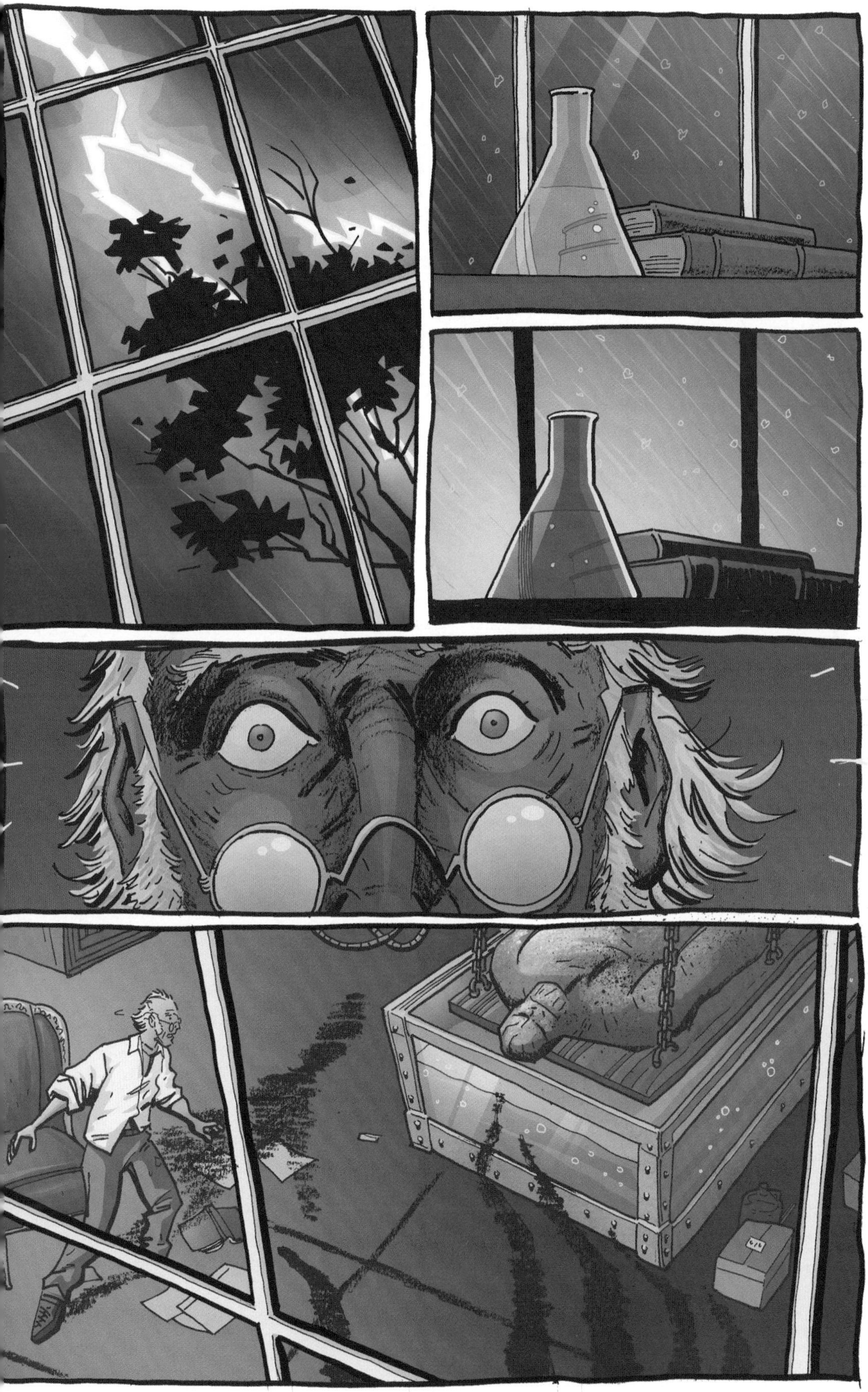

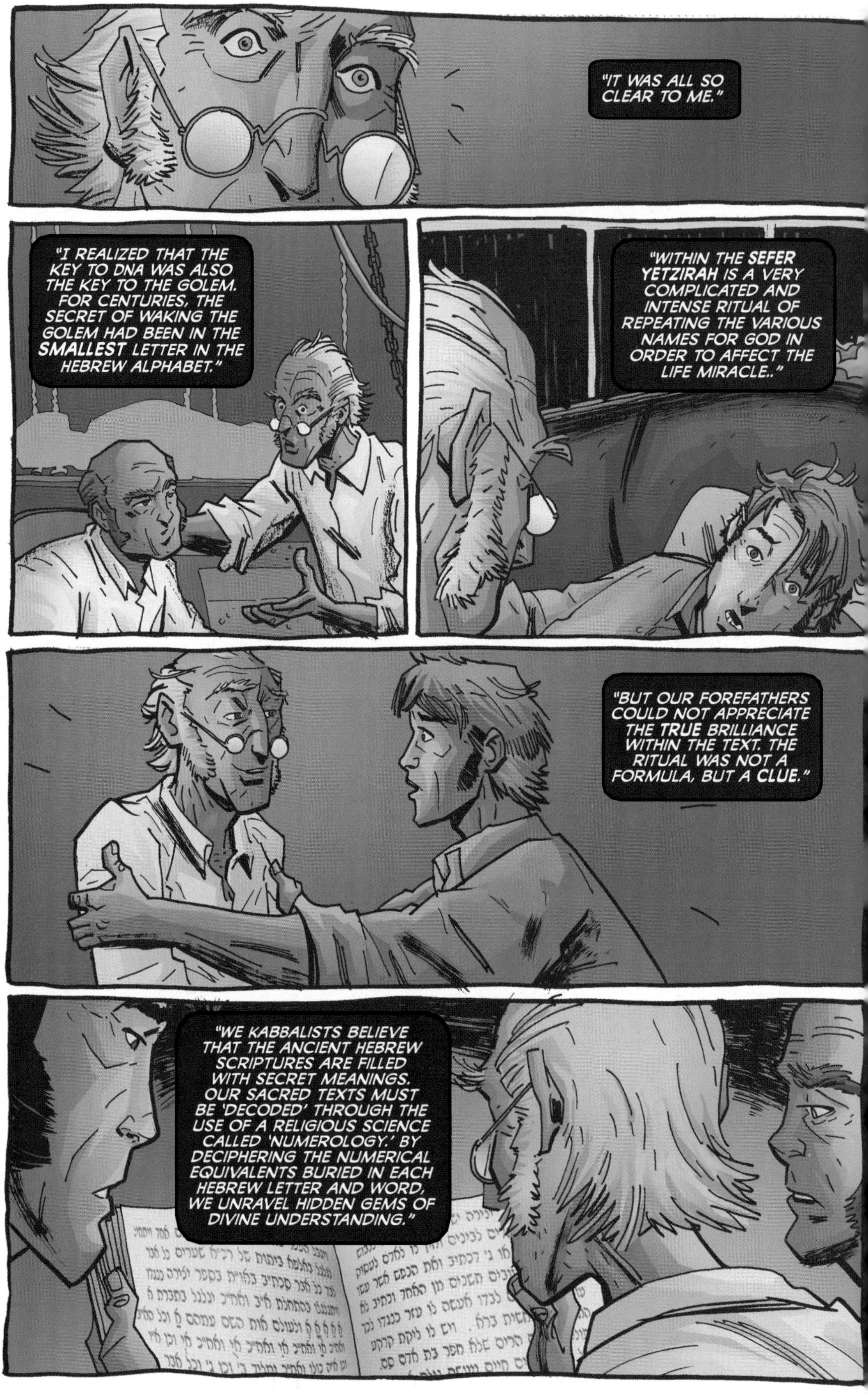
"IT WAS ALL SO CLEAR TO ME."
"I REALIZED THAT THE KEY TO DNA WAS ALSO THE KEY TO THE GOLEM. FOR CENTURIES, THE SECRET OF WAKING THE GOLEM HAD BEEN IN THE SMALLEST LETTER IN THE HEBREW ALPHABET."
"WITHIN THE SEFER YETZIRAH IS A VERY COMPLICATED AND INTENSE RITUAL OF REPEATING THE VARIOUS NAMES FOR GOD IN ORDER TO AFFECT THE LIFE MIRACLE.."
"BUT OUR FOREFATHERS COULD NOT APPRECIATE THE TRUE BRILLIANCE WITHIN THE TEXT. THE RITUAL WAS NOT A FORMULA, BUT A CLUE."
"WE KABBALISTS BELIEVE THAT THE ANCIENT HEBREW SCRIPTURES ARE FILLED WITH SECRET MEANINGS. OUR SACRED TEXTS MUST BE 'DECODED' THROUGH THE USE OF A RELIGIOUS SCIENCE CALLED 'NUMEROLOGY.' BY DECIPHERING THE NUMERICAL EQUIVALENTS BURIED IN EACH HEBREW LETTER AND WORD, WE UNRAVEL HIDDEN GEMS OF DIVINE UNDERSTANDING."

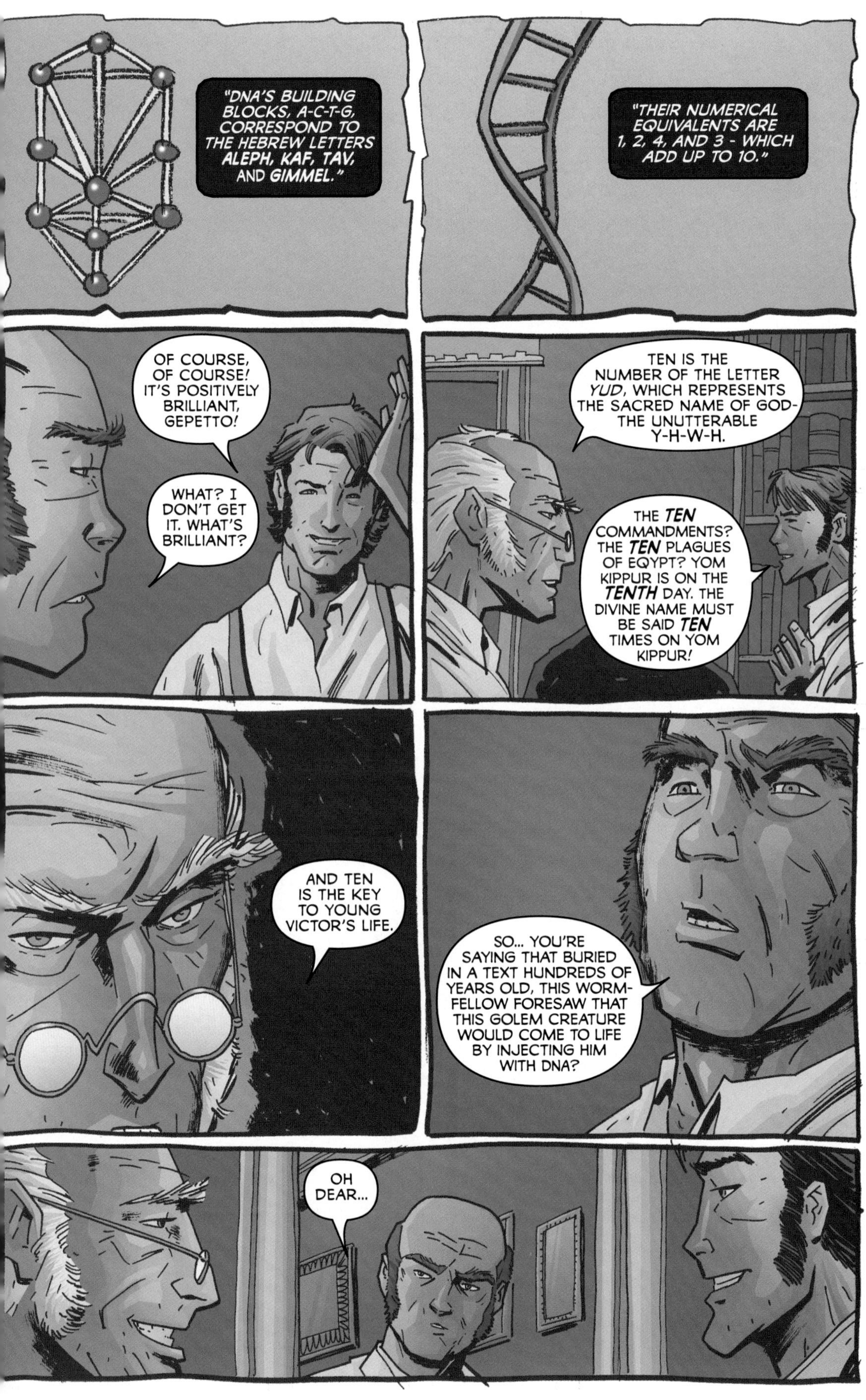
"DNA'S BUILDING BLOCKS, A-C-T-G, CORRESPOND TO THE HEBREW LETTERS ALEPH, KAF, TAV, AND GIMMEL."
"THEIR NUMERICAL EQUIVALENTS ARE 1, 2, 4, AND 3 - WHICH ADD UP TO 10."
OF COURSE, OF COURSE! IT'S POSITIVELY BRILLIANT, GEPETTO!
WHAT? I DON'T GET IT. WHAT'S BRILLIANT?
TEN IS THE NUMBER OF THE LETTER YUD, WHICH REPRESENTS THE SACRED NAME OF GOD- THE UNUTTERABLE Y-H-W-H.
THE TEN COMMANDMENTS? THE TEN PLAGUES OF EQYPT? YOM KIPPUR IS ON THE TENTH DAY. THE DIVINE NAME MUST BE SAID TEN TIMES ON YOM KIPPUR!
AND TEN IS THE KEY TO YOUNG VICTOR'S LIFE.
SO... YOU'RE SAYING THAT BURIED IN A TEXT HUNDREDS OF YEARS OLD, THIS WORM-FELLOW FORESAW THAT THIS GOLEM CREATURE WOULD COME TO LIFE BY INJECTING HIM WITH DNA?
OH DEAR...

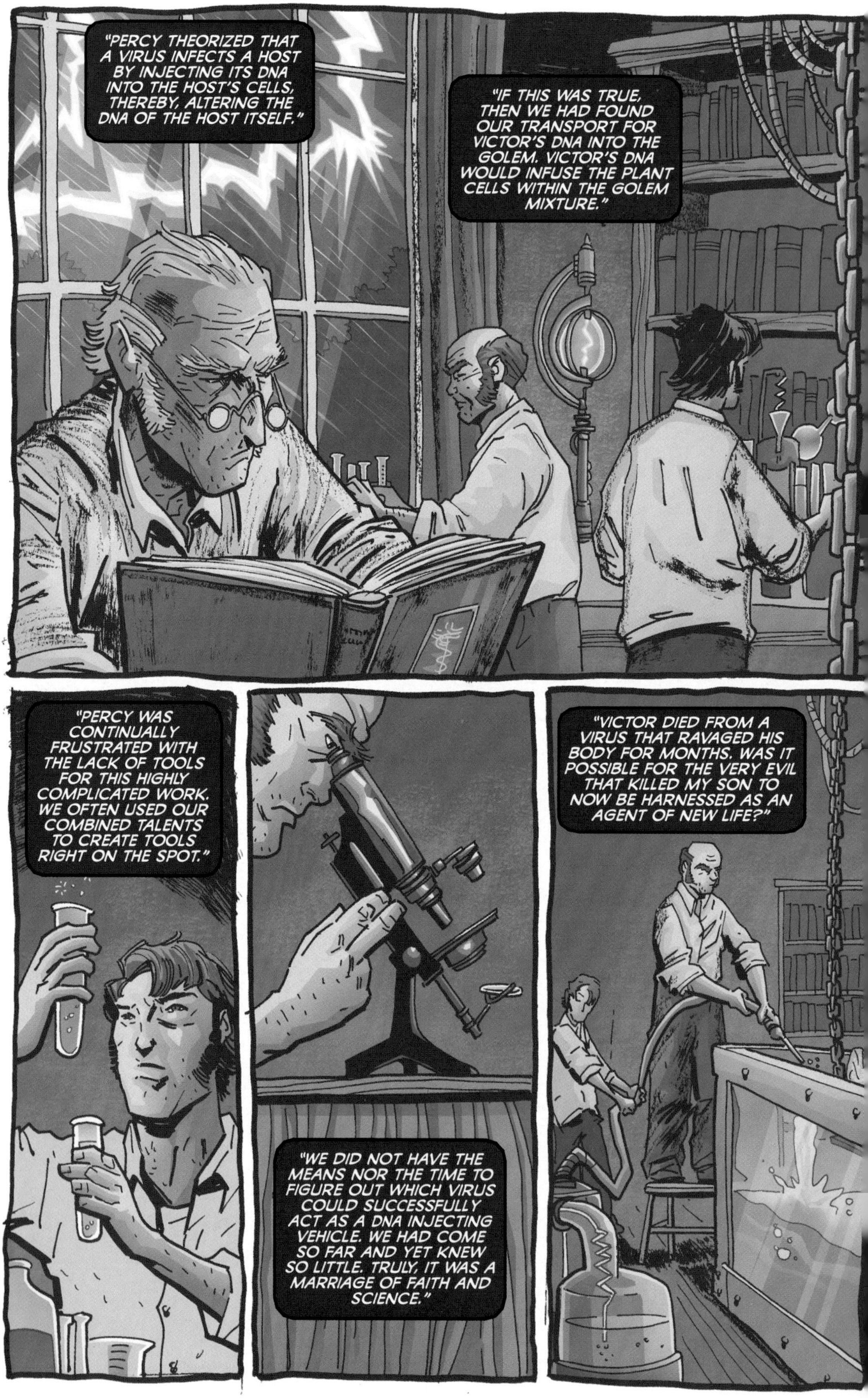
"PERCY THEORIZED THAT A VIRUS INFECTS A HOST BY INJECTING ITS DNA INTO THE HOST'S CELLS, THEREBY, ALTERING THE DNA OF THE HOST ITSELF."
"IF THIS WAS TRUE, THEN WE HAD FOUND OUR TRANSPORT FOR VICTOR'S DNA INTO THE GOLEM. VICTOR'S DNA WOULD INFUSE THE PLANT CELLS WITHIN THE GOLEM MIXTURE."
"PERCY WAS CONTINUALLY FRUSTRATED WITH THE LACK OF TOOLS FOR THIS HIGHLY COMPLICATED WORK. WE OFTEN USED OUR COMBINED TALENTS TO CREATE TOOLS RIGHT ON THE SPOT."
"WE DID NOT HAVE THE MEANS NOR THE TIME TO FIGURE OUT WHICH VIRUS COULD SUCCESSFULLY ACT AS A DNA INJECTING VEHICLE. WE HAD COME SO FAR AND YET KNEW SO LITTLE. TRULY, IT WAS A MARRIAGE OF FAITH AND SCIENCE."
"VICTOR DIED FROM A VIRUS THAT RAVAGED HIS BODY FOR MONTHS. WAS IT POSSIBLE FOR THE VERY EVIL THAT KILLED MY SON TO NOW BE HARNESSED AS AN AGENT OF NEW LIFE?"

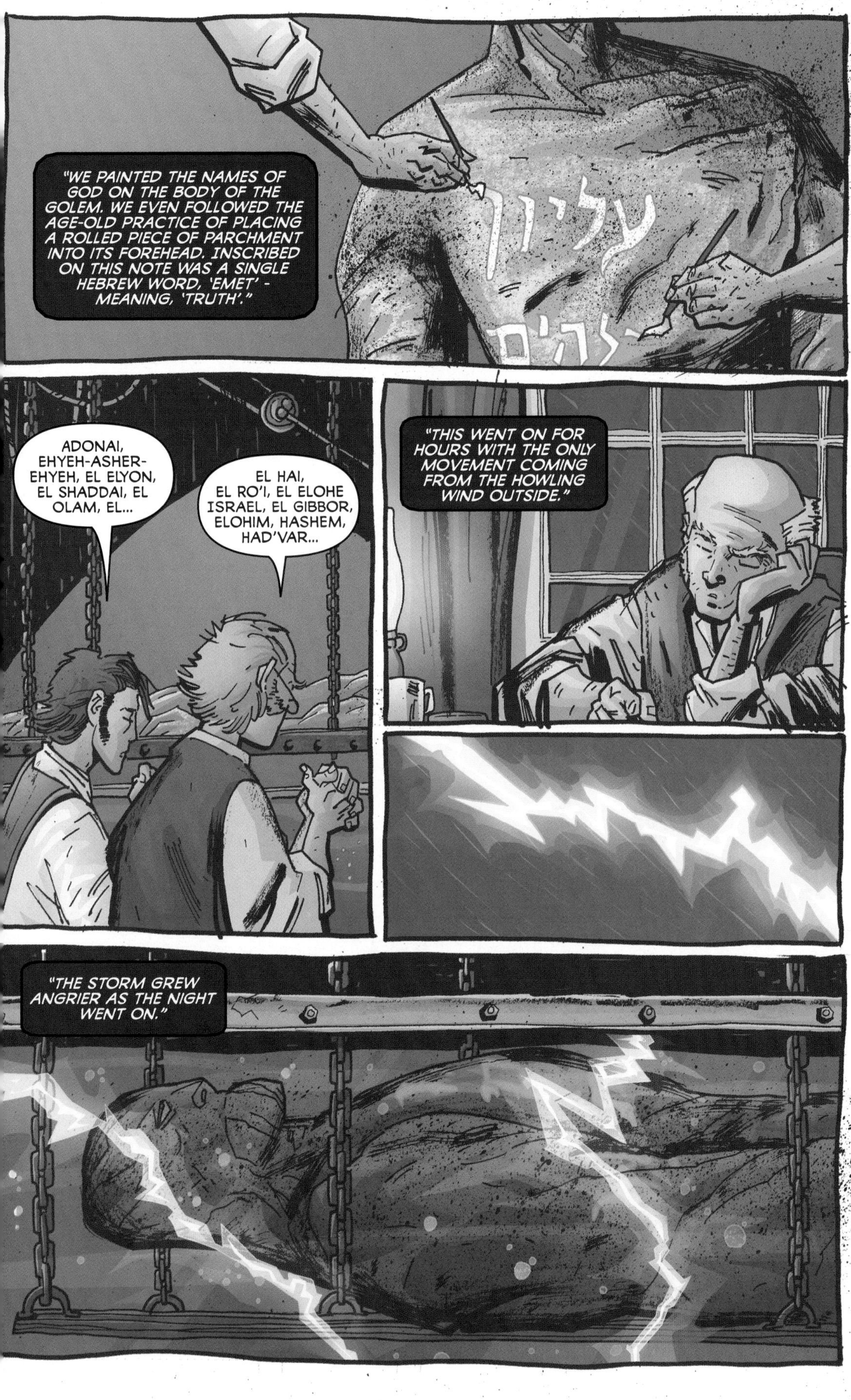
"WE PAINTED THE NAMES OF GOD ON THE BODY OF THE GOLEM. WE EVEN FOLLOWED THE AGE-OLD PRACTICE OF PLACING A ROLLED PIECE OF PARCHMENT INTO ITS FOREHEAD. INSCRIBED ON THIS NOTE WAS A SINGLE HEBREW WORD, 'EMET' - MEANING, 'TRUTH'."
עליון
ADONAI, EHYEH-ASHER-EHYEH, EL ELYON, EL SHADDAI, EL OLAM, EL...
EL HAI, EL RO'I, EL ELOHE ISRAEL, EL GIBBOR, ELOHIM, HASHEM, HAD'VAR...
"THIS WENT ON FOR HOURS WITH THE ONLY MOVEMENT COMING FROM THE HOWLING WIND OUTSIDE."
"THE STORM GREW ANGRIER AS THE NIGHT WENT ON."

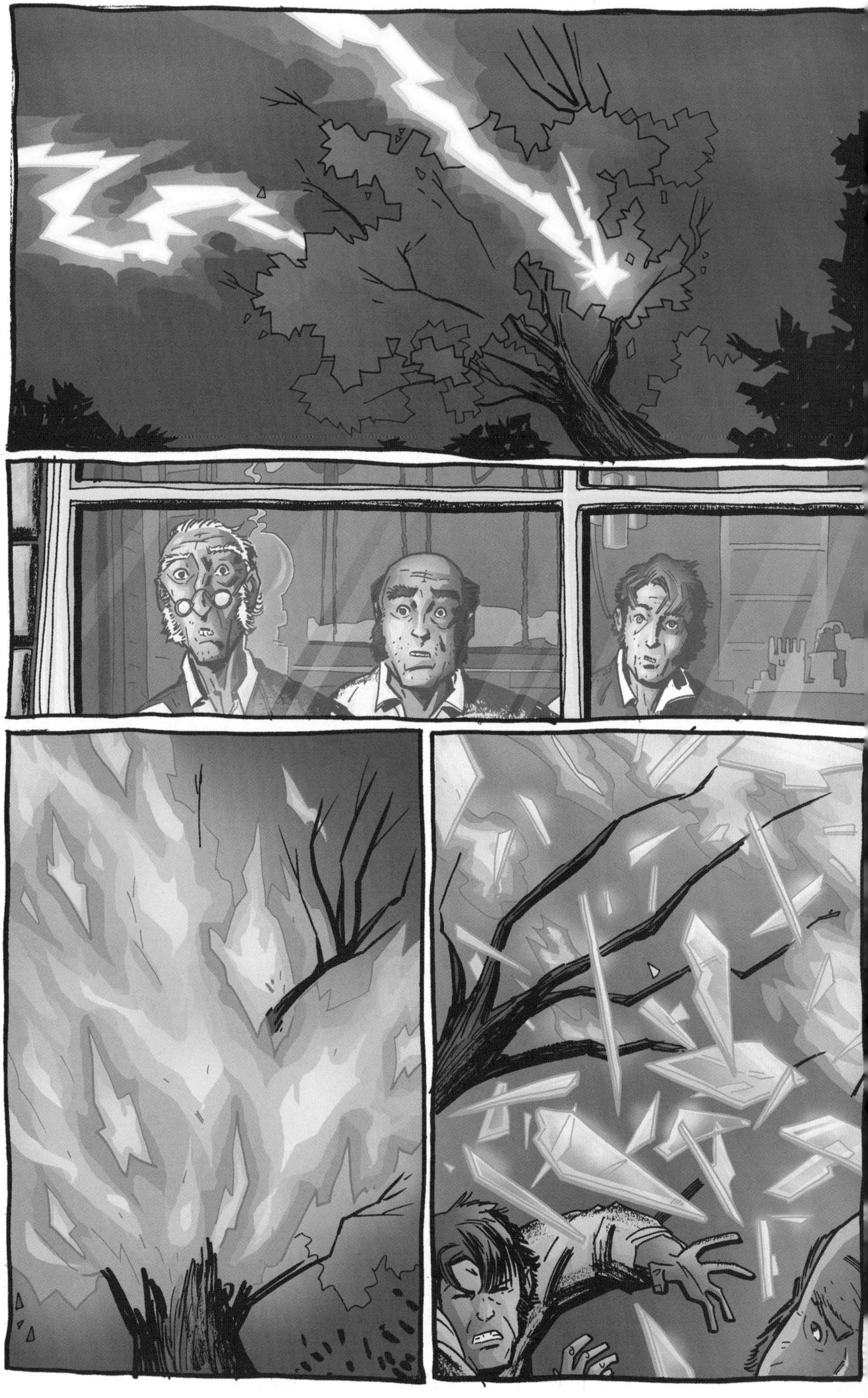

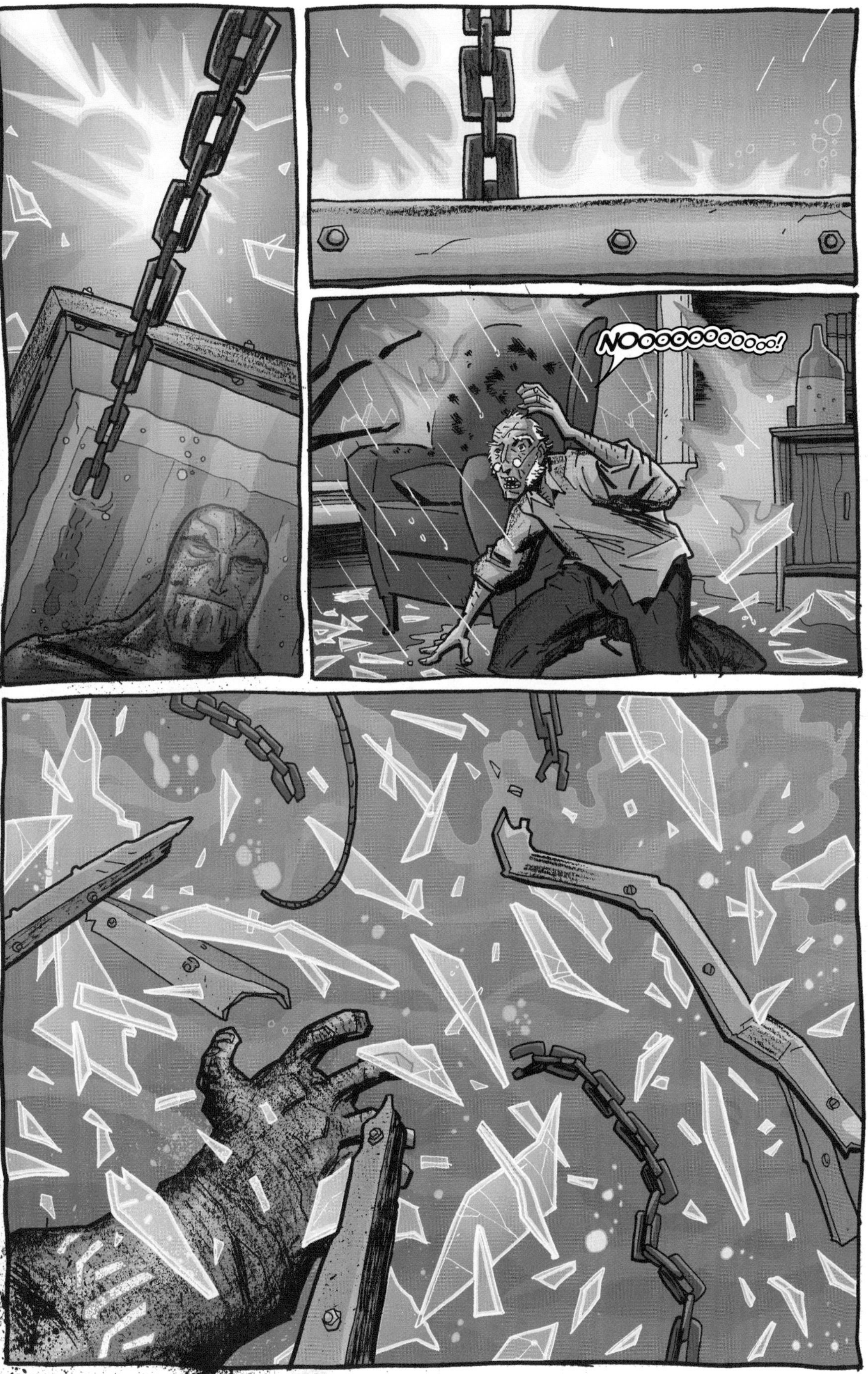
NOooooooooooo!

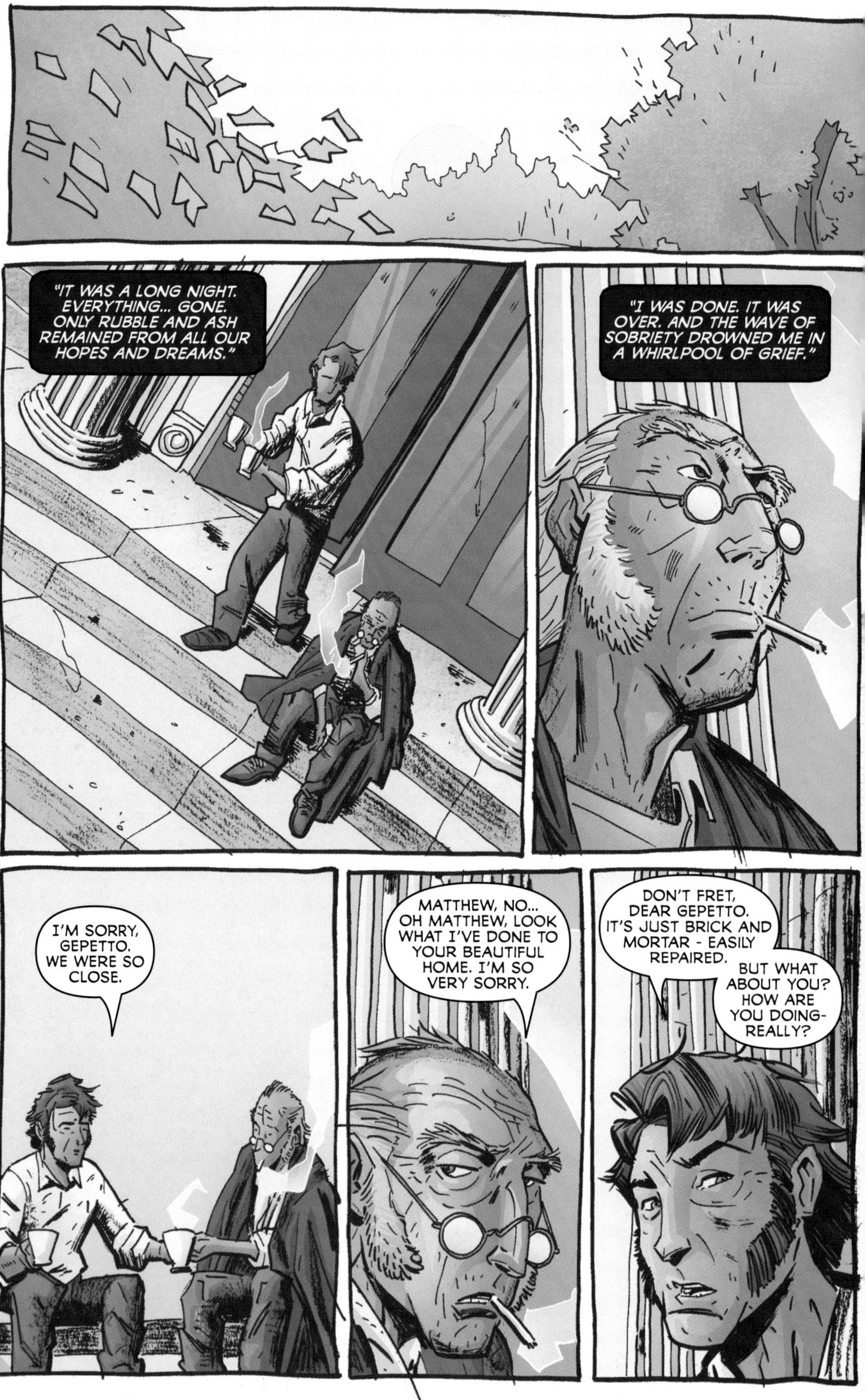
"IT WAS A LONG NIGHT. EVERYTHING... GONE. ONLY RUBBLE AND ASH REMAINED FROM ALL OUR HOPES AND DREAMS."
"I WAS DONE. IT WAS OVER. AND THE WAVE OF SOBRIETY DROWNED ME IN A WHIRLPOOL OF GRIEF."
I'M SORRY, GEPETTO. WE WERE SO CLOSE.
MATTHEW, NO... OH MATTHEW, LOOK WHAT I'VE DONE TO YOUR BEAUTIFUL HOME. I'M SO VERY SORRY.
DON'T FRET, DEAR GEPETTO. IT'S JUST BRICK AND MORTAR - EASILY REPAIRED.
BUT WHAT ABOUT YOU? HOW ARE YOU DOING-REALLY?

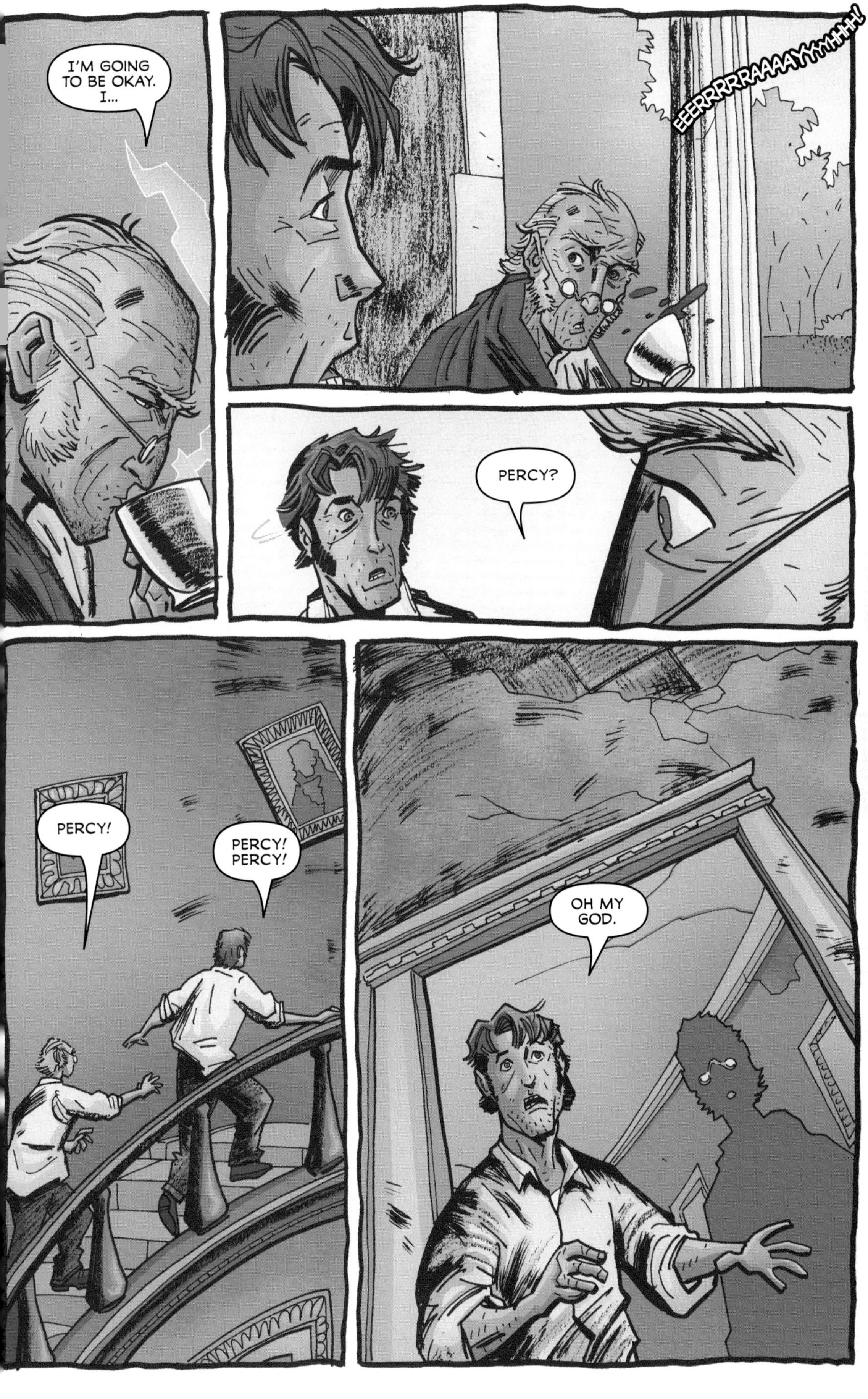
I'M GOING TO BE OKAY. I...
EEERRRRRAAAAYYYHHH!
PERCY?
PERCY!
PERCY! PERCY!
OH MY GOD.

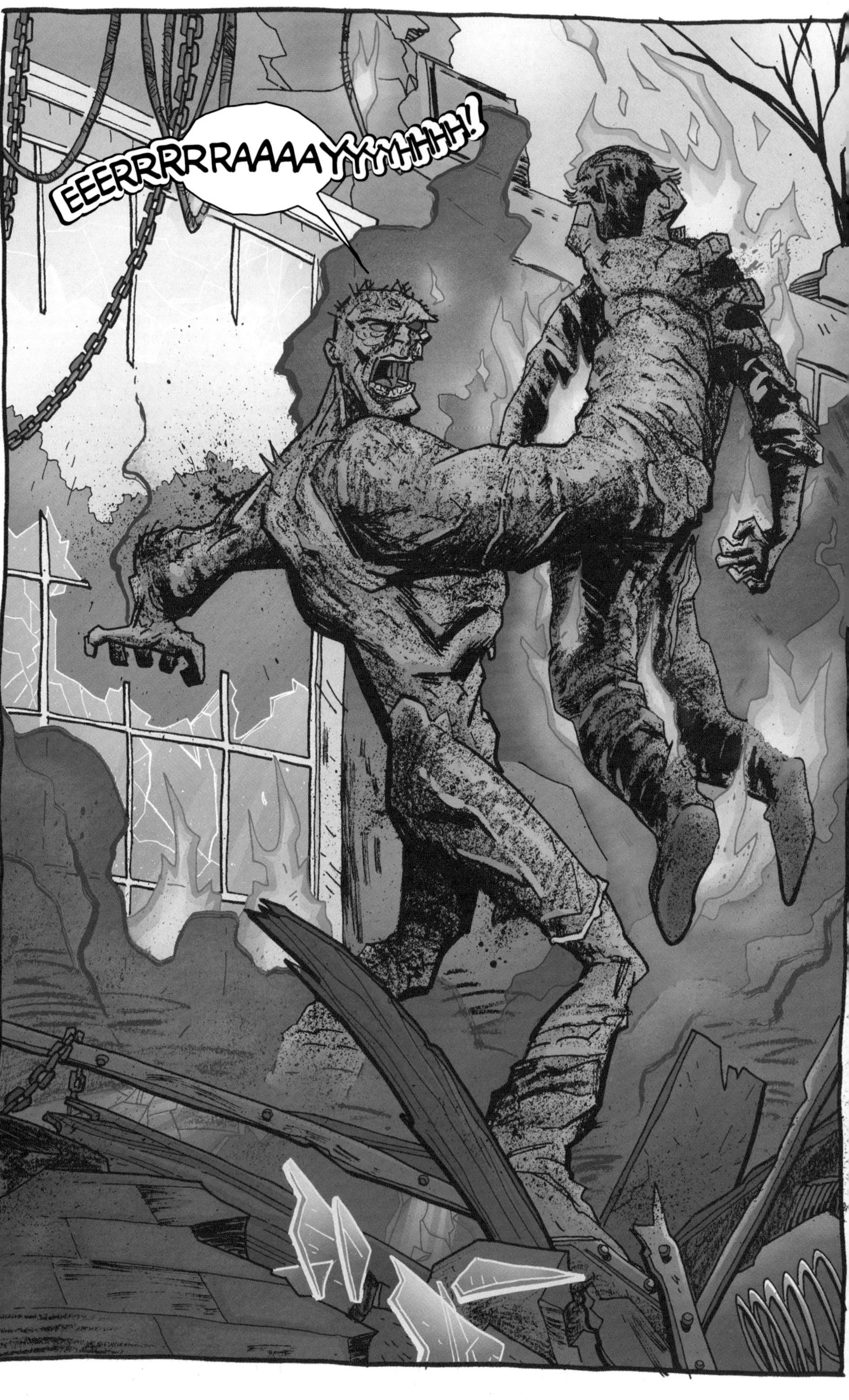
EEERRRRRRAAAAAYYYYHHHH!

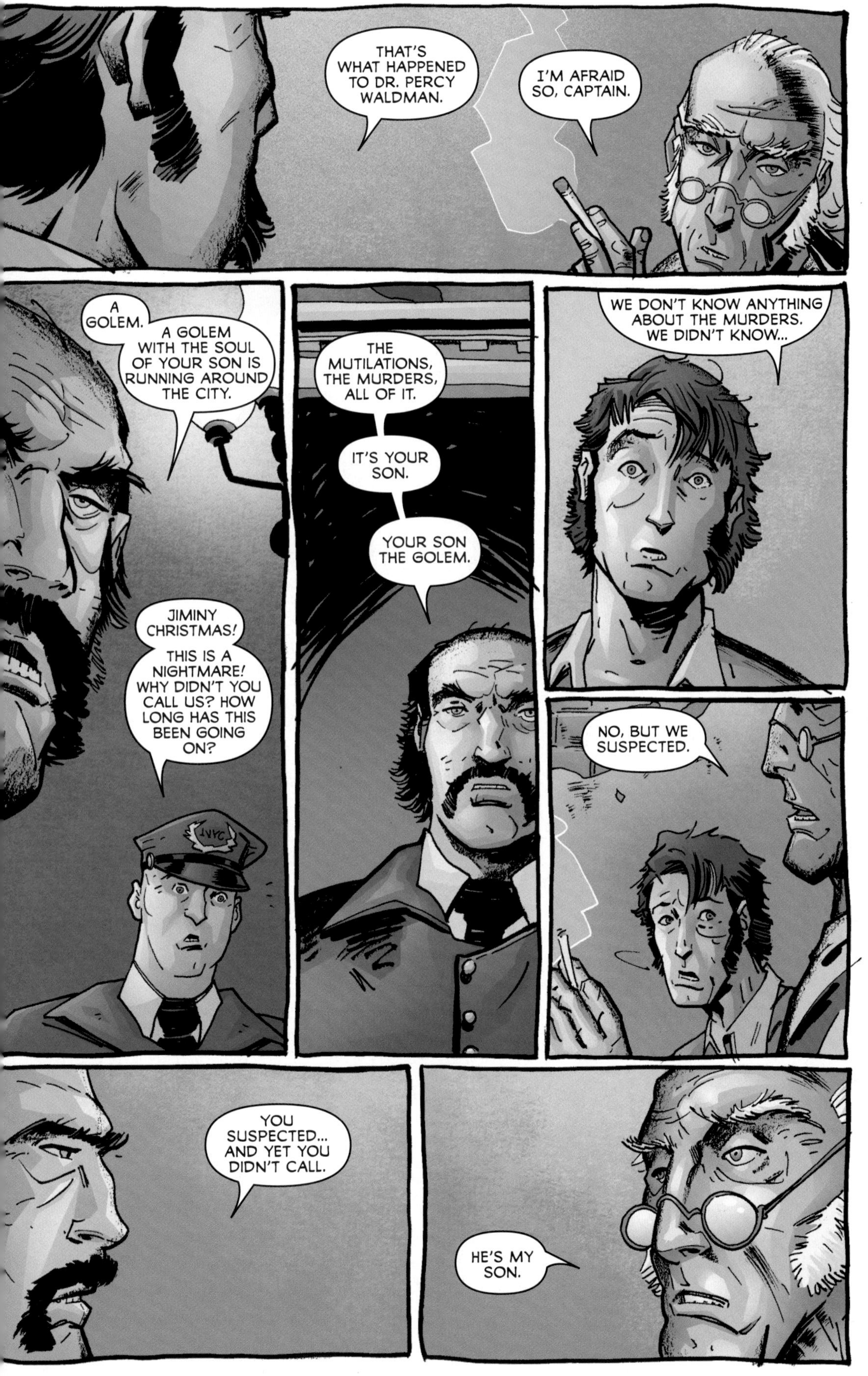
THAT'S WHAT HAPPENED TO DR. PERCY WALDMAN.
I'M AFRAID SO, CAPTAIN.
A GOLEM.
A GOLEM WITH THE SOUL OF YOUR SON IS RUNNING AROUND THE CITY.
JIMINY CHRISTMAS!
THIS IS A NIGHTMARE! WHY DIDN'T YOU CALL US? HOW LONG HAS THIS BEEN GOING ON?
THE MUTILATIONS, THE MURDERS, ALL OF IT.
IT'S YOUR SON.
YOUR SON THE GOLEM.
WE DON'T KNOW ANYTHING ABOUT THE MURDERS. WE DIDN'T KNOW...
NO, BUT WE SUSPECTED.
YOU SUSPECTED... AND YET YOU DIDN'T CALL.
HE'S MY SON.

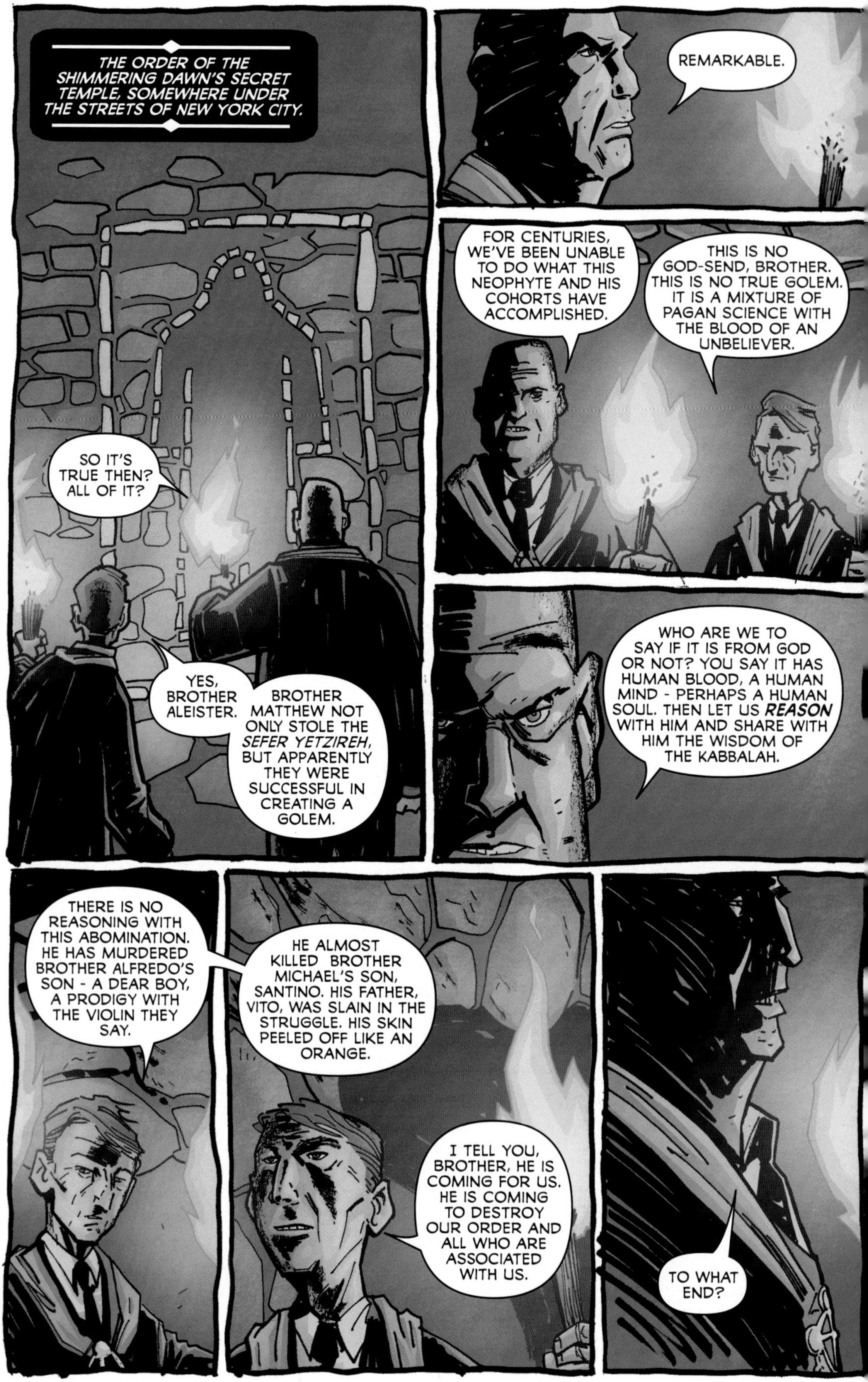
THE ORDER OF THE SHIMMERING DAWN'S SECRET TEMPLE, SOMEWHERE UNDER THE STREETS OF NEW YORK CITY.
SO IT'S TRUE THEN? ALL OF IT?
YES, BROTHER ALEISTER.
BROTHER MATTHEW NOT ONLY STOLE THE *SEFER YETZIREH*, BUT APPARENTLY THEY WERE SUCCESSFUL IN CREATING A GOLEM.
REMARKABLE.
FOR CENTURIES, WE'VE BEEN UNABLE TO DO WHAT THIS NEOPHYTE AND HIS COHORTS HAVE ACCOMPLISHED.
THIS IS NO GOD-SEND, BROTHER. THIS IS NO TRUE GOLEM. IT IS A MIXTURE OF PAGAN SCIENCE WITH THE BLOOD OF AN UNBELIEVER.
WHO ARE WE TO SAY IF IT IS FROM GOD OR NOT? YOU SAY IT HAS HUMAN BLOOD, A HUMAN MIND - PERHAPS A HUMAN SOUL. THEN LET US ***REASON*** WITH HIM AND SHARE WITH HIM THE WISDOM OF THE KABBALAH.
THERE IS NO REASONING WITH THIS ABOMINATION. HE HAS MURDERED BROTHER ALFREDO'S SON - A DEAR BOY, A PRODIGY WITH THE VIOLIN THEY SAY.
HE ALMOST KILLED BROTHER MICHAEL'S SON, SANTINO. HIS FATHER, VITO, WAS SLAIN IN THE STRUGGLE. HIS SKIN PEELED OFF LIKE AN ORANGE.
I TELL YOU, BROTHER, HE IS COMING FOR US. HE IS COMING TO DESTROY OUR ORDER AND ALL WHO ARE ASSOCIATED WITH US.
TO WHAT END?

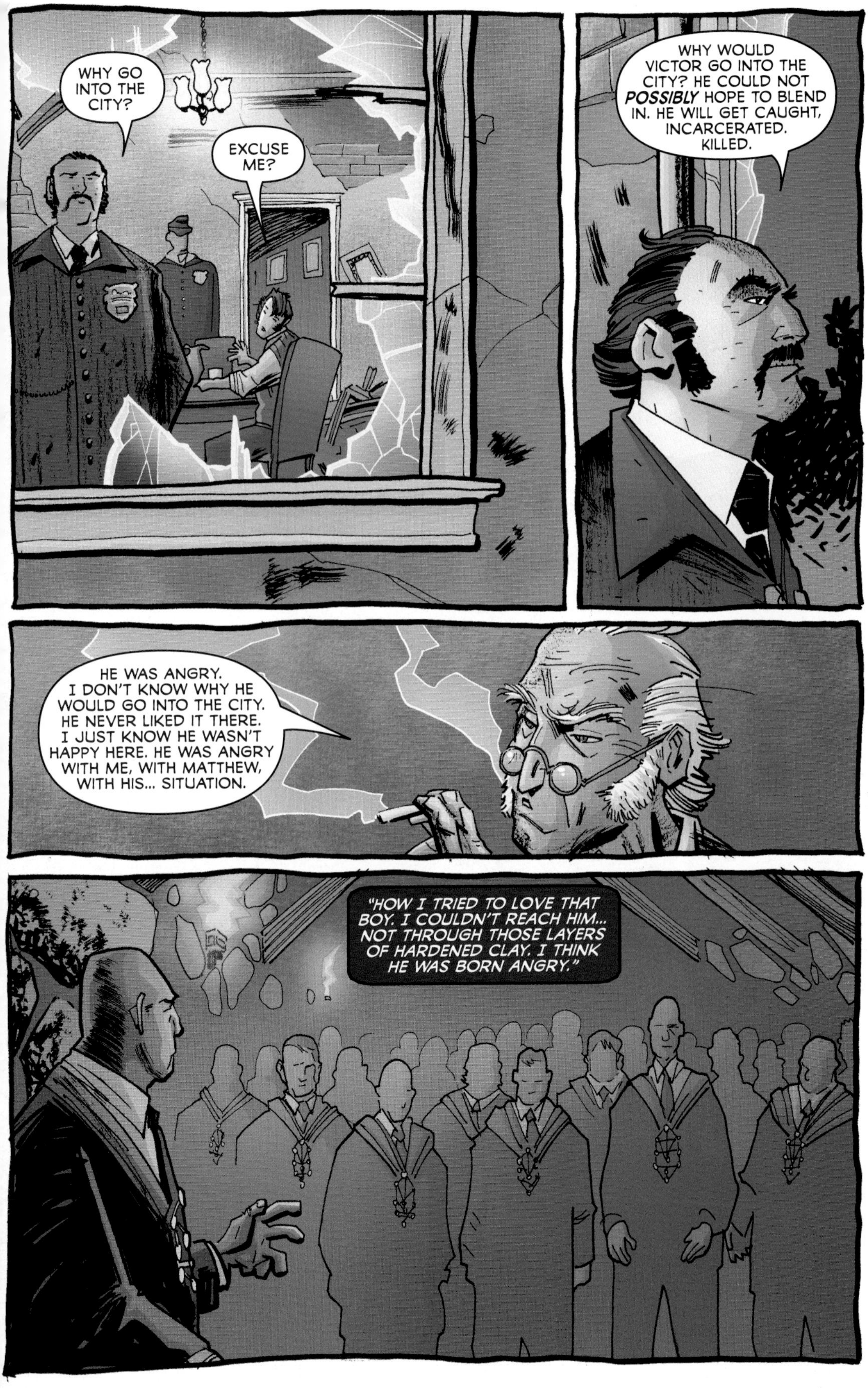
WHY GO INTO THE CITY?
EXCUSE ME?
WHY WOULD VICTOR GO INTO THE CITY? HE COULD NOT POSSIBLY HOPE TO BLEND IN. HE WILL GET CAUGHT, INCARCERATED. KILLED.
HE WAS ANGRY. I DON'T KNOW WHY HE WOULD GO INTO THE CITY. HE NEVER LIKED IT THERE. I JUST KNOW HE WASN'T HAPPY HERE. HE WAS ANGRY WITH ME, WITH MATTHEW, WITH HIS... SITUATION.
"HOW I TRIED TO LOVE THAT BOY. I COULDN'T REACH HIM... NOT THROUGH THOSE LAYERS OF HARDENED CLAY. I THINK HE WAS BORN ANGRY."

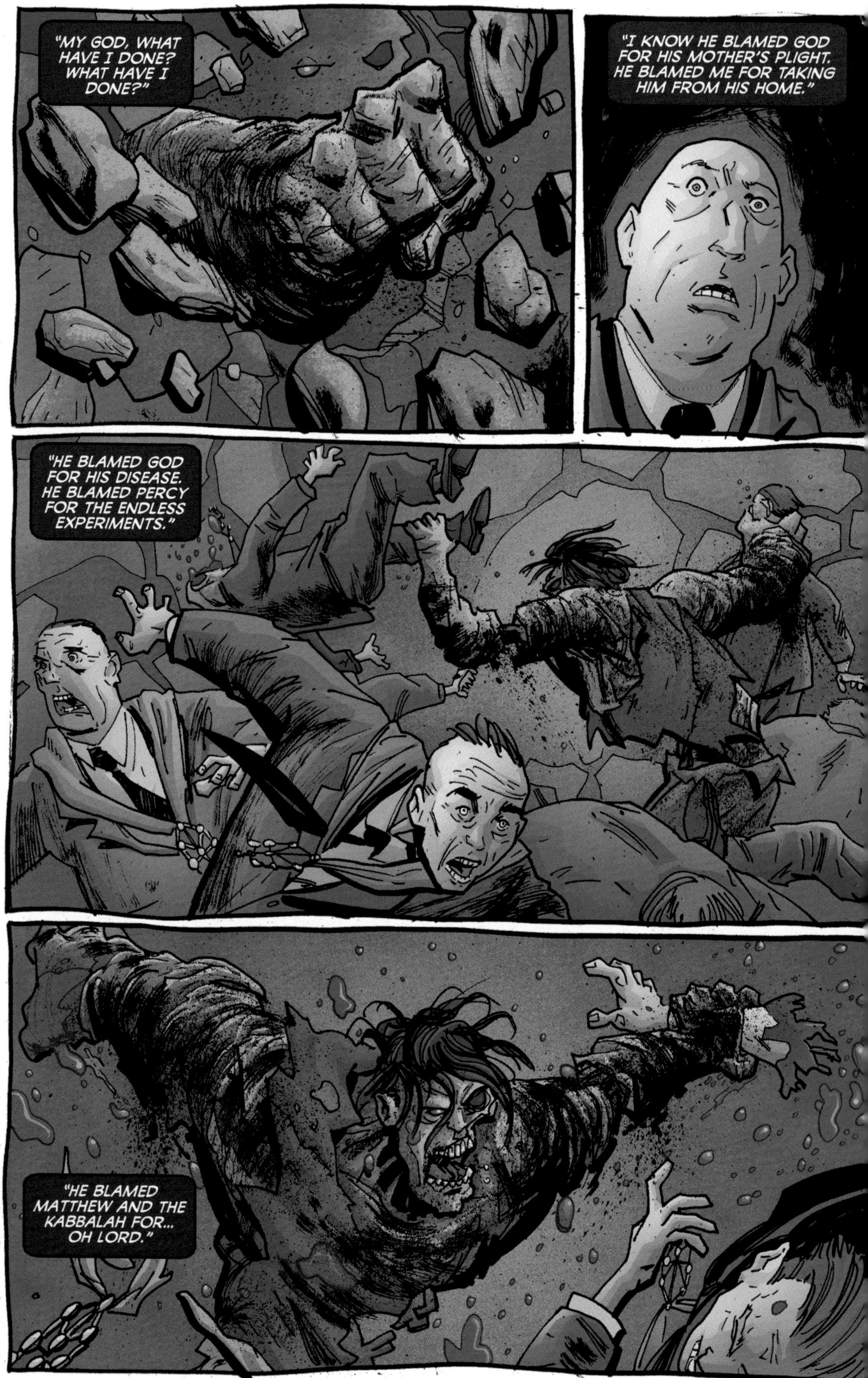
"MY GOD, WHAT HAVE I DONE? WHAT HAVE I DONE?"
"I KNOW HE BLAMED GOD FOR HIS MOTHER'S PLIGHT. HE BLAMED ME FOR TAKING HIM FROM HIS HOME."
"HE BLAMED GOD FOR HIS DISEASE. HE BLAMED PERCY FOR THE ENDLESS EXPERIMENTS."
"HE BLAMED MATTHEW AND THE KABBALAH FOR... OH LORD."

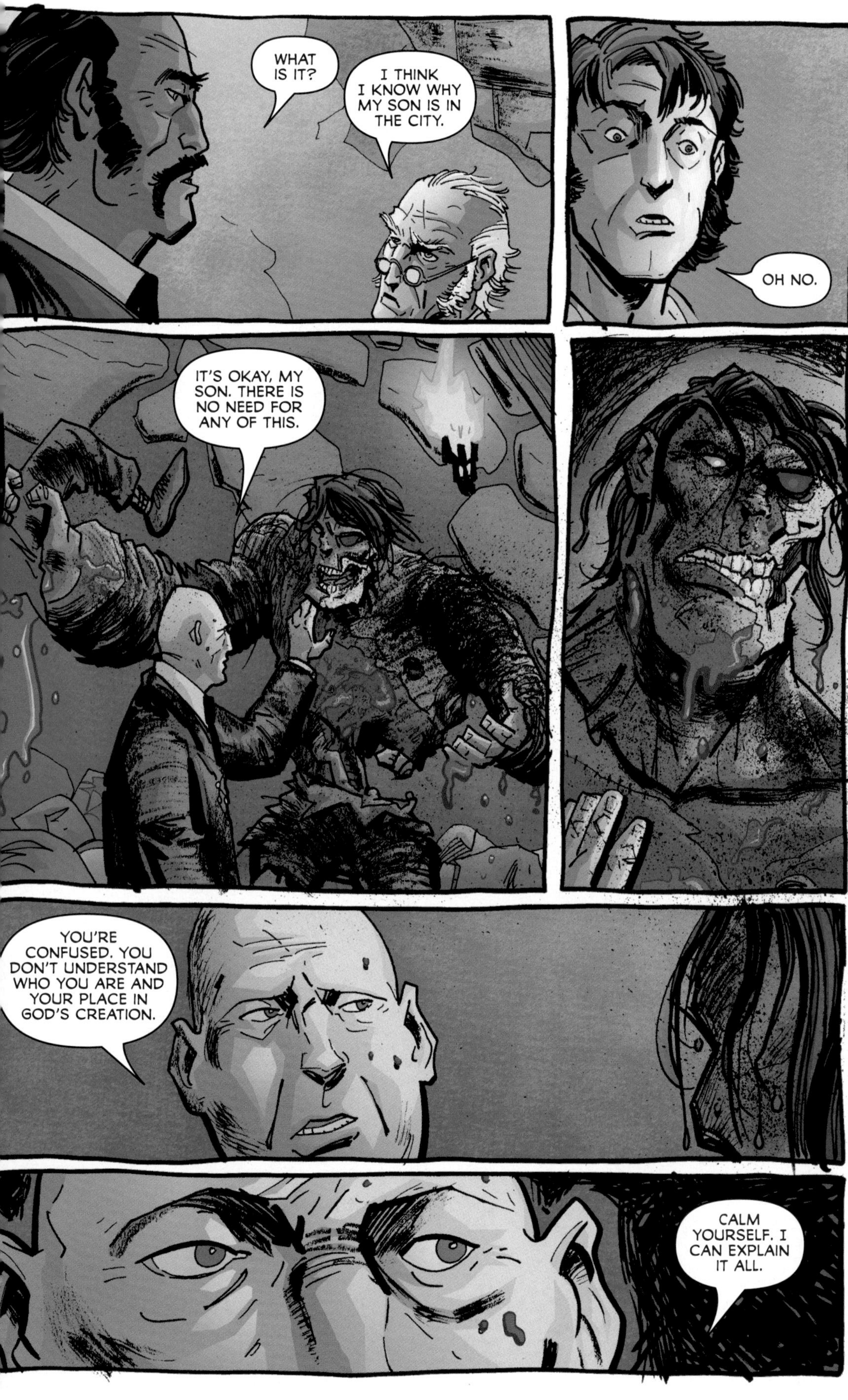
WHAT IS IT?
I THINK I KNOW WHY MY SON IS IN THE CITY.
OH NO.
IT'S OKAY, MY SON. THERE IS NO NEED FOR ANY OF THIS.
YOU'RE CONFUSED. YOU DON'T UNDERSTAND WHO YOU ARE AND YOUR PLACE IN GOD'S CREATION.
CALM YOURSELF. I CAN EXPLAIN IT ALL.

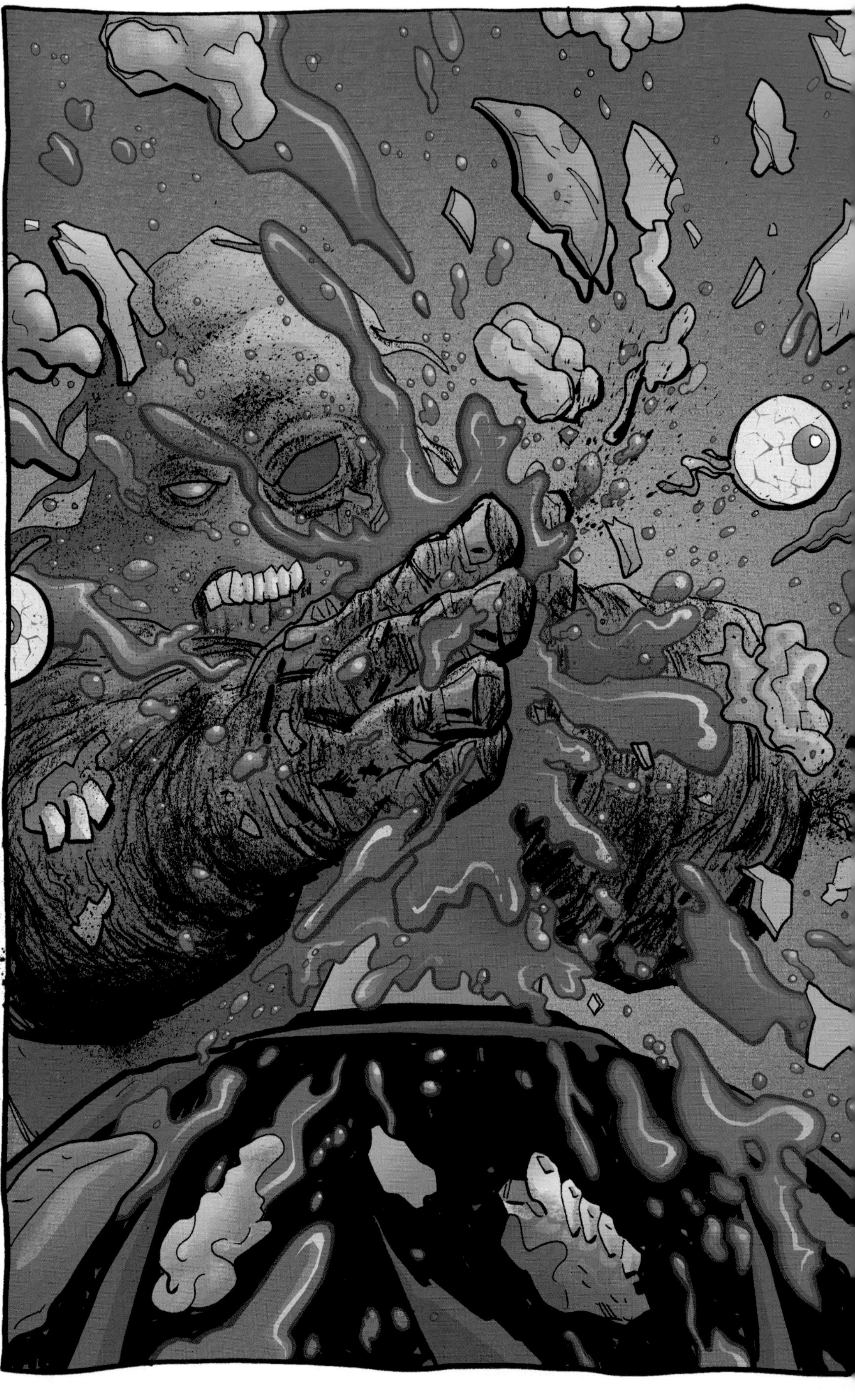

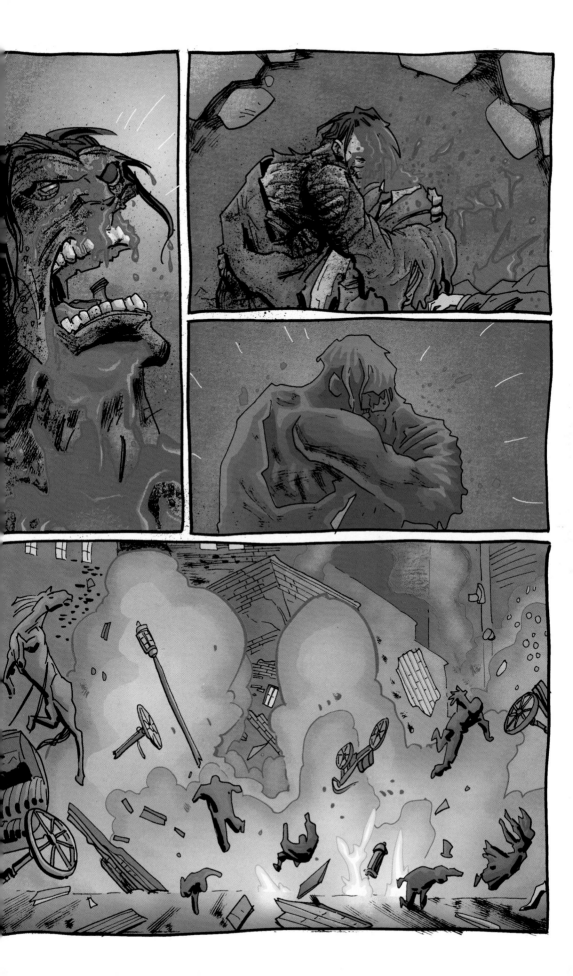

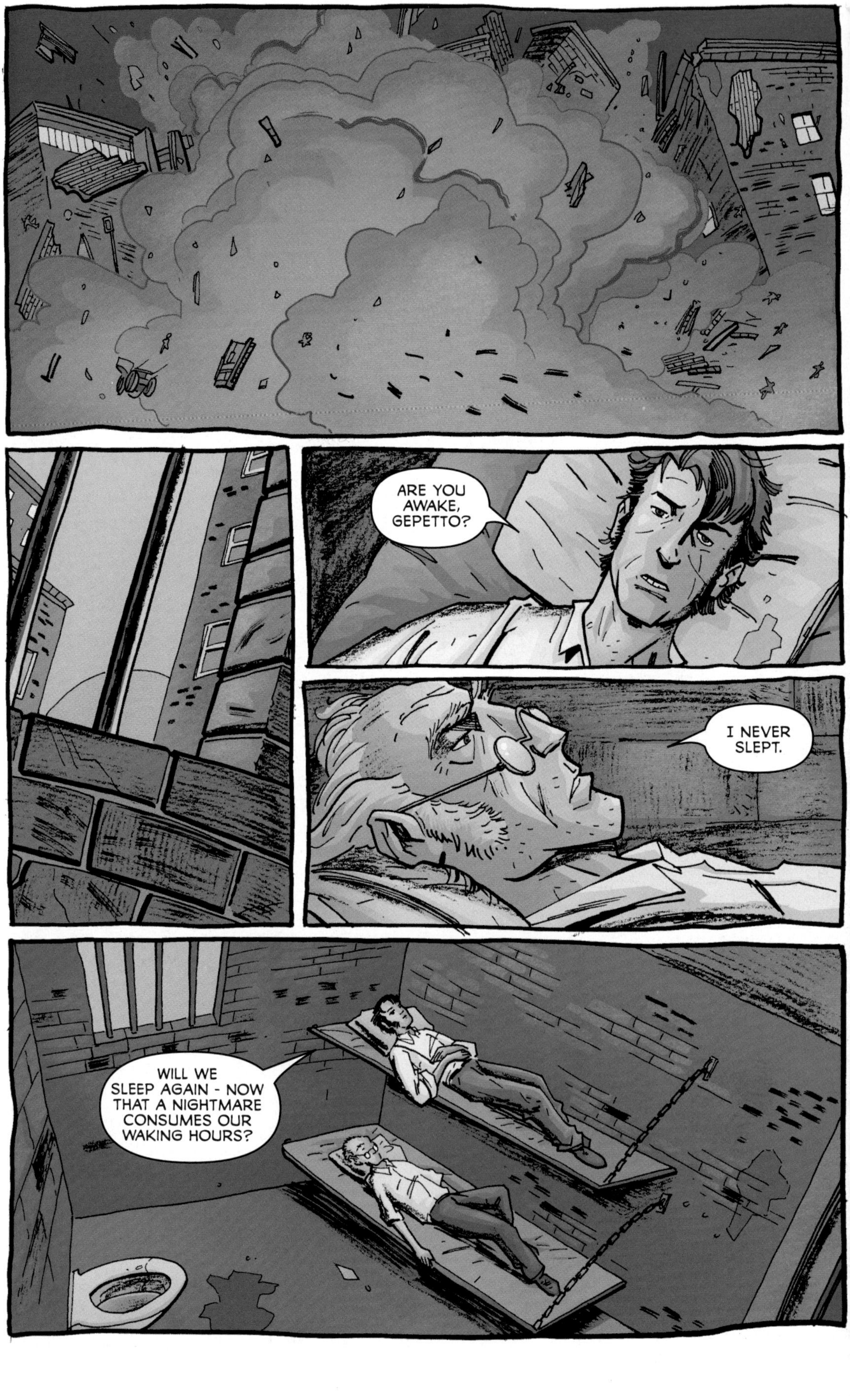
ARE YOU AWAKE, GEPETTO?
I NEVER SLEPT.
WILL WE SLEEP AGAIN - NOW THAT A NIGHTMARE CONSUMES OUR WAKING HOURS?

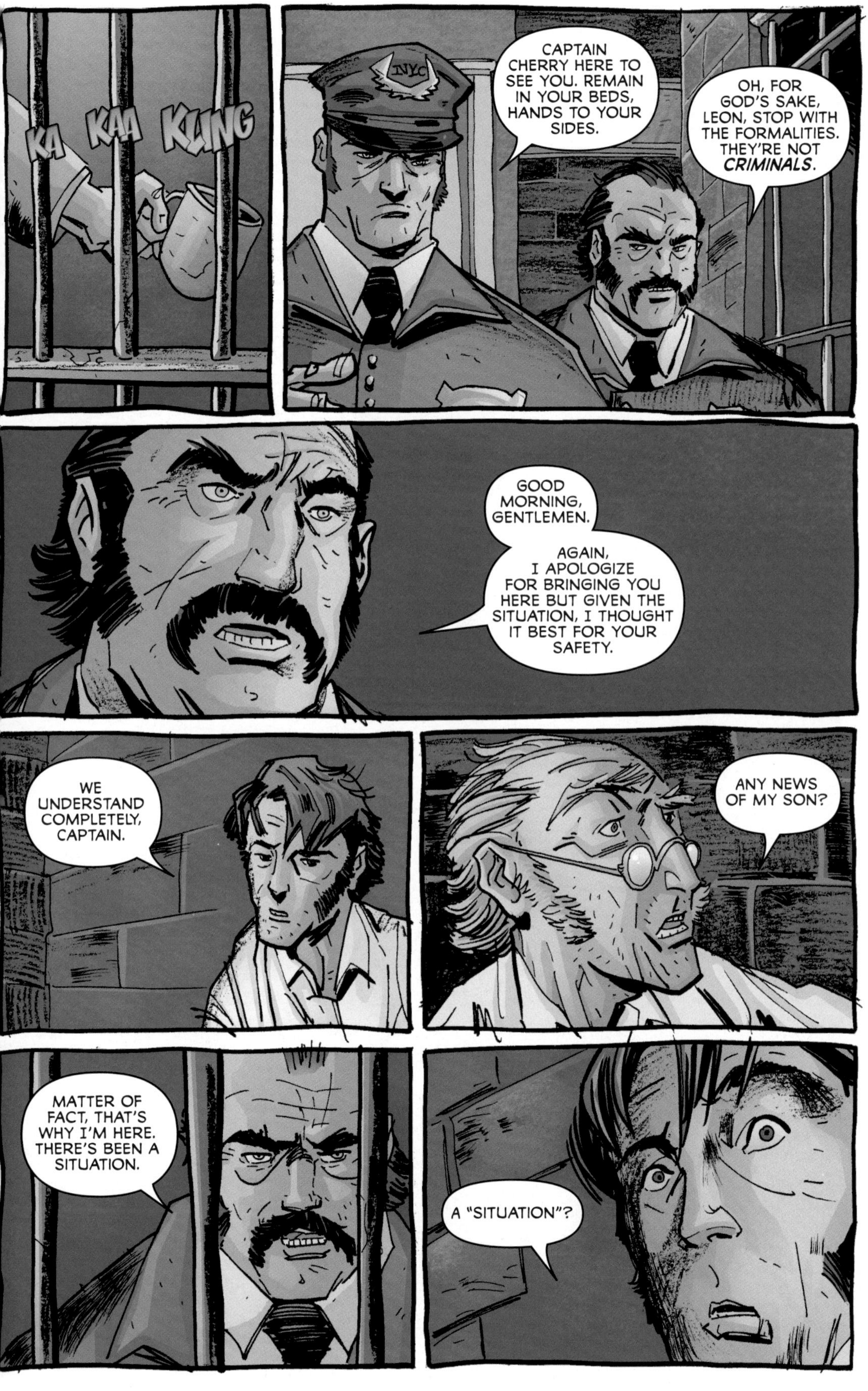
KA KAA KLING
CAPTAIN CHERRY HERE TO SEE YOU. REMAIN IN YOUR BEDS, HANDS TO YOUR SIDES.
OH, FOR GOD'S SAKE, LEON, STOP WITH THE FORMALITIES. THEY'RE NOT *CRIMINALS*.
GOOD MORNING, GENTLEMEN.
AGAIN, I APOLOGIZE FOR BRINGING YOU HERE BUT GIVEN THE SITUATION, I THOUGHT IT BEST FOR YOUR SAFETY.
WE UNDERSTAND COMPLETELY, CAPTAIN.
ANY NEWS OF MY SON?
MATTER OF FACT, THAT'S WHY I'M HERE. THERE'S BEEN A SITUATION.
A "SITUATION"?

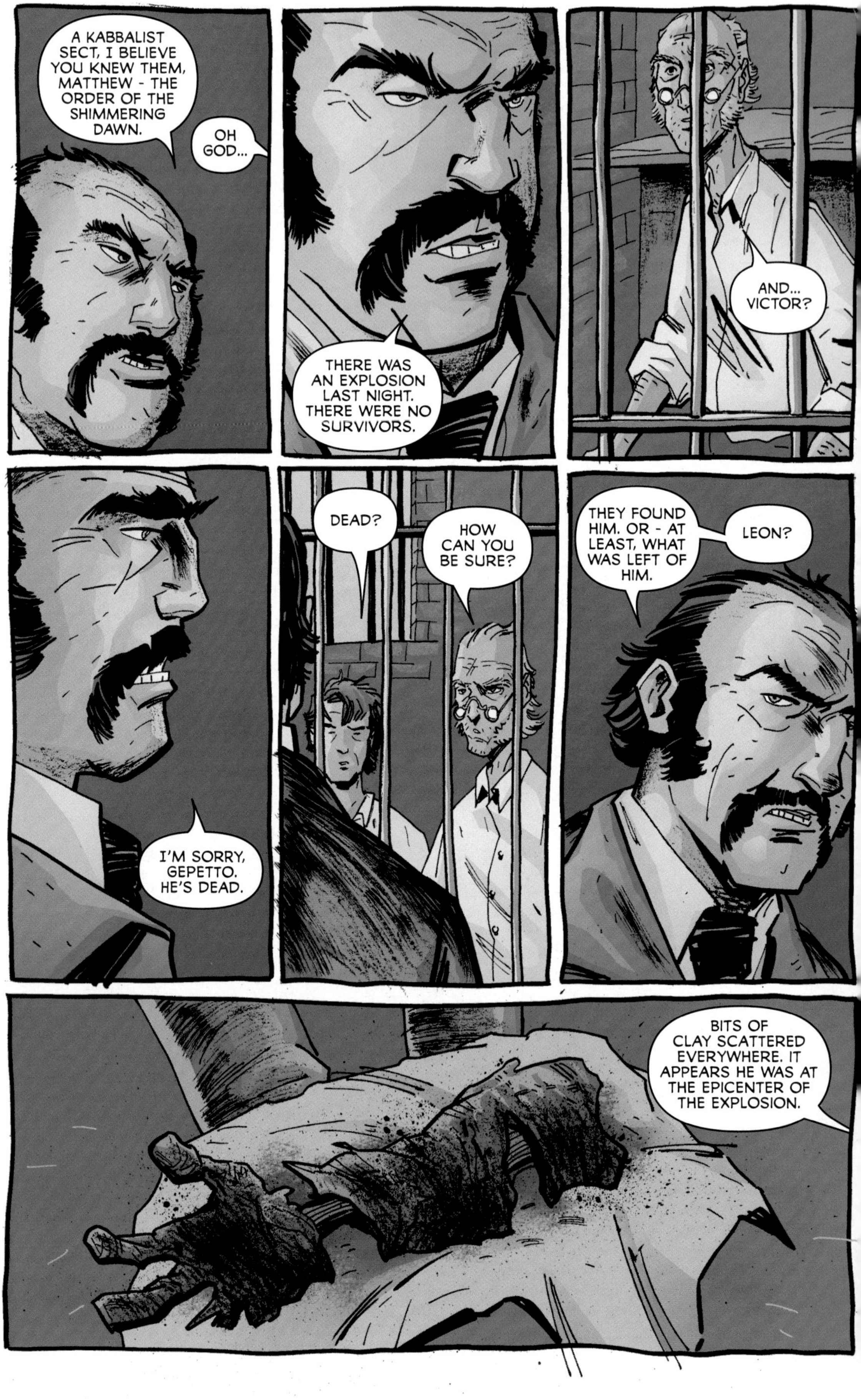
A KABBALIST SECT, I BELIEVE YOU KNEW THEM, MATTHEW - THE ORDER OF THE SHIMMERING DAWN.
OH GOD...
THERE WAS AN EXPLOSION LAST NIGHT. THERE WERE NO SURVIVORS.
AND... VICTOR?
I'M SORRY, GEPETTO. HE'S DEAD.
DEAD?
HOW CAN YOU BE SURE?
THEY FOUND HIM. OR - AT LEAST, WHAT WAS LEFT OF HIM.
LEON?
BITS OF CLAY SCATTERED EVERYWHERE. IT APPEARS HE WAS AT THE EPICENTER OF THE EXPLOSION.

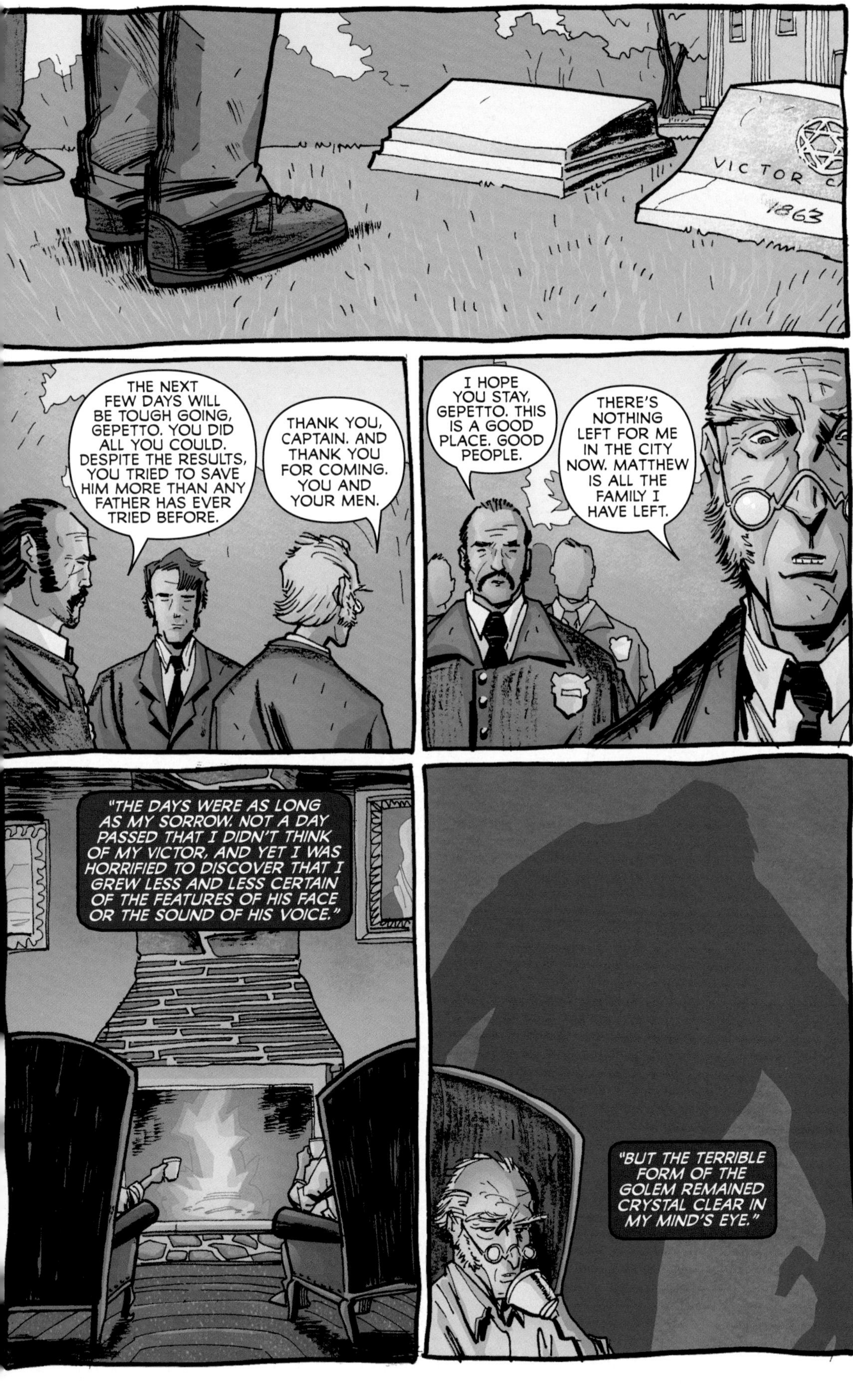
VICTOR C
1863
THE NEXT FEW DAYS WILL BE TOUGH GOING, GEPETTO. YOU DID ALL YOU COULD. DESPITE THE RESULTS, YOU TRIED TO SAVE HIM MORE THAN ANY FATHER HAS EVER TRIED BEFORE.
THANK YOU, CAPTAIN. AND THANK YOU FOR COMING. YOU AND YOUR MEN.
I HOPE YOU STAY, GEPETTO. THIS IS A GOOD PLACE. GOOD PEOPLE.
THERE'S NOTHING LEFT FOR ME IN THE CITY NOW. MATTHEW IS ALL THE FAMILY I HAVE LEFT.
"THE DAYS WERE AS LONG AS MY SORROW. NOT A DAY PASSED THAT I DIDN'T THINK OF MY VICTOR, AND YET I WAS HORRIFIED TO DISCOVER THAT I GREW LESS AND LESS CERTAIN OF THE FEATURES OF HIS FACE OR THE SOUND OF HIS VOICE."
"BUT THE TERRIBLE FORM OF THE GOLEM REMAINED CRYSTAL CLEAR IN MY MIND'S EYE."

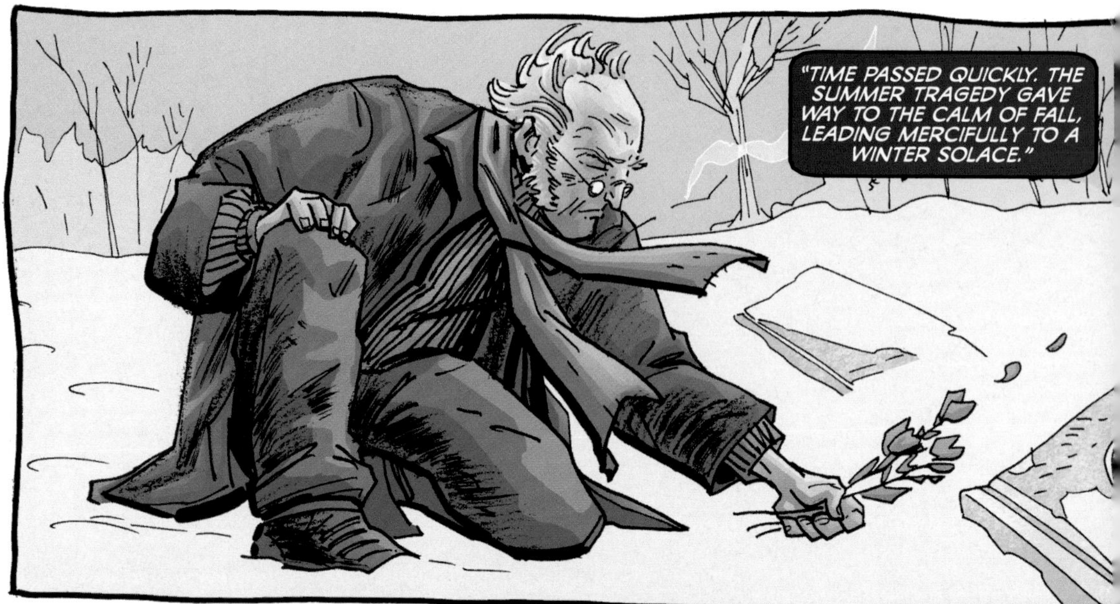
"TIME PASSED QUICKLY. THE SUMMER TRAGEDY GAVE WAY TO THE CALM OF FALL, LEADING MERCIFULLY TO A WINTER SOLACE."

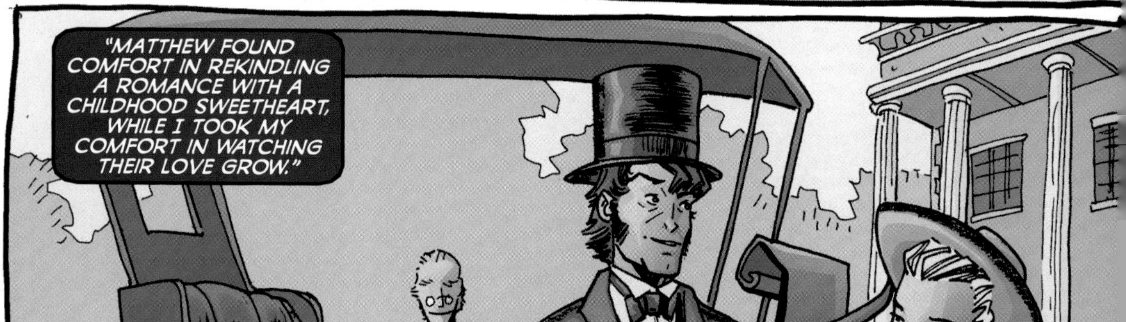
"MATTHEW FOUND COMFORT IN REKINDLING A ROMANCE WITH A CHILDHOOD SWEETHEART, WHILE I TOOK MY COMFORT IN WATCHING THEIR LOVE GROW."

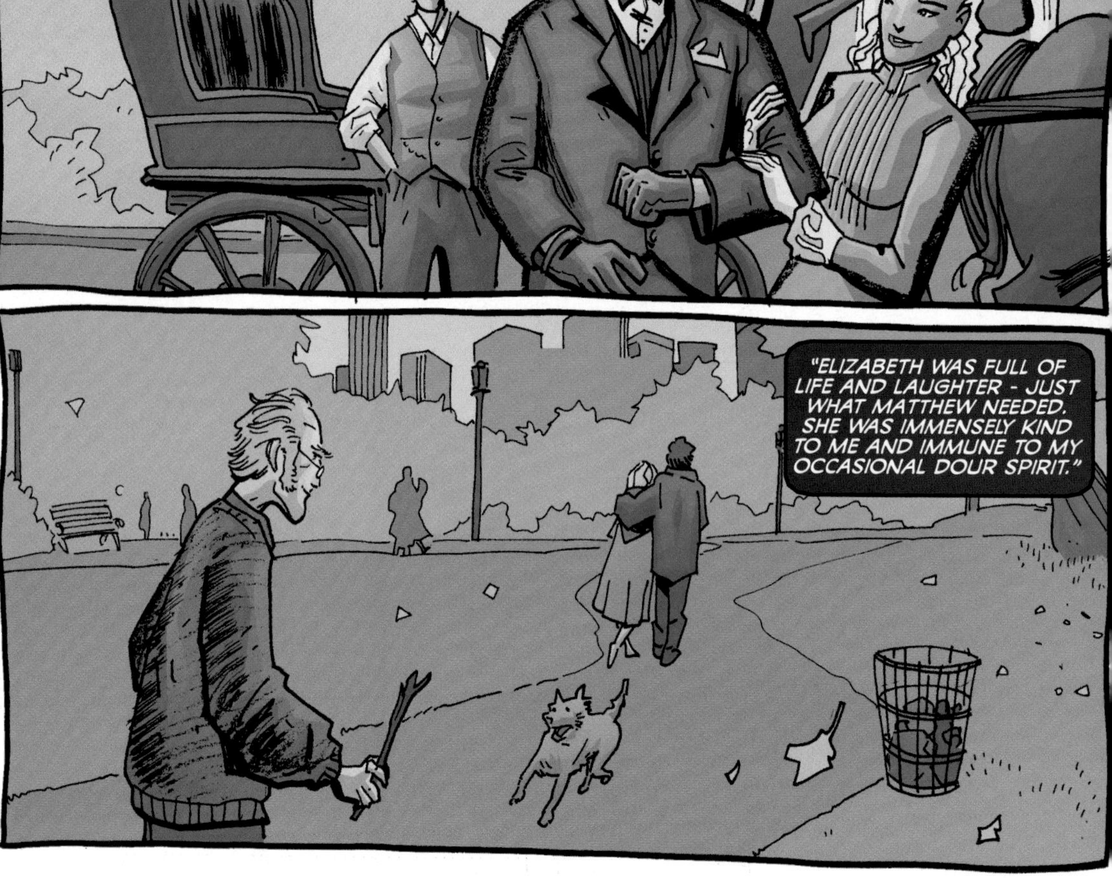
"ELIZABETH WAS FULL OF LIFE AND LAUGHTER - JUST WHAT MATTHEW NEEDED. SHE WAS IMMENSELY KIND TO ME AND IMMUNE TO MY OCCASIONAL DOUR SPIRIT."

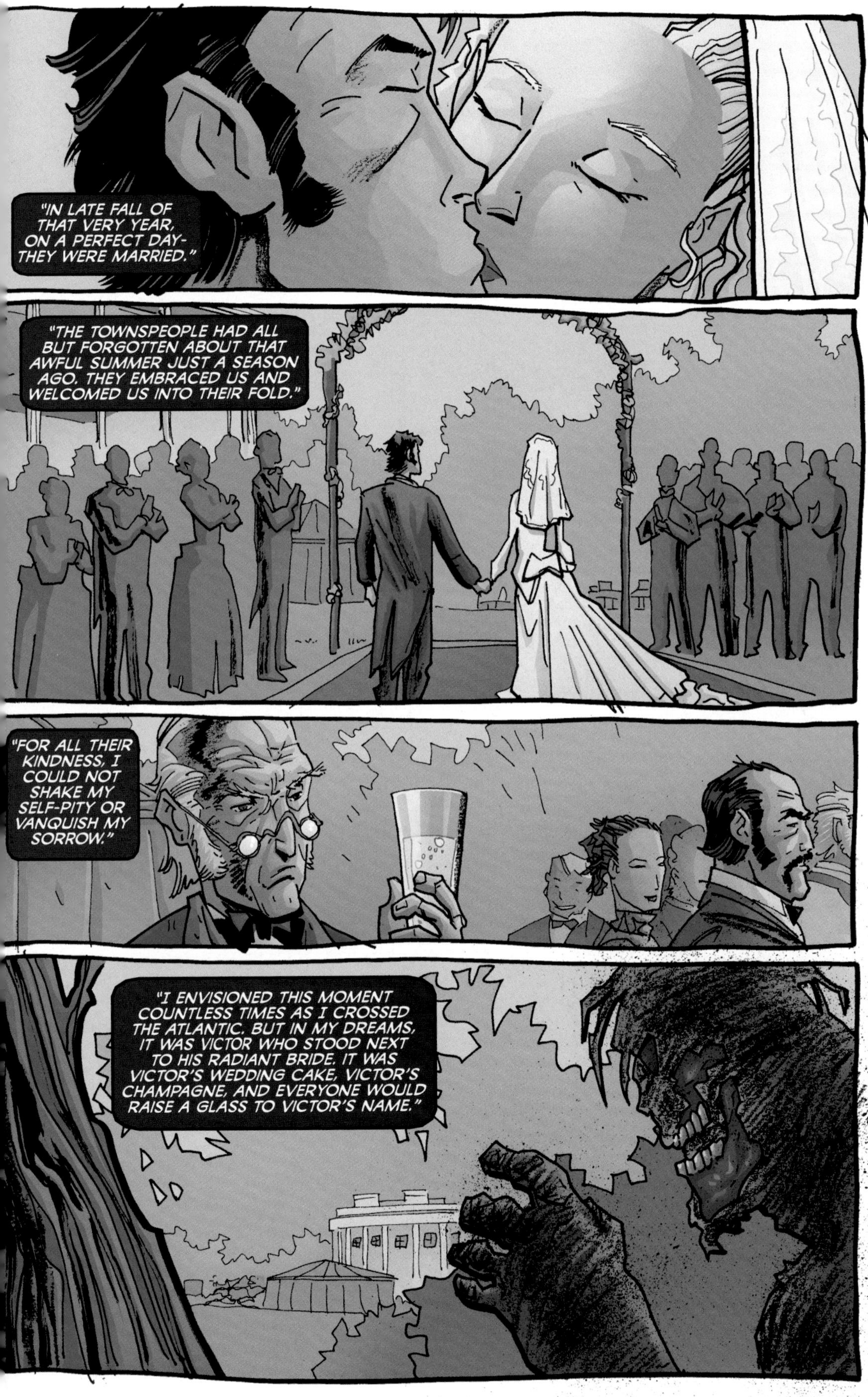
"IN LATE FALL OF THAT VERY YEAR, ON A PERFECT DAY- THEY WERE MARRIED."
"THE TOWNSPEOPLE HAD ALL BUT FORGOTTEN ABOUT THAT AWFUL SUMMER JUST A SEASON AGO. THEY EMBRACED US AND WELCOMED US INTO THEIR FOLD."
"FOR ALL THEIR KINDNESS, I COULD NOT SHAKE MY SELF-PITY OR VANQUISH MY SORROW."
"I ENVISIONED THIS MOMENT COUNTLESS TIMES AS I CROSSED THE ATLANTIC. BUT IN MY DREAMS, IT WAS VICTOR WHO STOOD NEXT TO HIS RADIANT BRIDE. IT WAS VICTOR'S WEDDING CAKE, VICTOR'S CHAMPAGNE, AND EVERYONE WOULD RAISE A GLASS TO VICTOR'S NAME."

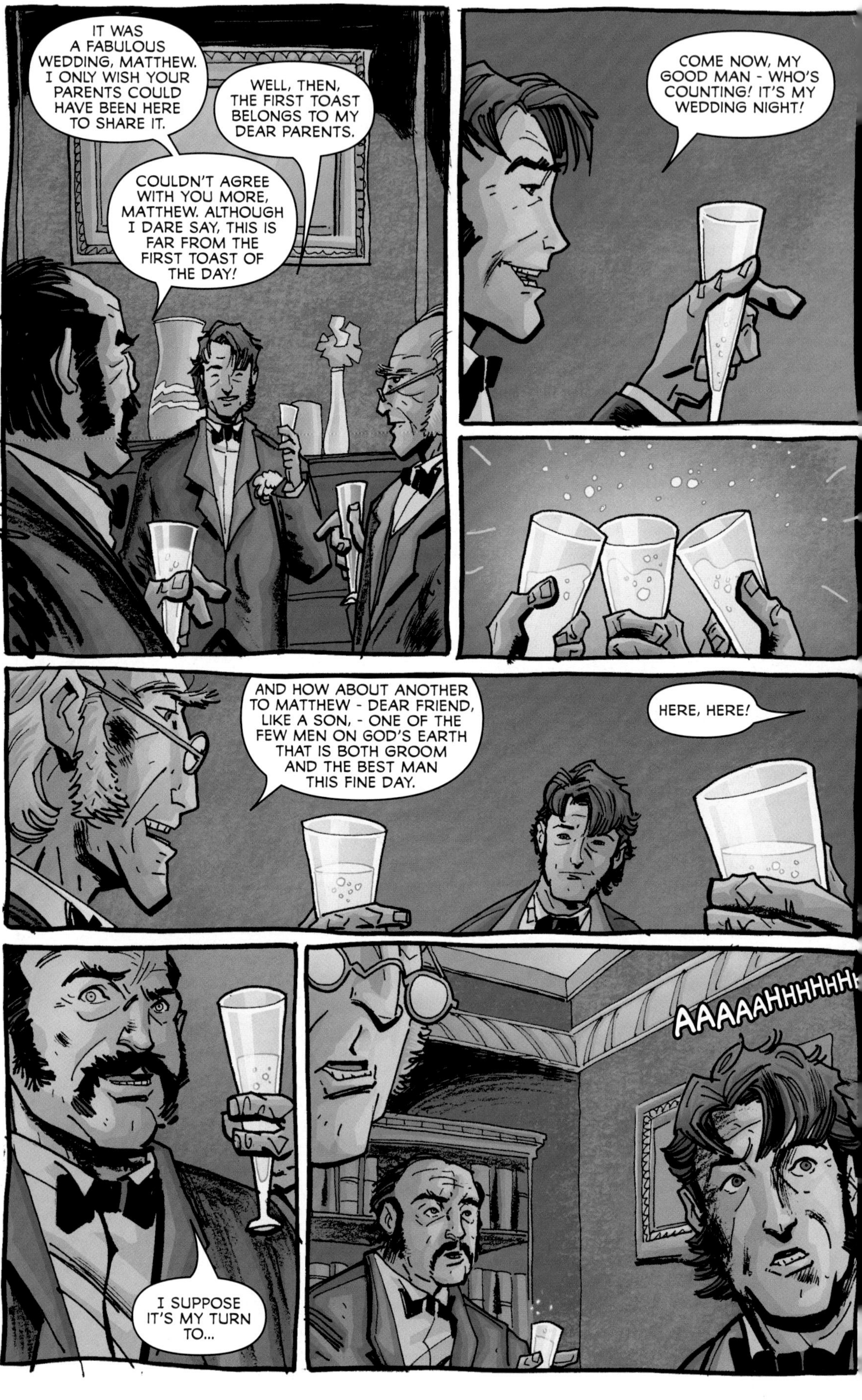
IT WAS A FABULOUS WEDDING, MATTHEW. I ONLY WISH YOUR PARENTS COULD HAVE BEEN HERE TO SHARE IT.
WELL, THEN, THE FIRST TOAST BELONGS TO MY DEAR PARENTS.
COULDN'T AGREE WITH YOU MORE, MATTHEW. ALTHOUGH I DARE SAY, THIS IS FAR FROM THE FIRST TOAST OF THE DAY!
COME NOW, MY GOOD MAN - WHO'S COUNTING! IT'S MY WEDDING NIGHT!
AND HOW ABOUT ANOTHER TO MATTHEW - DEAR FRIEND, LIKE A SON, - ONE OF THE FEW MEN ON GOD'S EARTH THAT IS BOTH GROOM AND THE BEST MAN THIS FINE DAY.
HERE, HERE!
I SUPPOSE IT'S MY TURN TO...
AAAAAHHHHHH

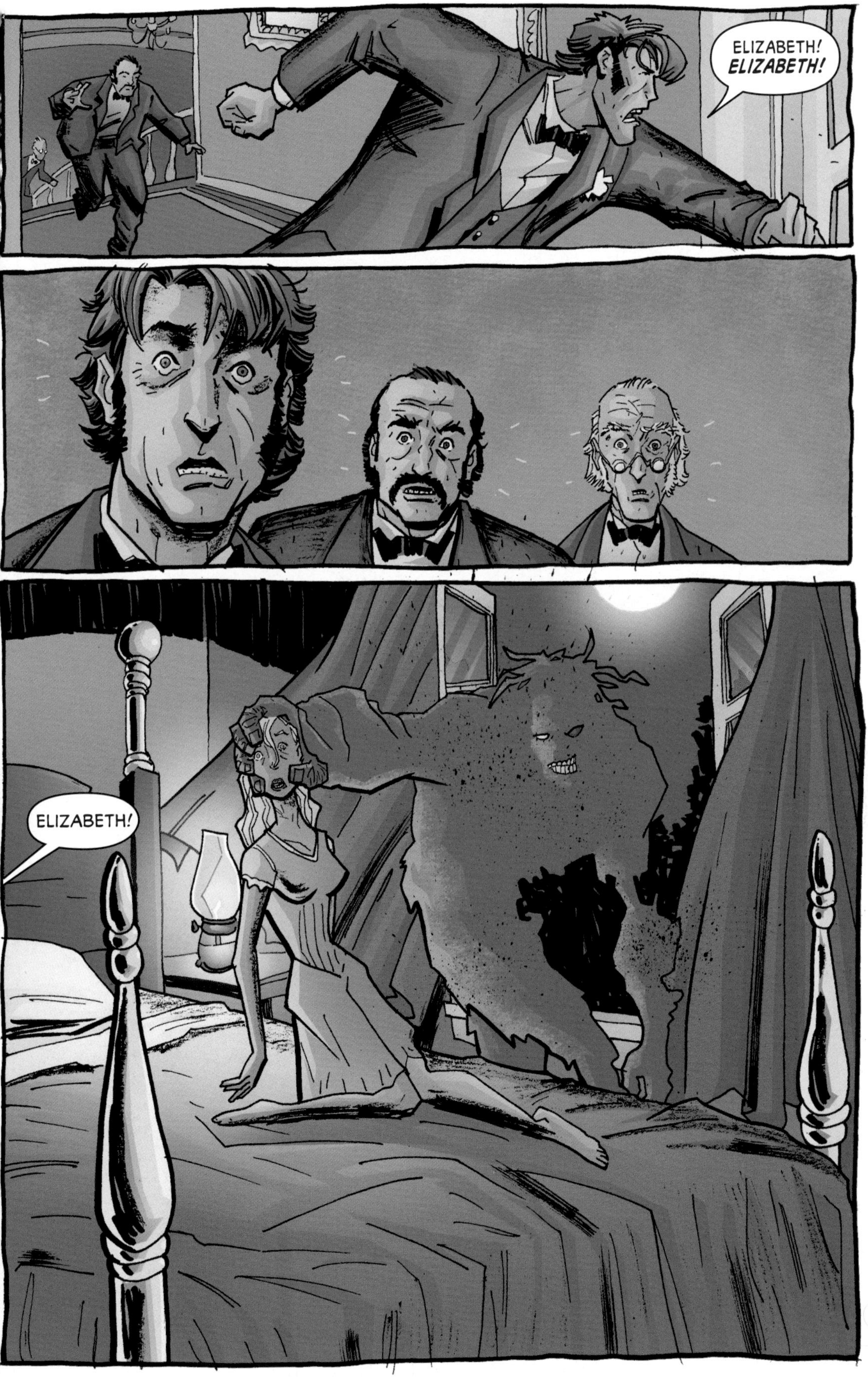
ELIZABETH!
ELIZABETH!
ELIZABETH!

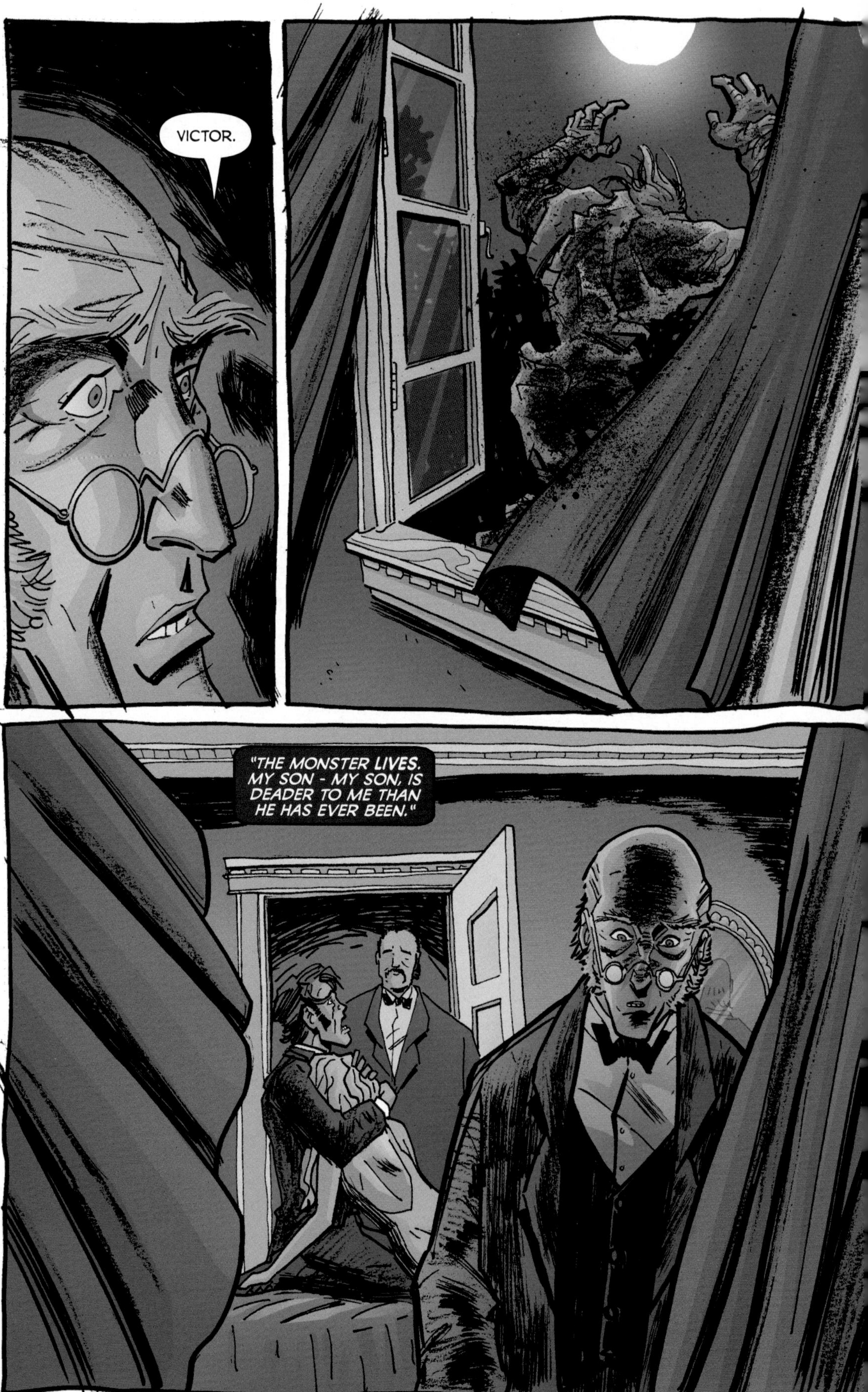
VICTOR.
"THE MONSTER LIVES. MY SON - MY SON, IS DEADER TO ME THAN HE HAS EVER BEEN."

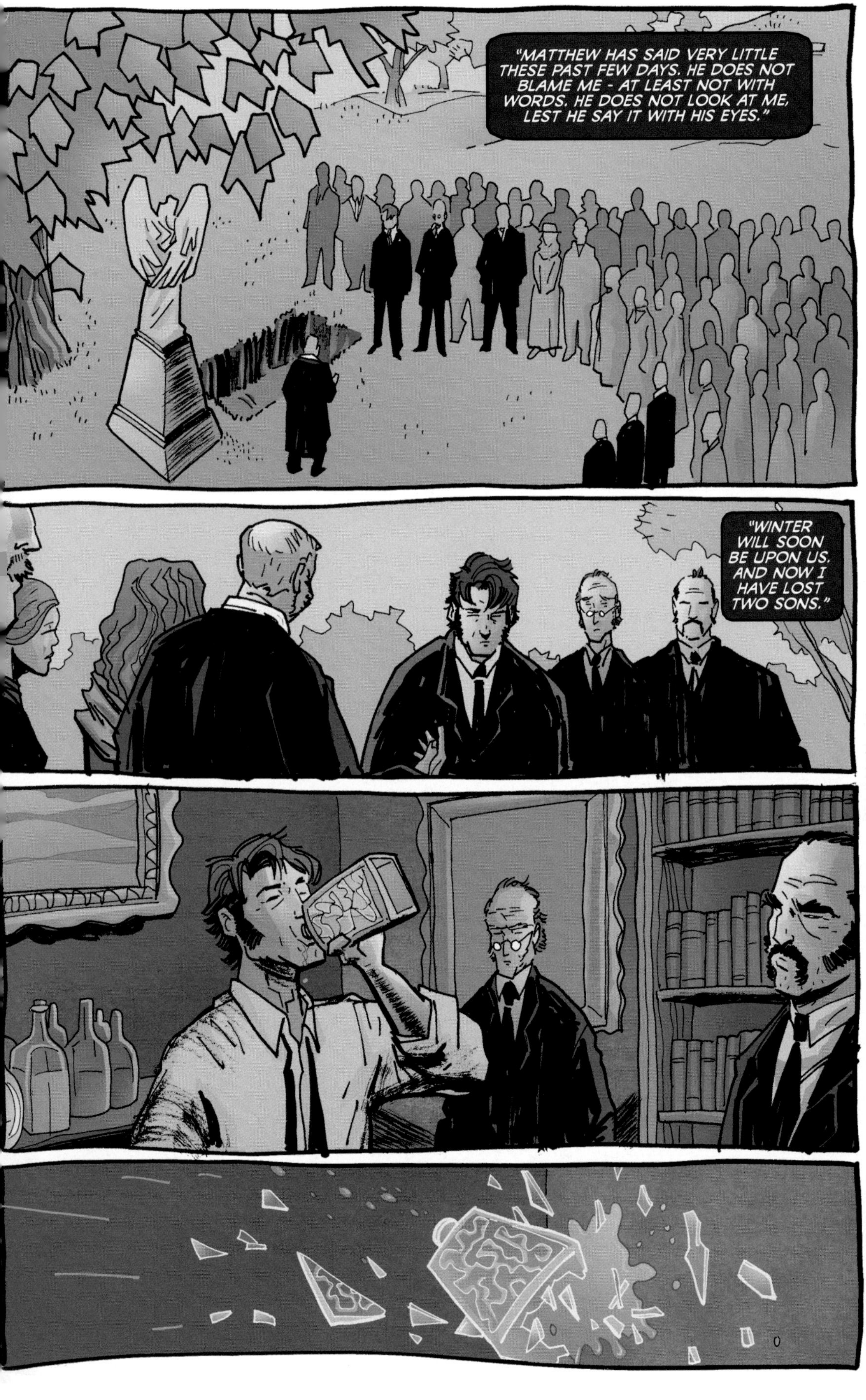
"MATTHEW HAS SAID VERY LITTLE THESE PAST FEW DAYS. HE DOES NOT BLAME ME - AT LEAST NOT WITH WORDS. HE DOES NOT LOOK AT ME, LEST HE SAY IT WITH HIS EYES."
"WINTER WILL SOON BE UPON US. AND NOW I HAVE LOST TWO SONS."

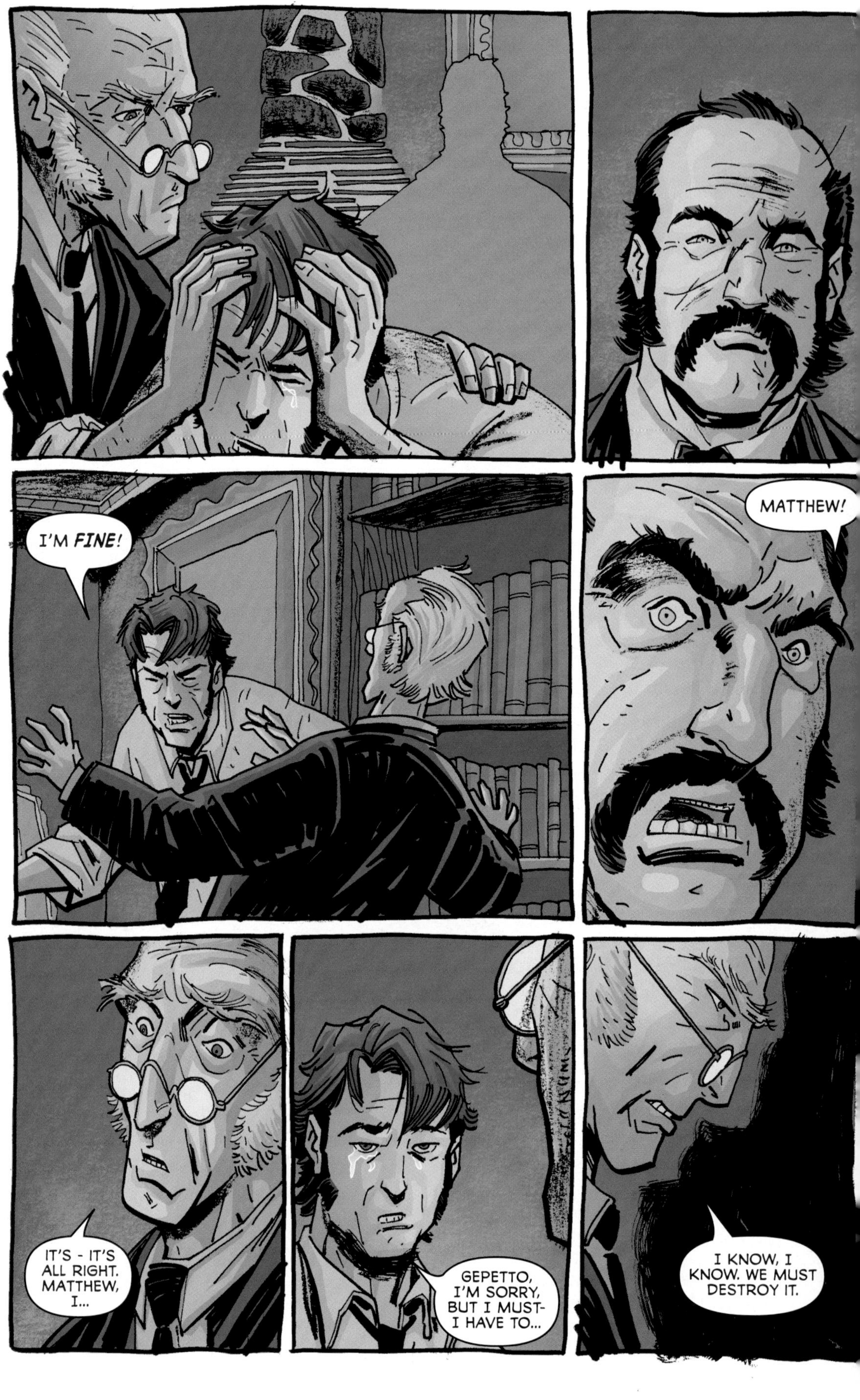
I'M *FINE*!
MATTHEW!
IT'S - IT'S ALL RIGHT. MATTHEW, I...
GEPETTO, I'M SORRY, BUT I MUST- I HAVE TO...
I KNOW, I KNOW. WE MUST DESTROY IT.

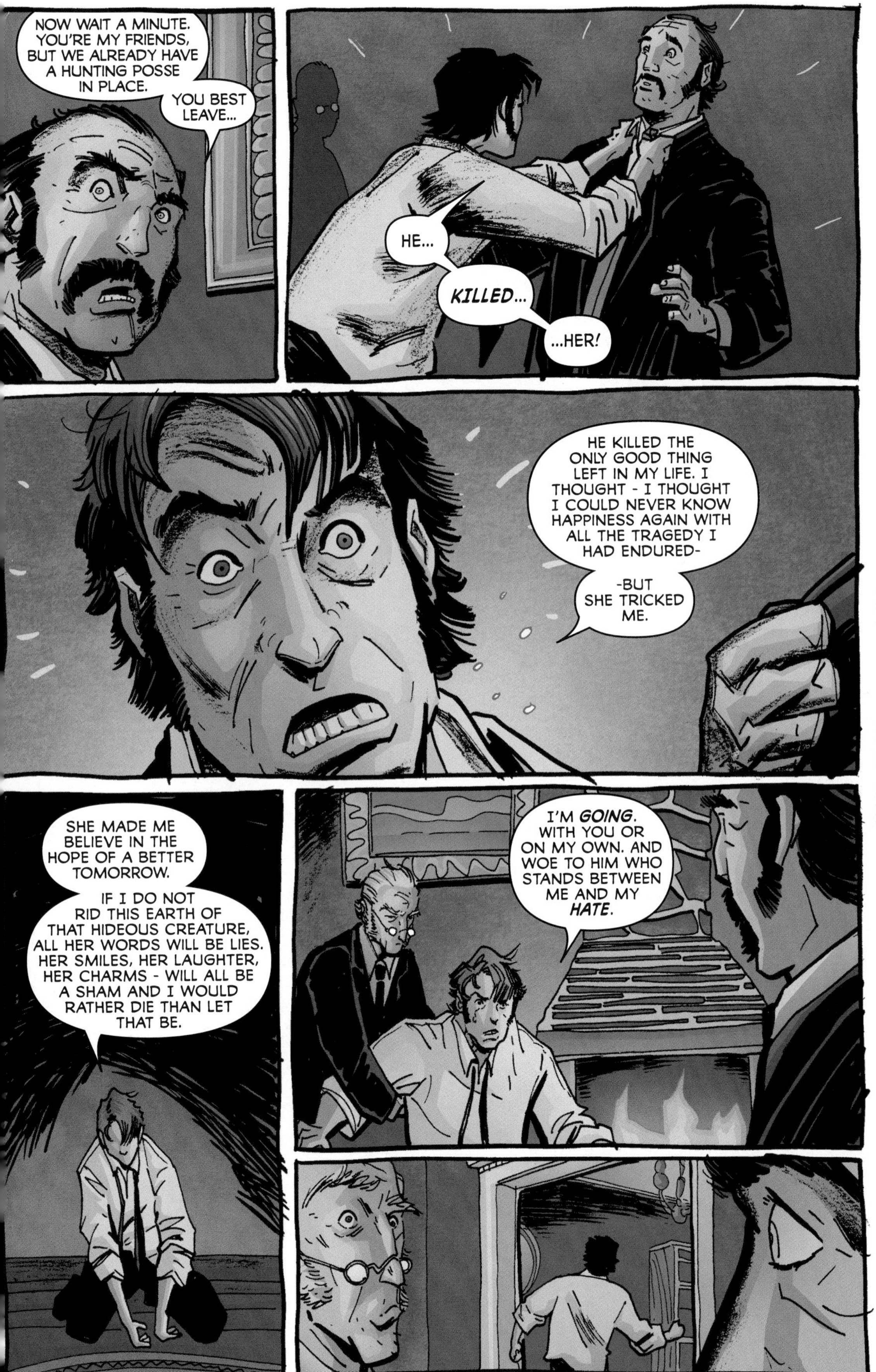
NOW WAIT A MINUTE. YOU'RE MY FRIENDS, BUT WE ALREADY HAVE A HUNTING POSSE IN PLACE.
YOU BEST LEAVE...
HE...
KILLED...
...HER!
HE KILLED THE ONLY GOOD THING LEFT IN MY LIFE. I THOUGHT - I THOUGHT I COULD NEVER KNOW HAPPINESS AGAIN WITH ALL THE TRAGEDY I HAD ENDURED-
-BUT SHE TRICKED ME.
SHE MADE ME BELIEVE IN THE HOPE OF A BETTER TOMORROW.
IF I DO NOT RID THIS EARTH OF THAT HIDEOUS CREATURE, ALL HER WORDS WILL BE LIES. HER SMILES, HER LAUGHTER, HER CHARMS - WILL ALL BE A SHAM AND I WOULD RATHER DIE THAN LET THAT BE.
I'M GOING. WITH YOU OR ON MY OWN. AND WOE TO HIM WHO STANDS BETWEEN ME AND MY HATE.

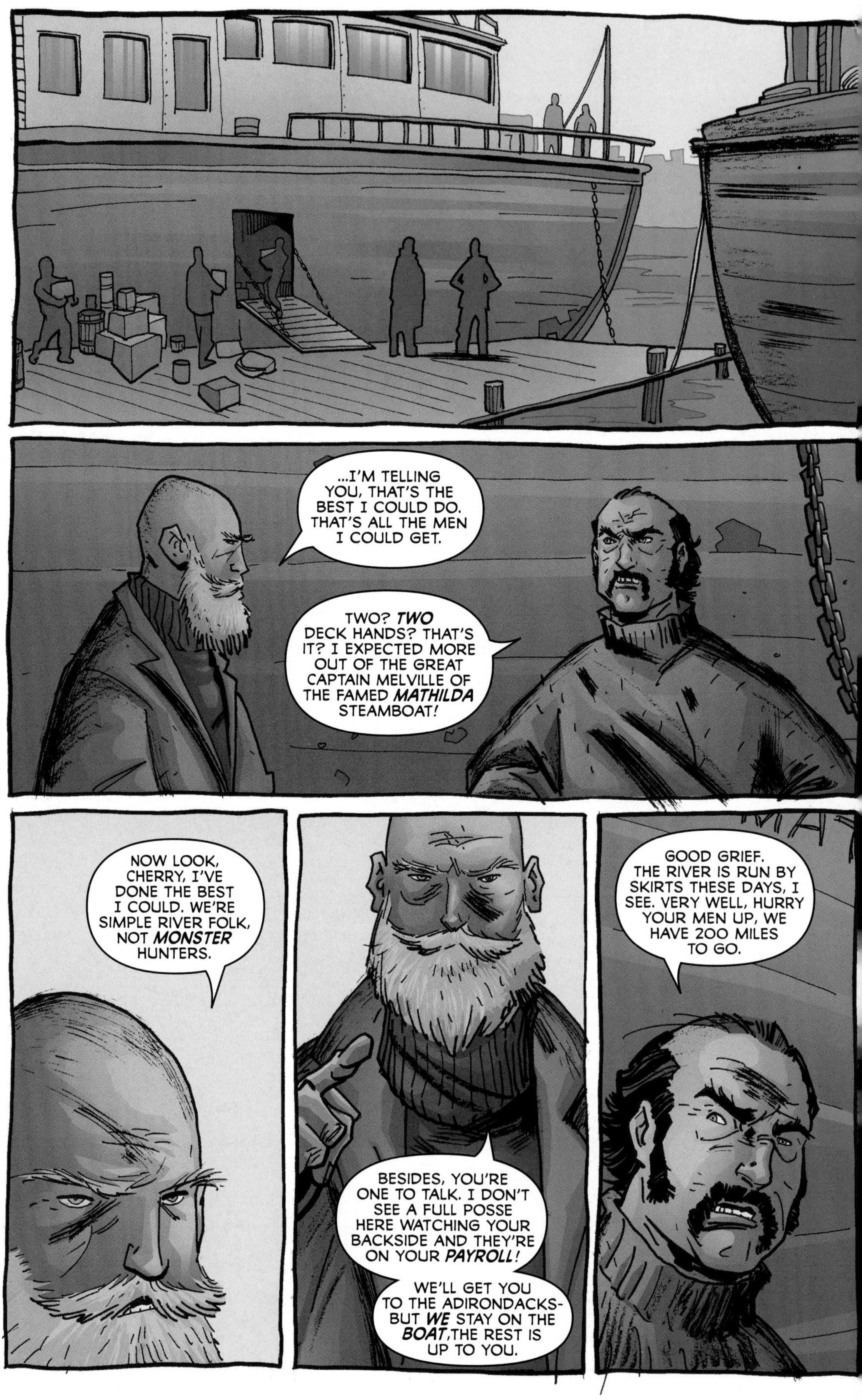

...I'M TELLING YOU, THAT'S THE BEST I COULD DO. THAT'S ALL THE MEN I COULD GET.
TWO? *TWO* DECK HANDS? THAT'S IT? I EXPECTED MORE OUT OF THE GREAT CAPTAIN MELVILLE OF THE FAMED *MATHILDA* STEAMBOAT!
NOW LOOK, CHERRY, I'VE DONE THE BEST I COULD. WE'RE SIMPLE RIVER FOLK, NOT *MONSTER* HUNTERS.
BESIDES, YOU'RE ONE TO TALK. I DON'T SEE A FULL POSSE HERE WATCHING YOUR BACKSIDE AND THEY'RE ON YOUR *PAYROLL!*
WE'LL GET YOU TO THE ADIRONDACKS- BUT *WE* STAY ON THE *BOAT*, THE REST IS UP TO YOU.
GOOD GRIEF. THE RIVER IS RUN BY SKIRTS THESE DAYS, I SEE. VERY WELL, HURRY YOUR MEN UP, WE HAVE 200 MILES TO GO.

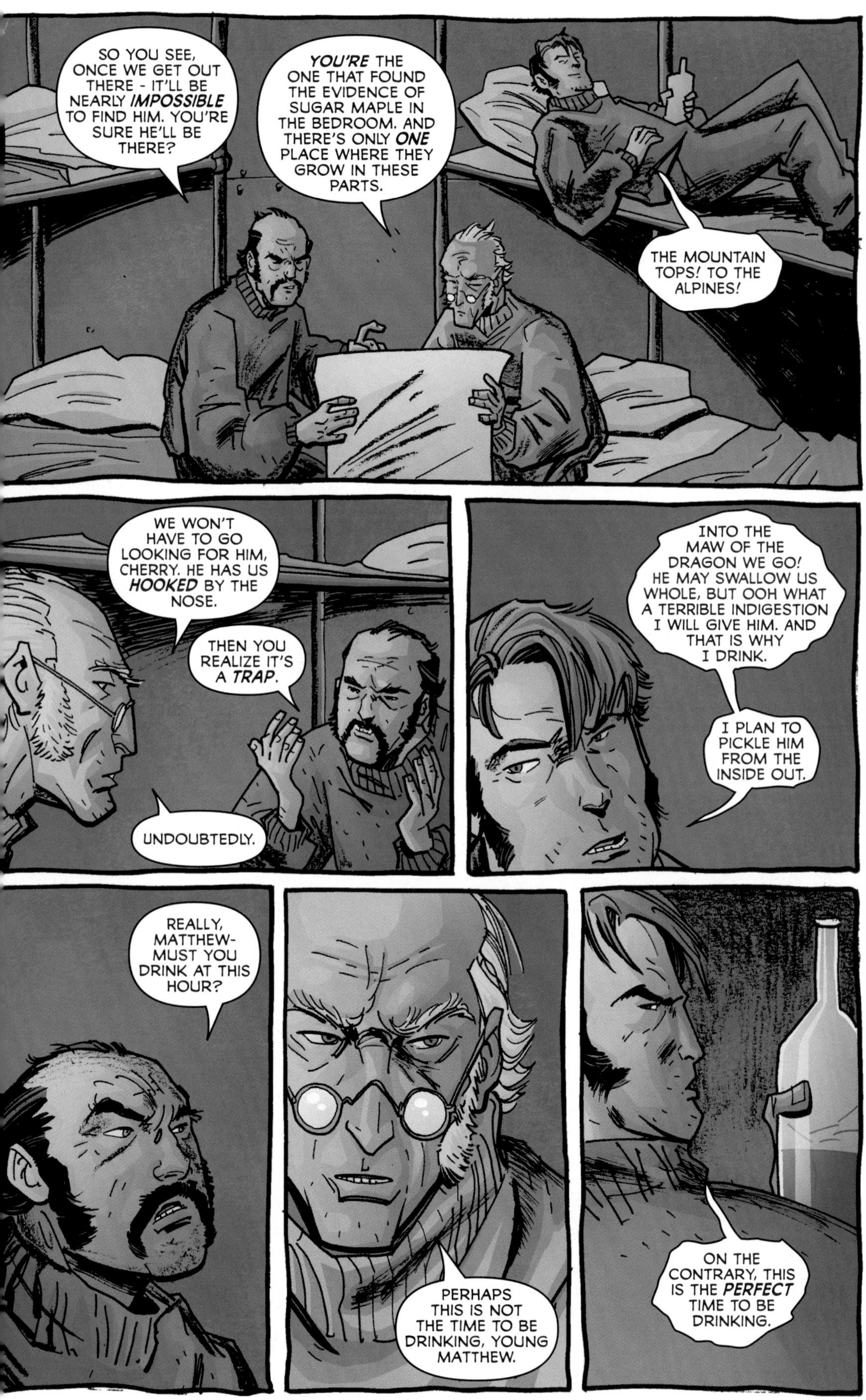
SO YOU SEE, ONCE WE GET OUT THERE - IT'LL BE NEARLY IMPOSSIBLE TO FIND HIM. YOU'RE SURE HE'LL BE THERE?
YOU'RE THE ONE THAT FOUND THE EVIDENCE OF SUGAR MAPLE IN THE BEDROOM. AND THERE'S ONLY ONE PLACE WHERE THEY GROW IN THESE PARTS.
THE MOUNTAIN TOPS! TO THE ALPINES!
WE WON'T HAVE TO GO LOOKING FOR HIM, CHERRY. HE HAS US HOOKED BY THE NOSE.
THEN YOU REALIZE IT'S A TRAP.
UNDOUBTEDLY.
INTO THE MAW OF THE DRAGON WE GO! HE MAY SWALLOW US WHOLE, BUT OOH WHAT A TERRIBLE INDIGESTION I WILL GIVE HIM. AND THAT IS WHY I DRINK.
I PLAN TO PICKLE HIM FROM THE INSIDE OUT.
REALLY, MATTHEW- MUST YOU DRINK AT THIS HOUR?
PERHAPS THIS IS NOT THE TIME TO BE DRINKING, YOUNG MATTHEW.
ON THE CONTRARY, THIS IS THE PERFECT TIME TO BE DRINKING.

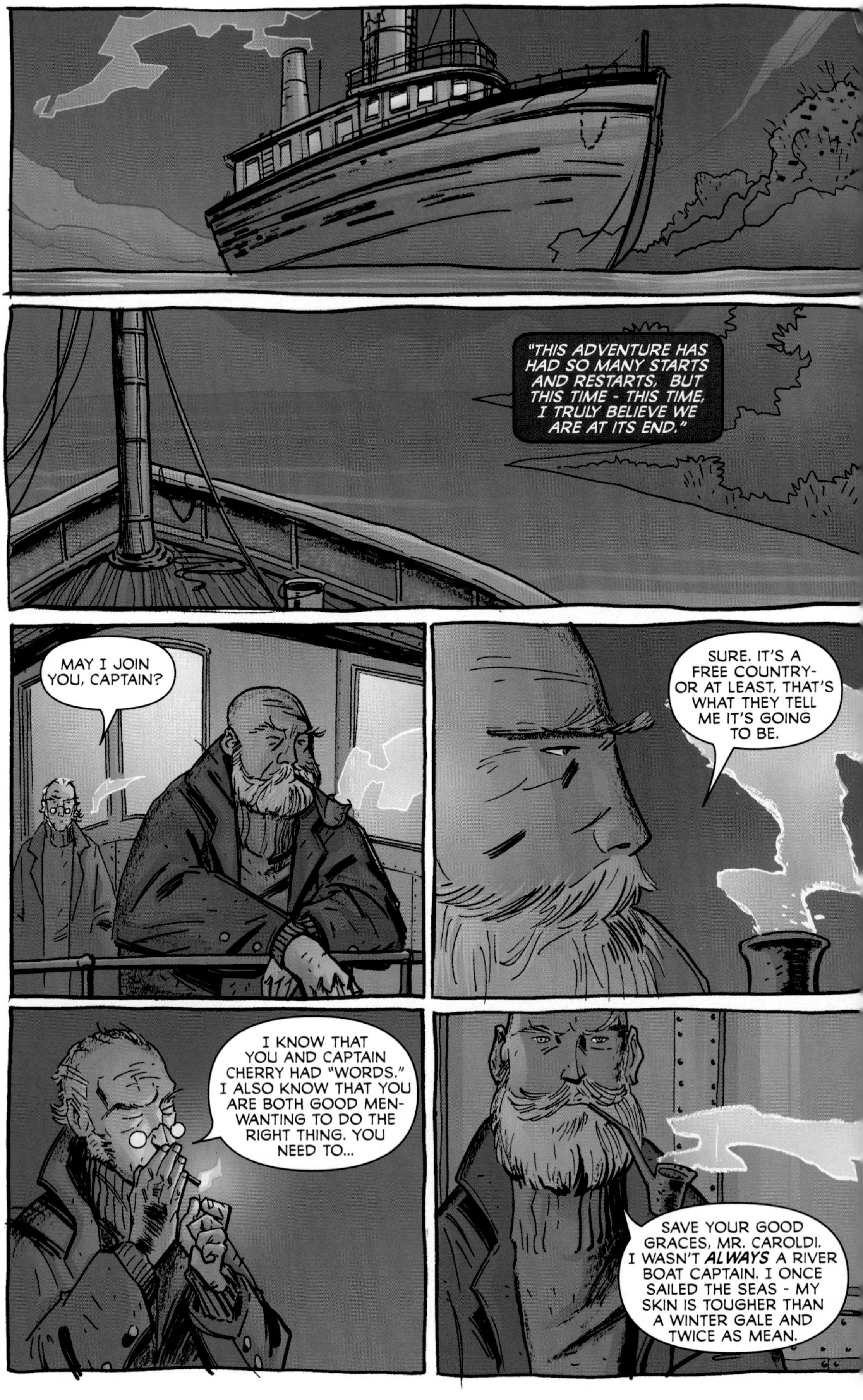
"THIS ADVENTURE HAS HAD SO MANY STARTS AND RESTARTS, BUT THIS TIME - THIS TIME, I TRULY BELIEVE WE ARE AT ITS END."
MAY I JOIN YOU, CAPTAIN?
SURE. IT'S A FREE COUNTRY- OR AT LEAST, THAT'S WHAT THEY TELL ME IT'S GOING TO BE.
I KNOW THAT YOU AND CAPTAIN CHERRY HAD "WORDS." I ALSO KNOW THAT YOU ARE BOTH GOOD MEN- WANTING TO DO THE RIGHT THING. YOU NEED TO...
SAVE YOUR GOOD GRACES, MR. CAROLDI. I WASN'T ***ALWAYS*** A RIVER BOAT CAPTAIN. I ONCE SAILED THE SEAS - MY SKIN IS TOUGHER THAN A WINTER GALE AND TWICE AS MEAN.

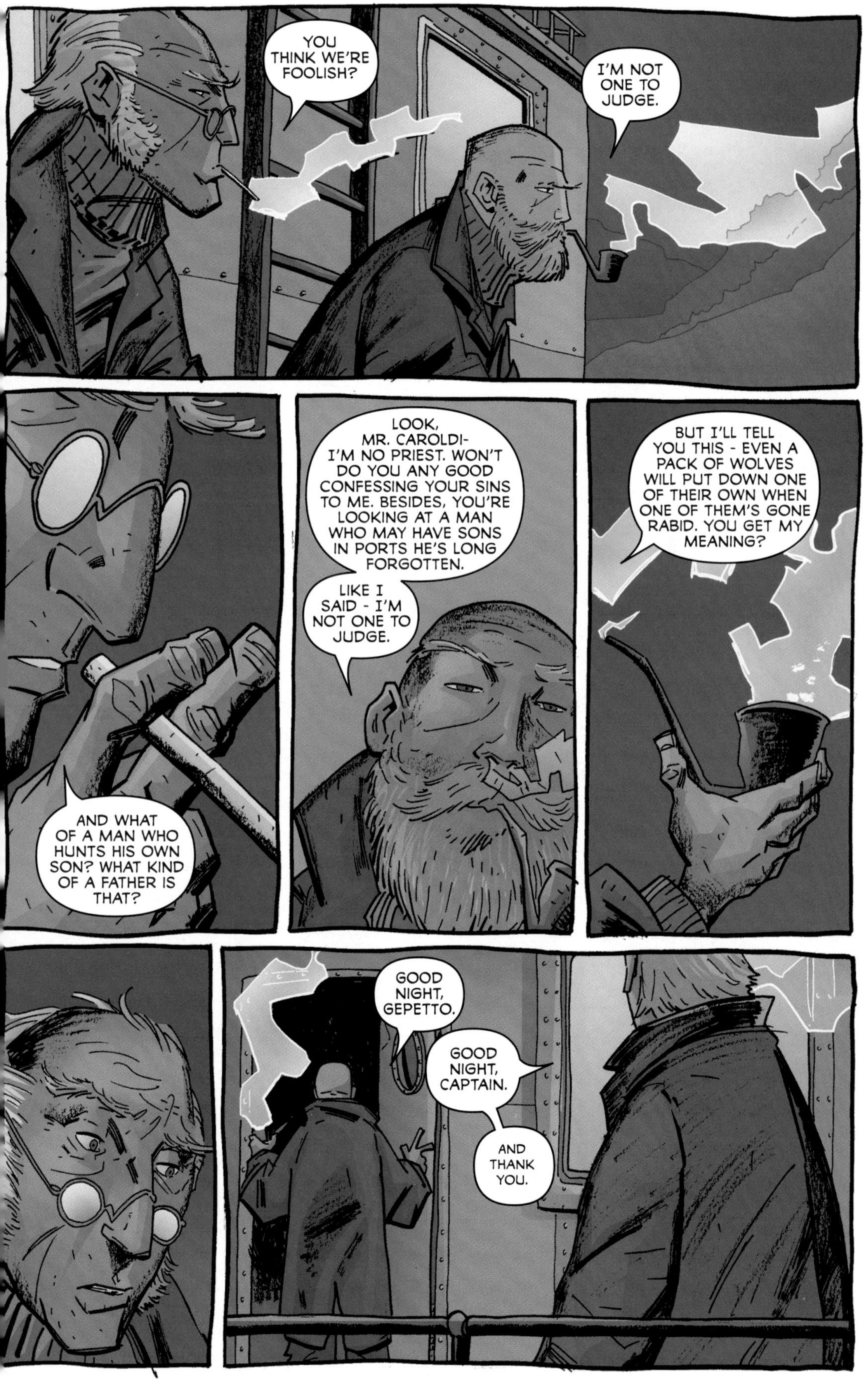
YOU THINK WE'RE FOOLISH?
I'M NOT ONE TO JUDGE.
LOOK, MR. CAROLDI- I'M NO PRIEST. WON'T DO YOU ANY GOOD CONFESSING YOUR SINS TO ME. BESIDES, YOU'RE LOOKING AT A MAN WHO MAY HAVE SONS IN PORTS HE'S LONG FORGOTTEN.
LIKE I SAID - I'M NOT ONE TO JUDGE.
AND WHAT OF A MAN WHO HUNTS HIS OWN SON? WHAT KIND OF A FATHER IS THAT?
BUT I'LL TELL YOU THIS - EVEN A PACK OF WOLVES WILL PUT DOWN ONE OF THEIR OWN WHEN ONE OF THEM'S GONE RABID. YOU GET MY MEANING?
GOOD NIGHT, GEPETTO.
GOOD NIGHT, CAPTAIN.
AND THANK YOU.

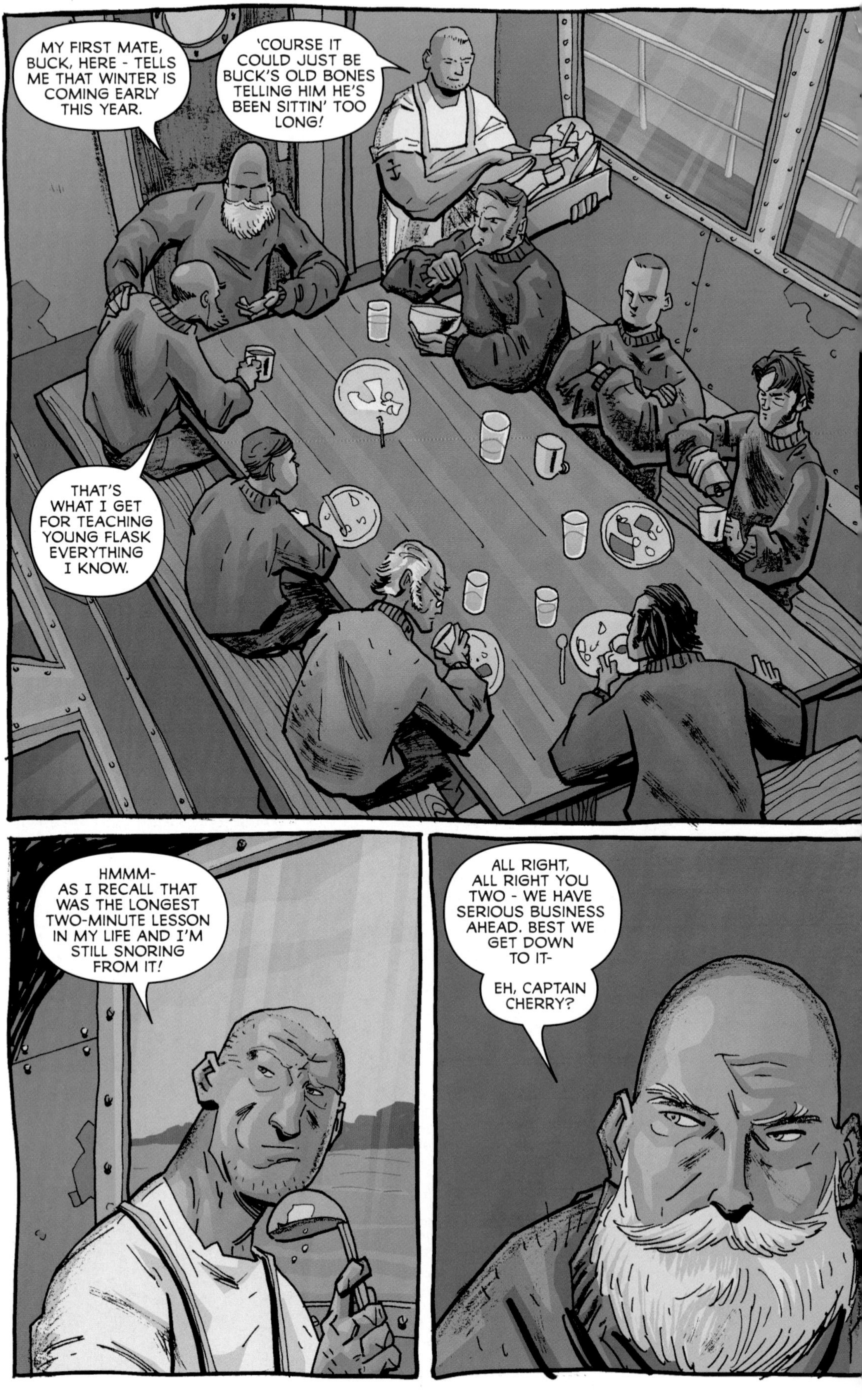
MY FIRST MATE, BUCK, HERE - TELLS ME THAT WINTER IS COMING EARLY THIS YEAR.
'COURSE IT COULD JUST BE BUCK'S OLD BONES TELLING HIM HE'S BEEN SITTIN' TOO LONG!
THAT'S WHAT I GET FOR TEACHING YOUNG FLASK EVERYTHING I KNOW.
HMMM- AS I RECALL THAT WAS THE LONGEST TWO-MINUTE LESSON IN MY LIFE AND I'M STILL SNORING FROM IT!
ALL RIGHT, ALL RIGHT YOU TWO - WE HAVE SERIOUS BUSINESS AHEAD. BEST WE GET DOWN TO IT-
EH, CAPTAIN CHERRY?

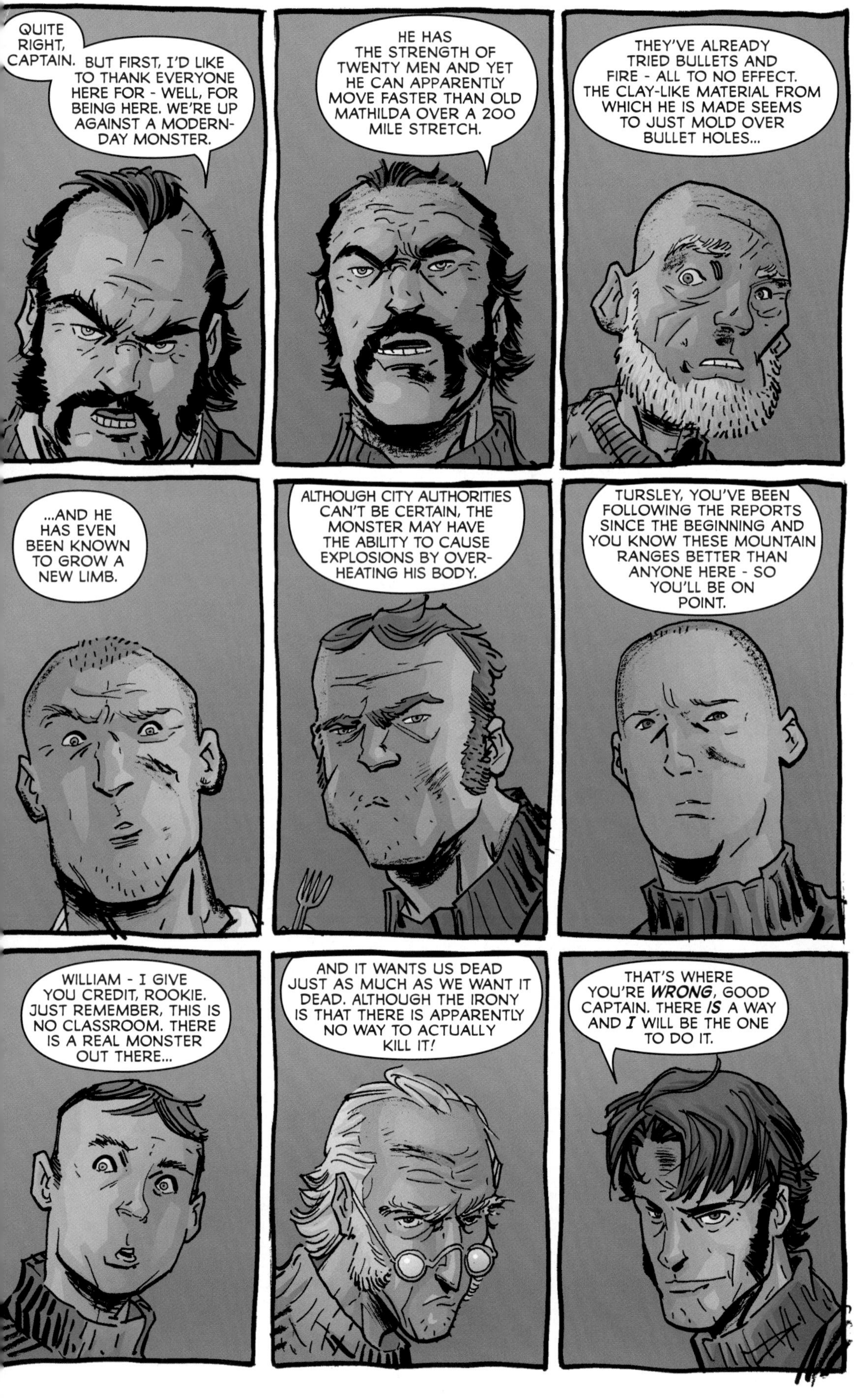
QUITE RIGHT, CAPTAIN.
BUT FIRST, I'D LIKE TO THANK EVERYONE HERE FOR - WELL, FOR BEING HERE. WE'RE UP AGAINST A MODERN-DAY MONSTER.
HE HAS THE STRENGTH OF TWENTY MEN AND YET HE CAN APPARENTLY MOVE FASTER THAN OLD MATHILDA OVER A 200 MILE STRETCH.
THEY'VE ALREADY TRIED BULLETS AND FIRE - ALL TO NO EFFECT. THE CLAY-LIKE MATERIAL FROM WHICH HE IS MADE SEEMS TO JUST MOLD OVER BULLET HOLES...
...AND HE HAS EVEN BEEN KNOWN TO GROW A NEW LIMB.
ALTHOUGH CITY AUTHORITIES CAN'T BE CERTAIN, THE MONSTER MAY HAVE THE ABILITY TO CAUSE EXPLOSIONS BY OVER-HEATING HIS BODY.
TURSLEY, YOU'VE BEEN FOLLOWING THE REPORTS SINCE THE BEGINNING AND YOU KNOW THESE MOUNTAIN RANGES BETTER THAN ANYONE HERE - SO YOU'LL BE ON POINT.
WILLIAM - I GIVE YOU CREDIT, ROOKIE. JUST REMEMBER, THIS IS NO CLASSROOM. THERE IS A REAL MONSTER OUT THERE...
AND IT WANTS US DEAD JUST AS MUCH AS WE WANT IT DEAD. ALTHOUGH THE IRONY IS THAT THERE IS APPARENTLY NO WAY TO ACTUALLY KILL IT!
THAT'S WHERE YOU'RE *WRONG*, GOOD CAPTAIN. THERE *IS* A WAY AND *I* WILL BE THE ONE TO DO IT.

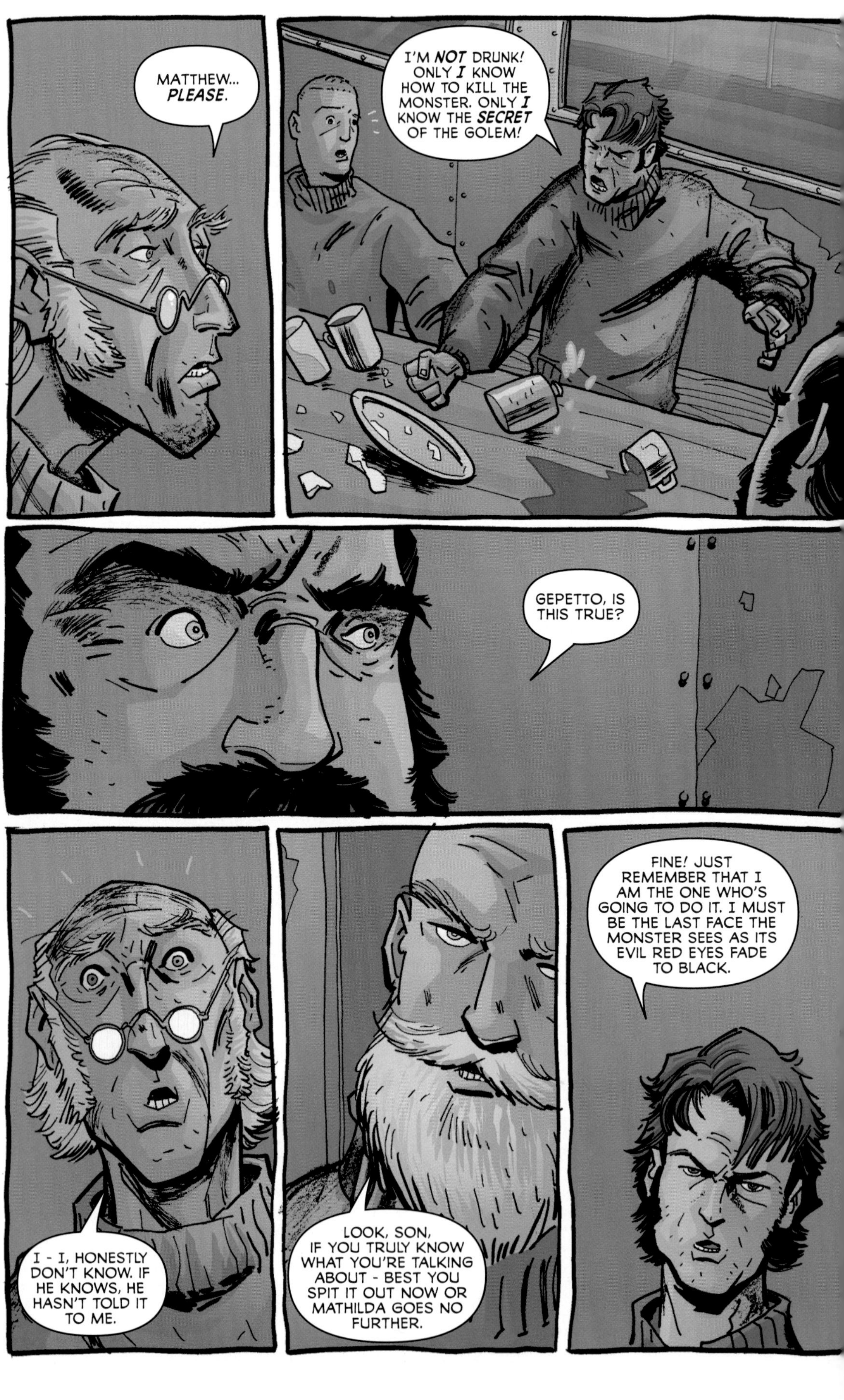
MATTHEW... *PLEASE*.
I'M *NOT* DRUNK! ONLY *I* KNOW HOW TO KILL THE MONSTER. ONLY *I* KNOW THE *SECRET* OF THE GOLEM!
GEPETTO, IS THIS TRUE?
I - I, HONESTLY DON'T KNOW. IF HE KNOWS, HE HASN'T TOLD IT TO ME.
LOOK, SON, IF YOU TRULY KNOW WHAT YOU'RE TALKING ABOUT - BEST YOU SPIT IT OUT NOW OR MATHILDA GOES NO FURTHER.
FINE! JUST REMEMBER THAT I AM THE ONE WHO'S GOING TO DO IT. I MUST BE THE LAST FACE THE MONSTER SEES AS ITS EVIL RED EYES FADE TO BLACK.

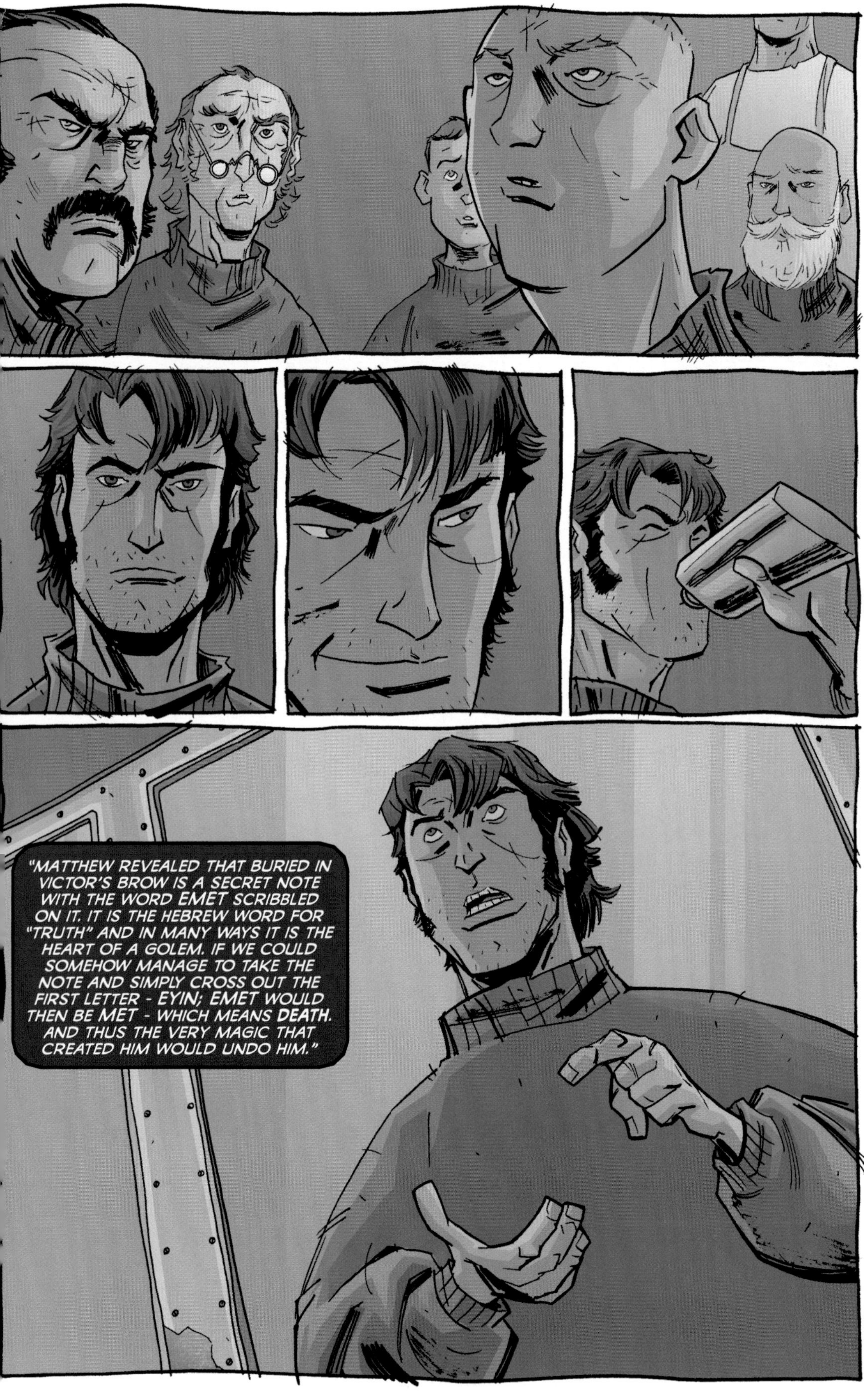
"MATTHEW REVEALED THAT BURIED IN VICTOR'S BROW IS A SECRET NOTE WITH THE WORD EMET SCRIBBLED ON IT. IT IS THE HEBREW WORD FOR "TRUTH" AND IN MANY WAYS IT IS THE HEART OF A GOLEM. IF WE COULD SOMEHOW MANAGE TO TAKE THE NOTE AND SIMPLY CROSS OUT THE FIRST LETTER - EYIN; EMET WOULD THEN BE MET - WHICH MEANS DEATH. AND THUS THE VERY MAGIC THAT CREATED HIM WOULD UNDO HIM."

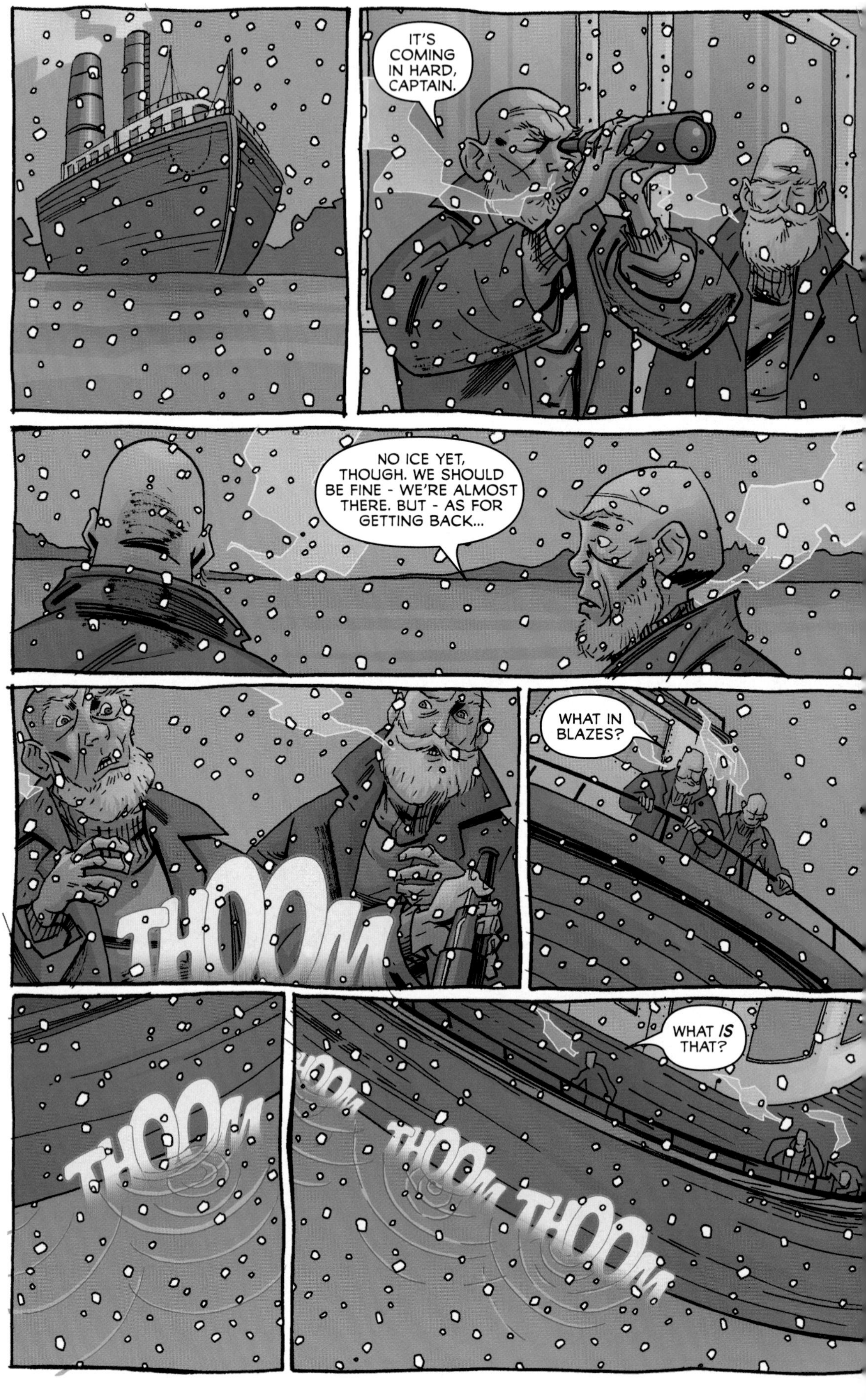
IT'S COMING IN HARD, CAPTAIN.
NO ICE YET, THOUGH. WE SHOULD BE FINE - WE'RE ALMOST THERE. BUT - AS FOR GETTING BACK...
THOOM
WHAT IN BLAZES?
THOOM
THOOM
THOOM
THOOM
WHAT *IS* THAT?
THOOM

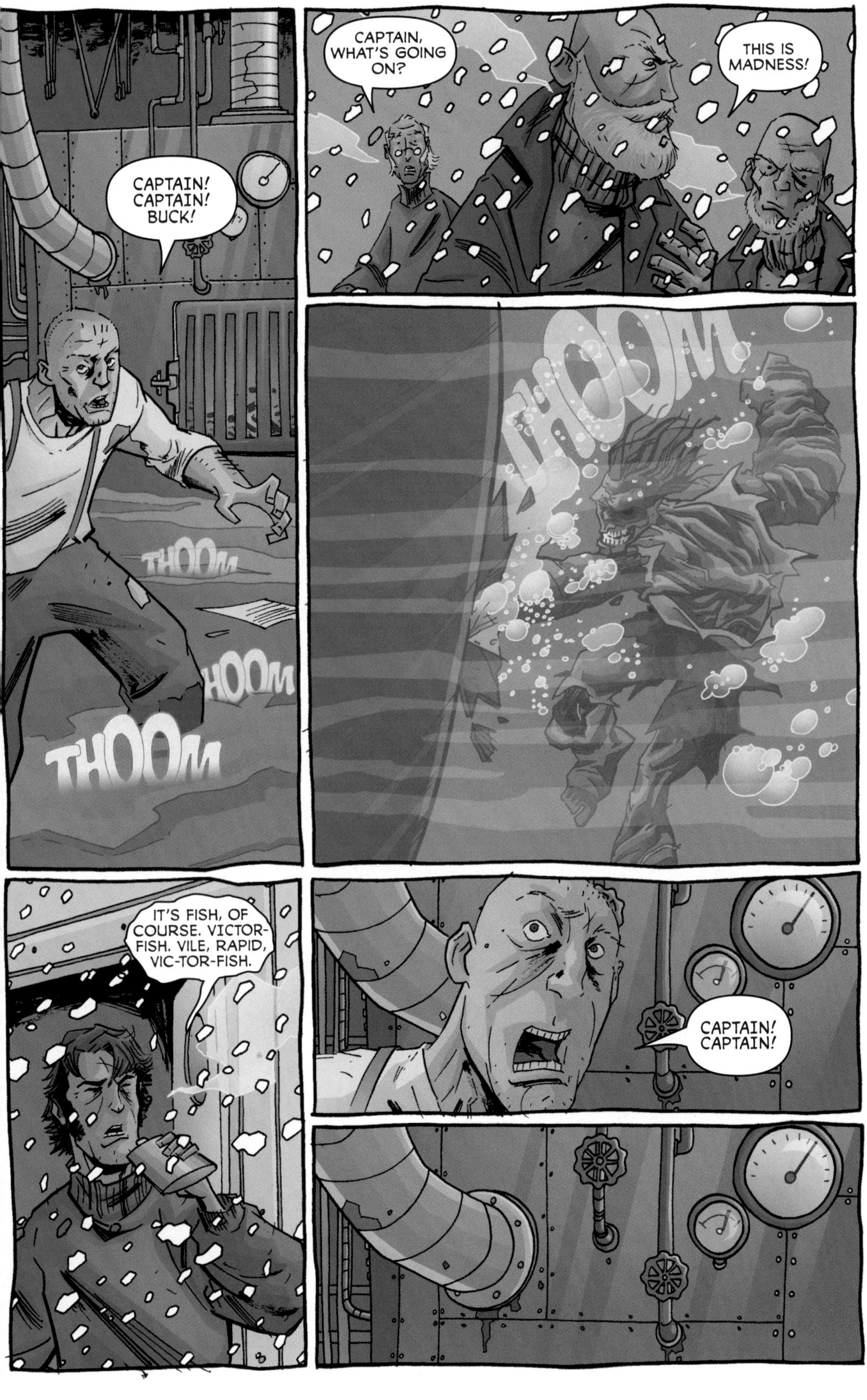
CAPTAIN! CAPTAIN! BUCK!
THOOM
THOOM
THOOM
CAPTAIN, WHAT'S GOING ON?
THIS IS MADNESS!
THOOM
IT'S FISH, OF COURSE. VICTOR-FISH. VILE, RAPID, VIC-TOR-FISH.
CAPTAIN! CAPTAIN!

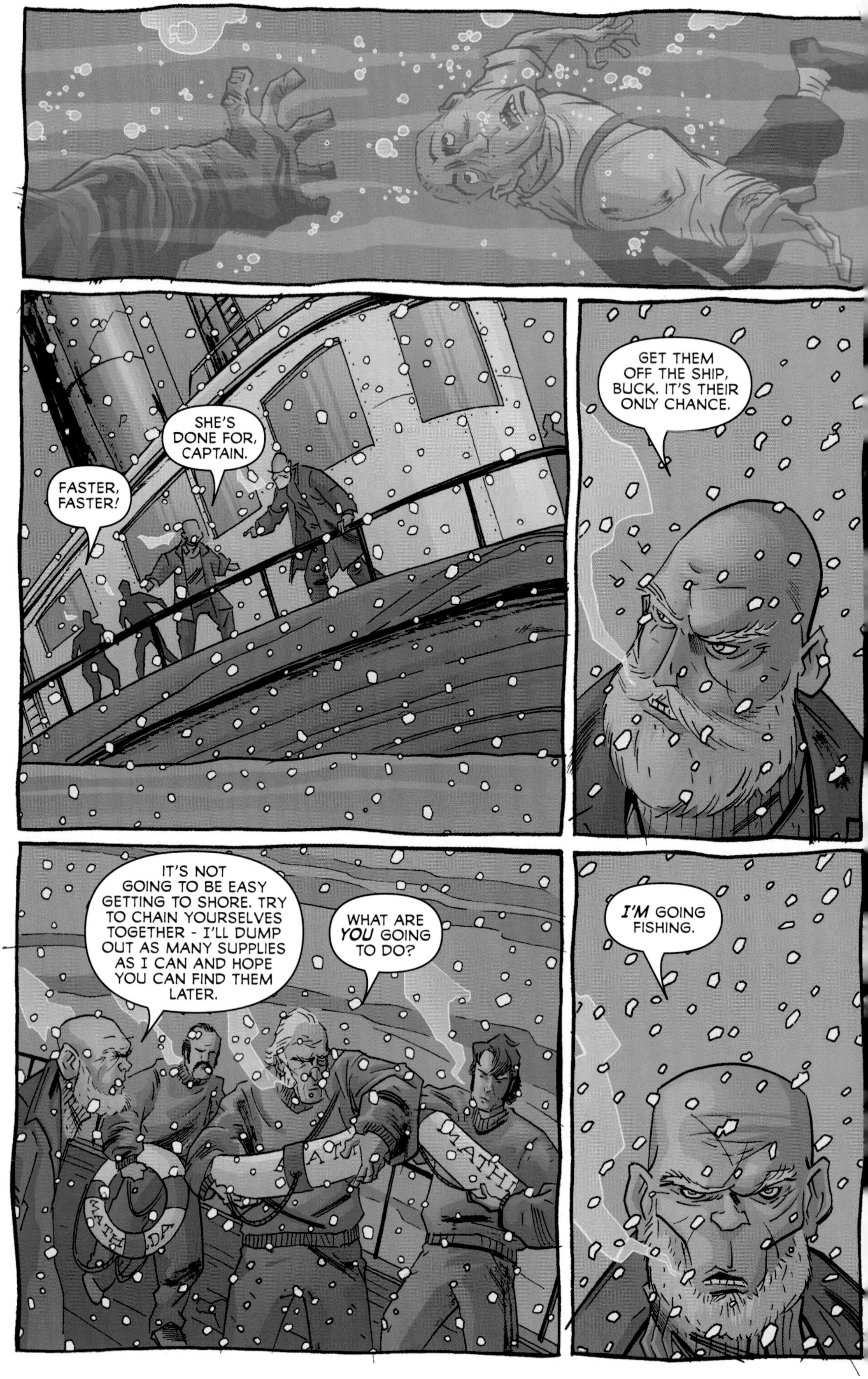
FASTER, FASTER!
SHE'S DONE FOR, CAPTAIN.
GET THEM OFF THE SHIP, BUCK. IT'S THEIR ONLY CHANCE.
IT'S NOT GOING TO BE EASY GETTING TO SHORE. TRY TO CHAIN YOURSELVES TOGETHER - I'LL DUMP OUT AS MANY SUPPLIES AS I CAN AND HOPE YOU CAN FIND THEM LATER.
WHAT ARE *YOU* GOING TO DO?
I'M GOING FISHING.

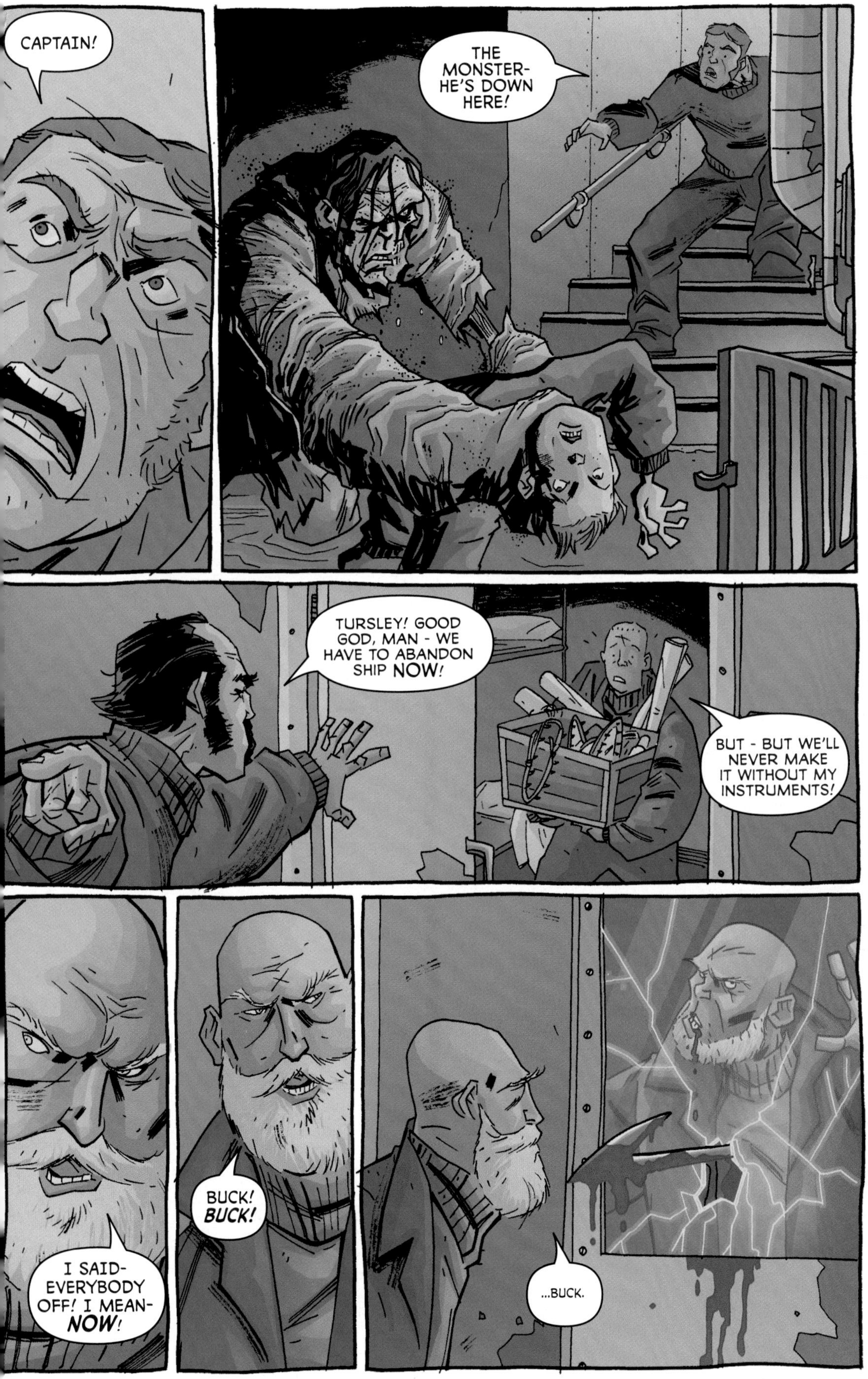
CAPTAIN!
THE MONSTER- HE'S DOWN HERE!
TURSLEY! GOOD GOD, MAN - WE HAVE TO ABANDON SHIP **NOW**!
BUT - BUT WE'LL NEVER MAKE IT WITHOUT MY INSTRUMENTS!
I SAID- EVERYBODY OFF! I MEAN- ***NOW***!
BUCK! ***BUCK!***
...BUCK.

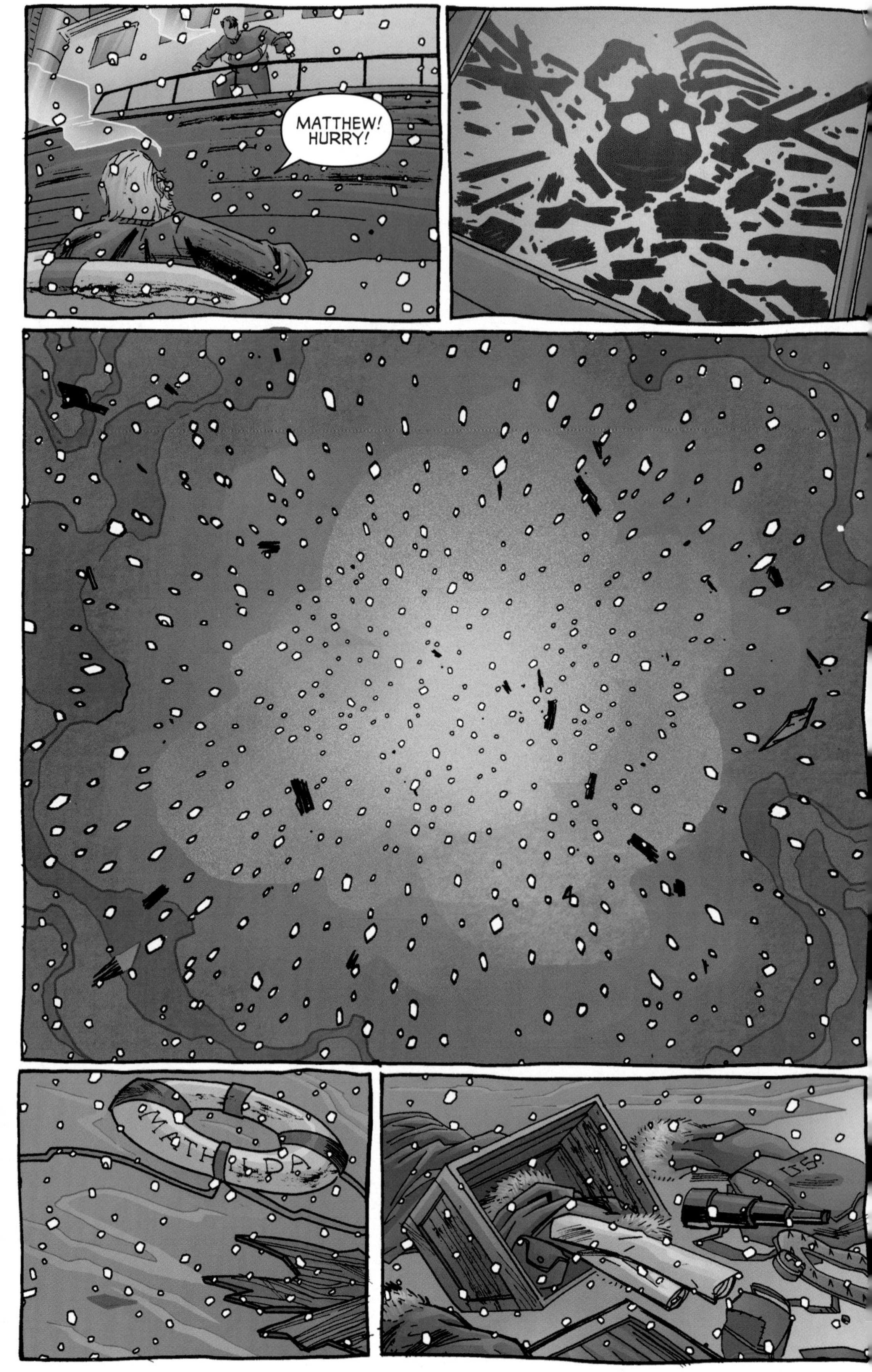
MATTHEW! HURRY!

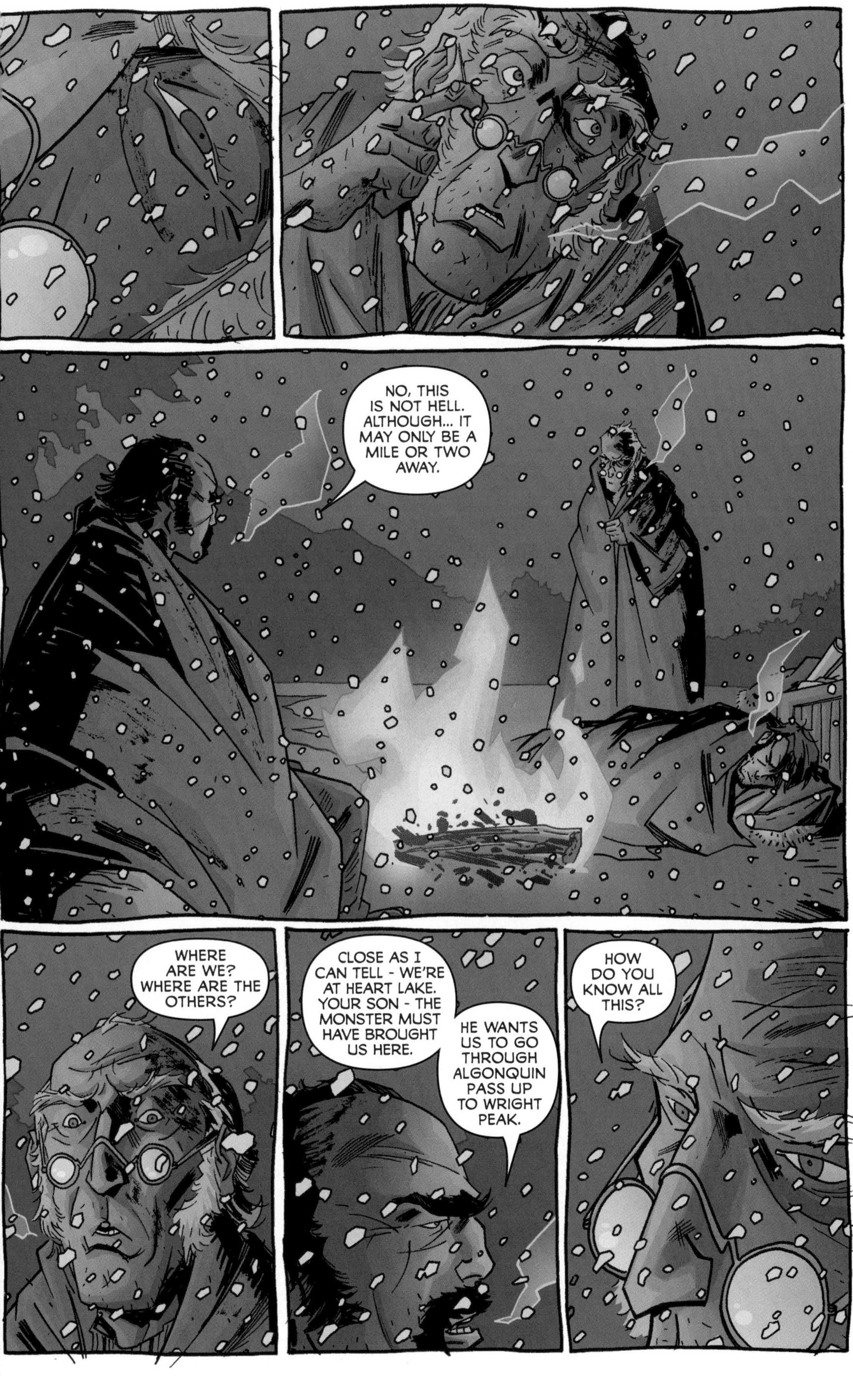
NO, THIS IS NOT HELL. ALTHOUGH... IT MAY ONLY BE A MILE OR TWO AWAY.
WHERE ARE WE? WHERE ARE THE OTHERS?
CLOSE AS I CAN TELL - WE'RE AT HEART LAKE. YOUR SON - THE MONSTER MUST HAVE BROUGHT US HERE.
HE WANTS US TO GO THROUGH ALGONQUIN PASS UP TO WRIGHT PEAK.
HOW DO YOU KNOW ALL THIS?

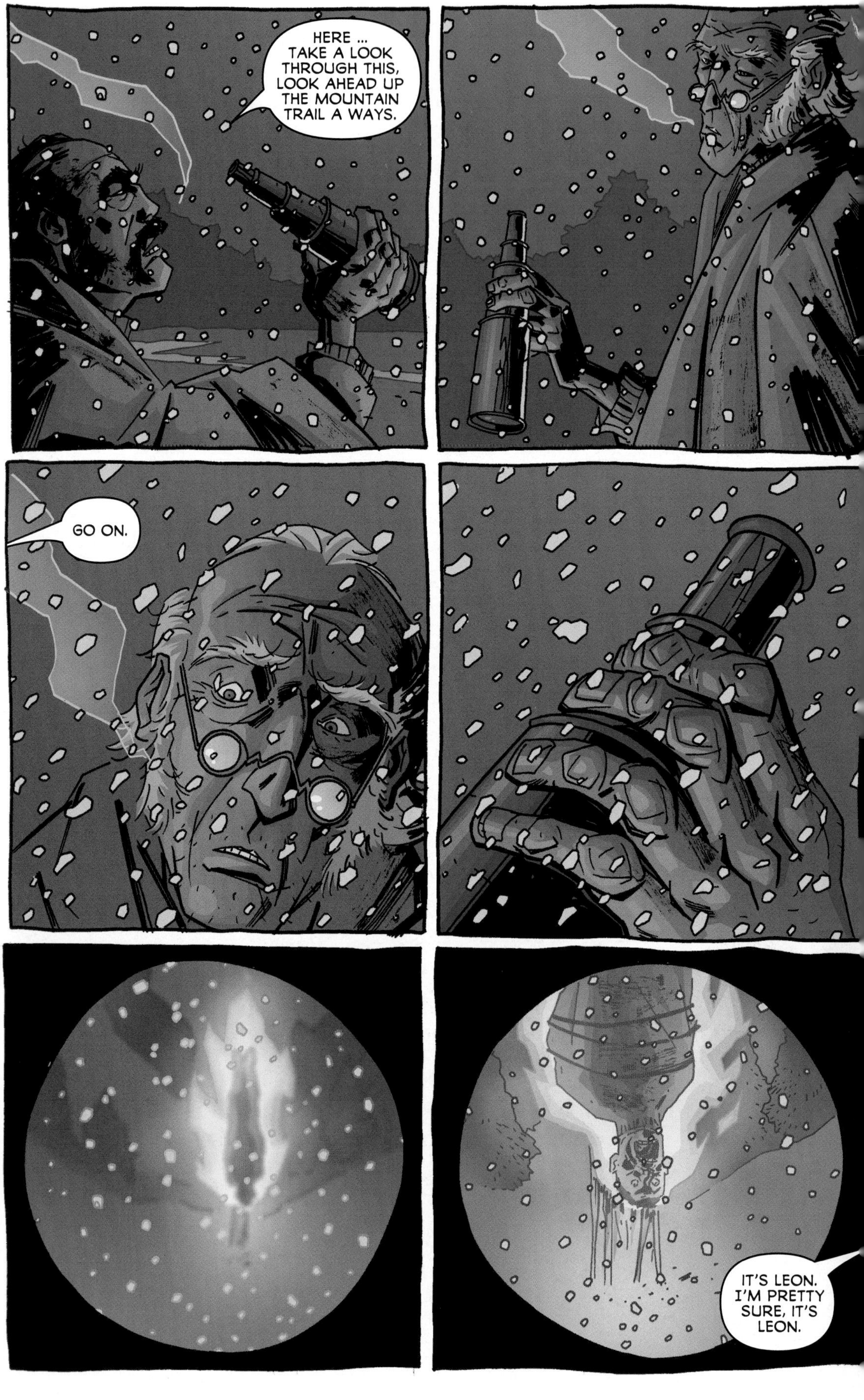
HERE ... TAKE A LOOK THROUGH THIS, LOOK AHEAD UP THE MOUNTAIN TRAIL A WAYS.
GO ON.
IT'S LEON. I'M PRETTY SURE, IT'S LEON.

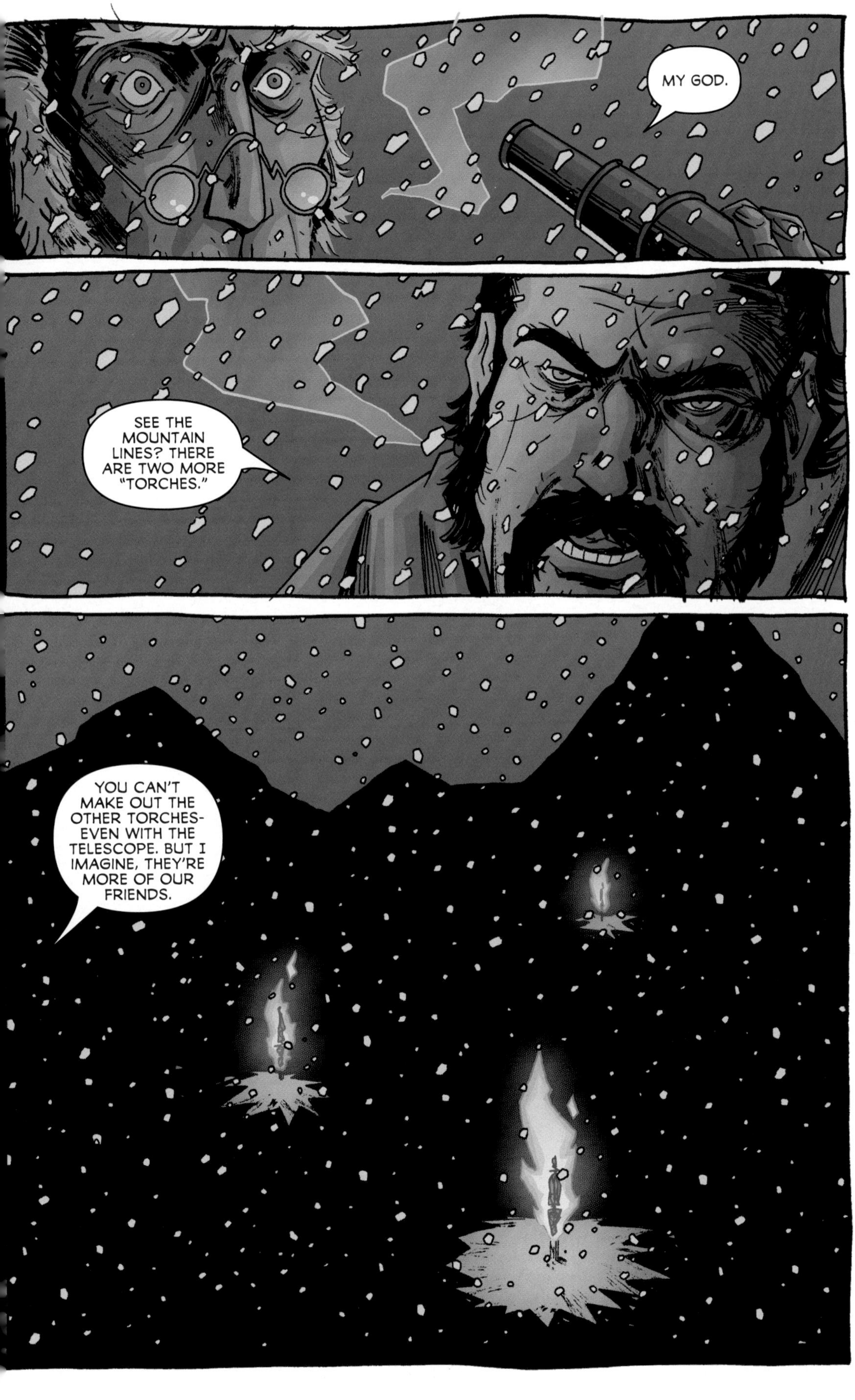
MY GOD.
SEE THE MOUNTAIN LINES? THERE ARE TWO MORE "TORCHES."
YOU CAN'T MAKE OUT THE OTHER TORCHES- EVEN WITH THE TELESCOPE. BUT I IMAGINE, THEY'RE MORE OF OUR FRIENDS.

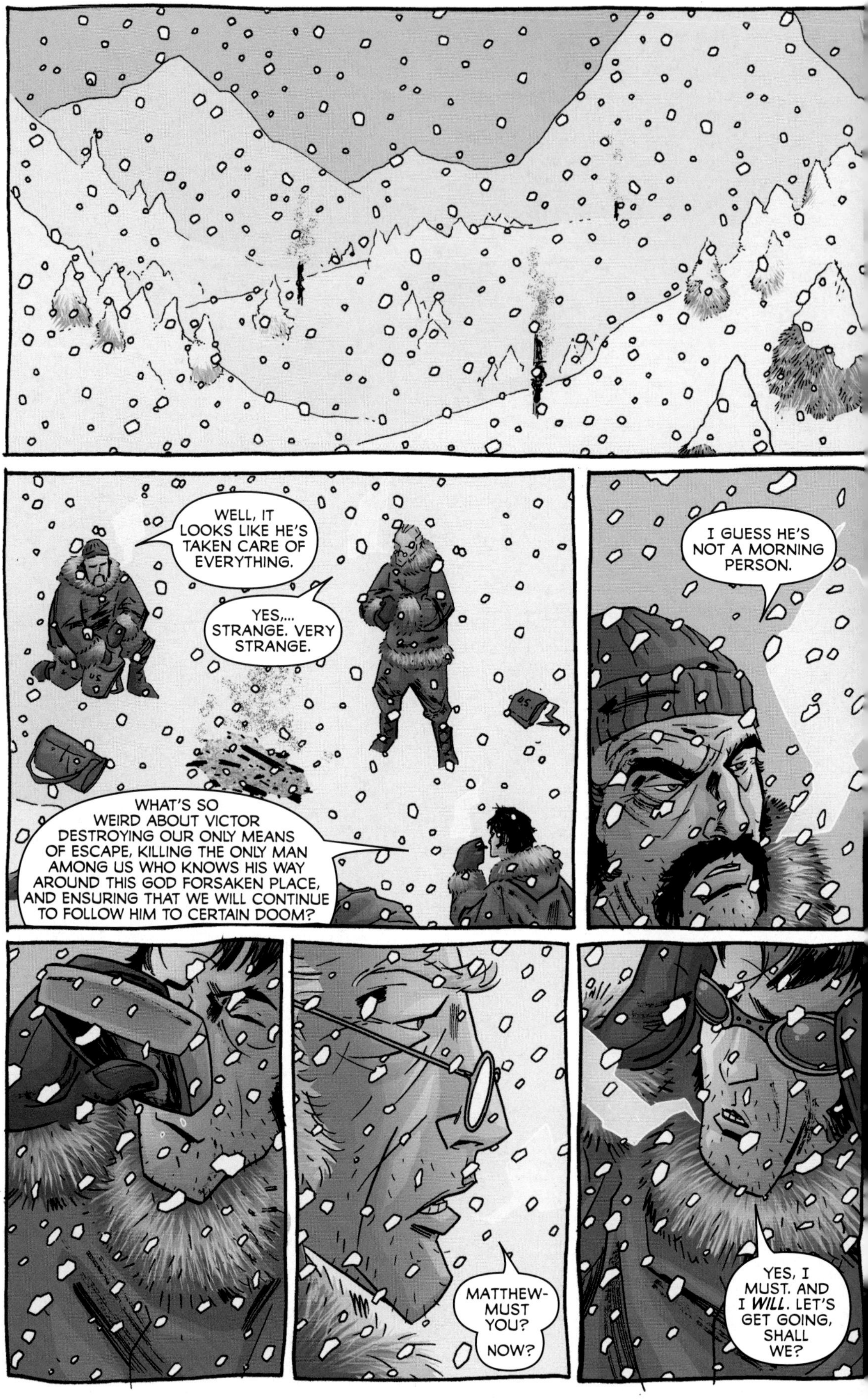

WELL, IT LOOKS LIKE HE'S TAKEN CARE OF EVERYTHING.
YES,... STRANGE. VERY STRANGE.
WHAT'S SO WEIRD ABOUT VICTOR DESTROYING OUR ONLY MEANS OF ESCAPE, KILLING THE ONLY MAN AMONG US WHO KNOWS HIS WAY AROUND THIS GOD FORSAKEN PLACE, AND ENSURING THAT WE WILL CONTINUE TO FOLLOW HIM TO CERTAIN DOOM?
I GUESS HE'S NOT A MORNING PERSON.
MATTHEW-MUST YOU? NOW?
YES, I MUST. AND I *WILL*. LET'S GET GOING, SHALL WE?

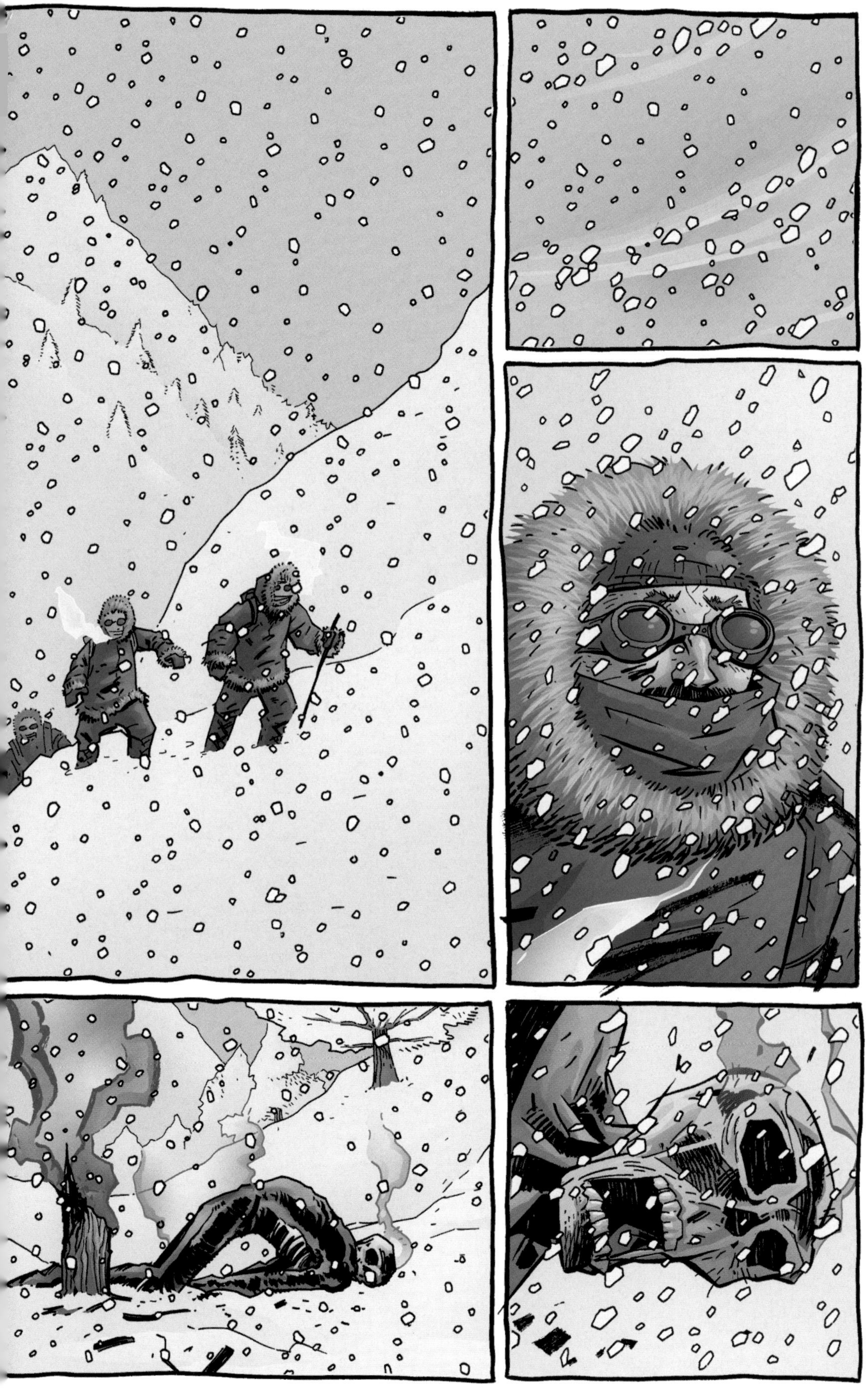

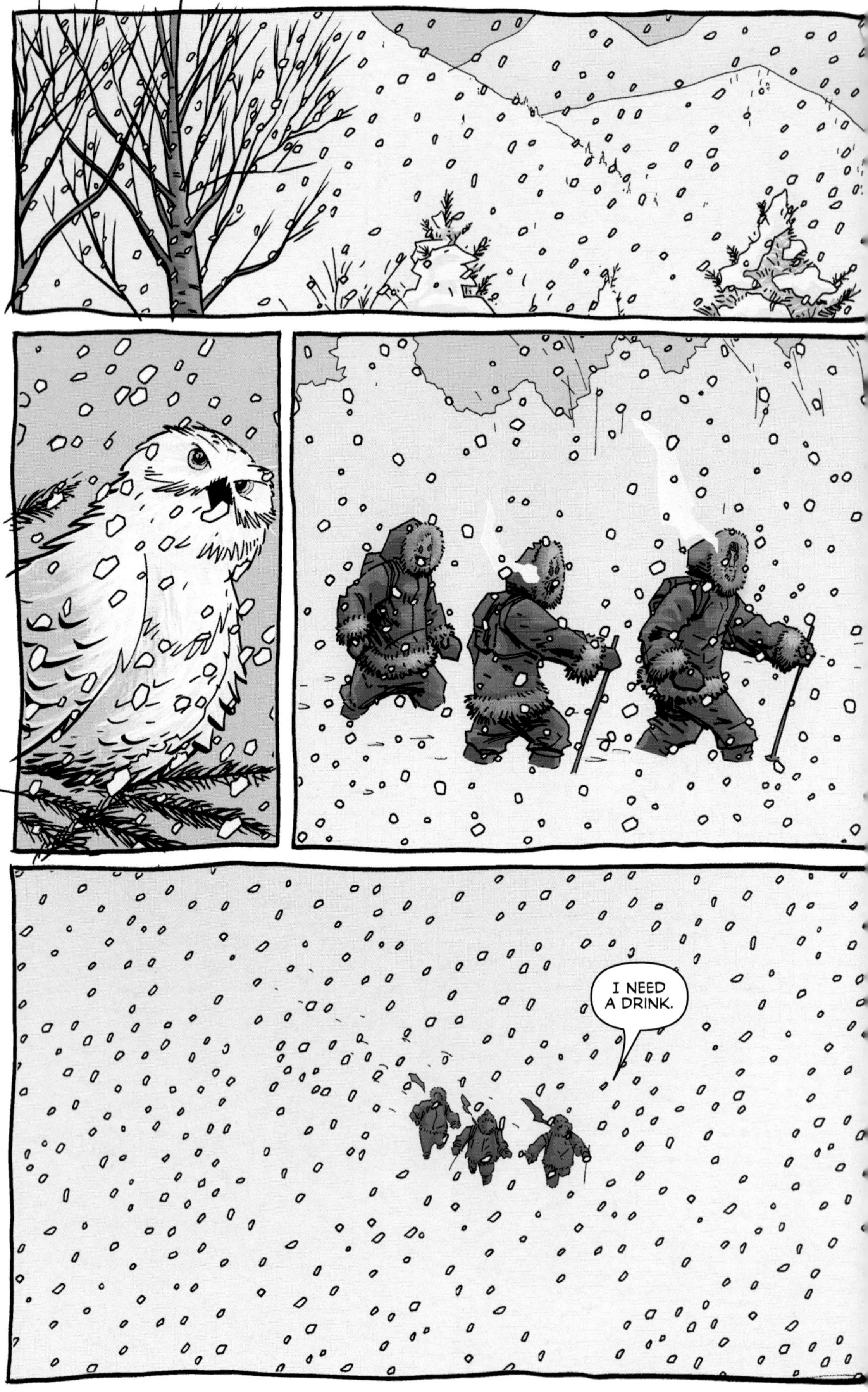
I NEED A DRINK.

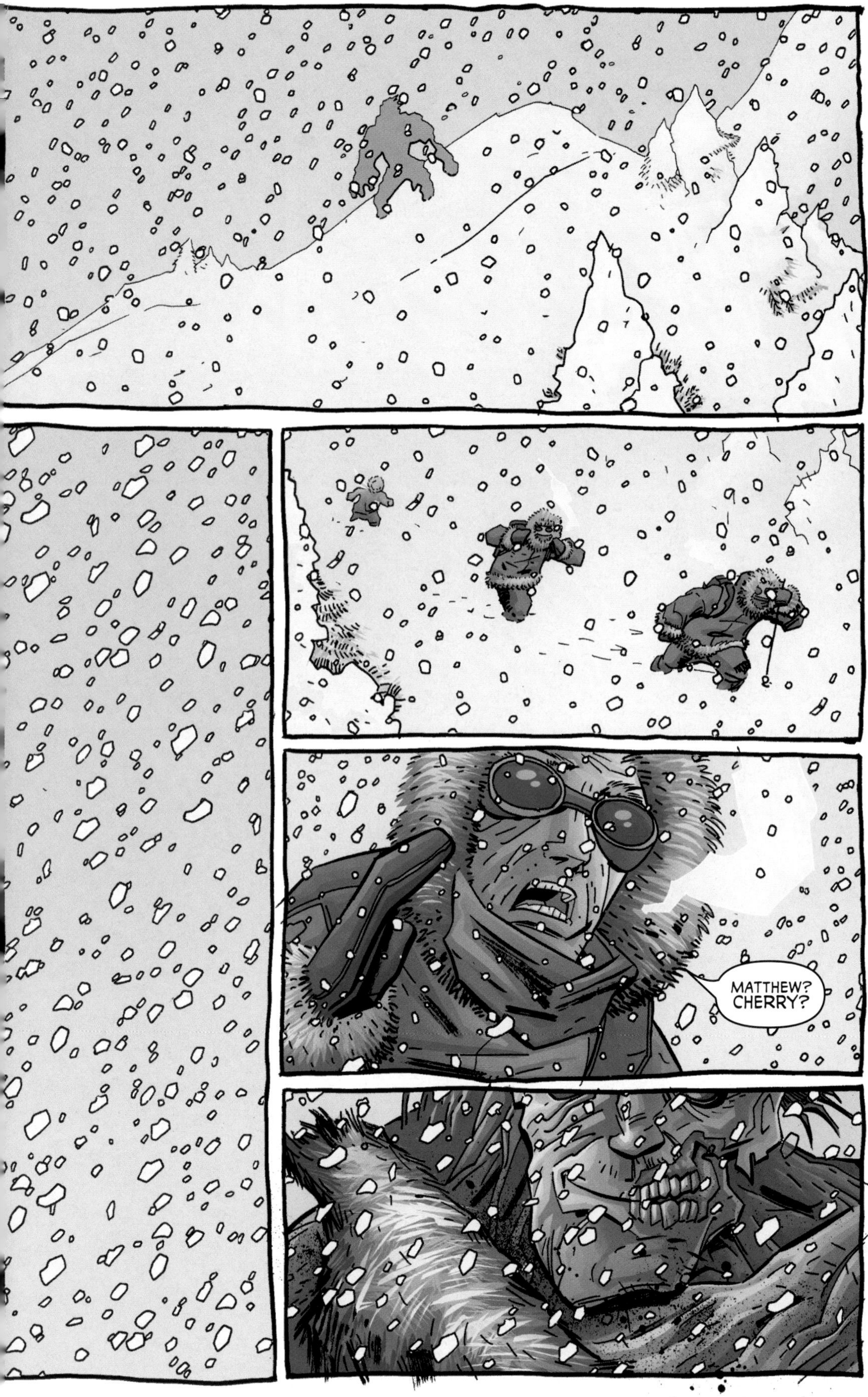
MATTHEW? CHERRY?

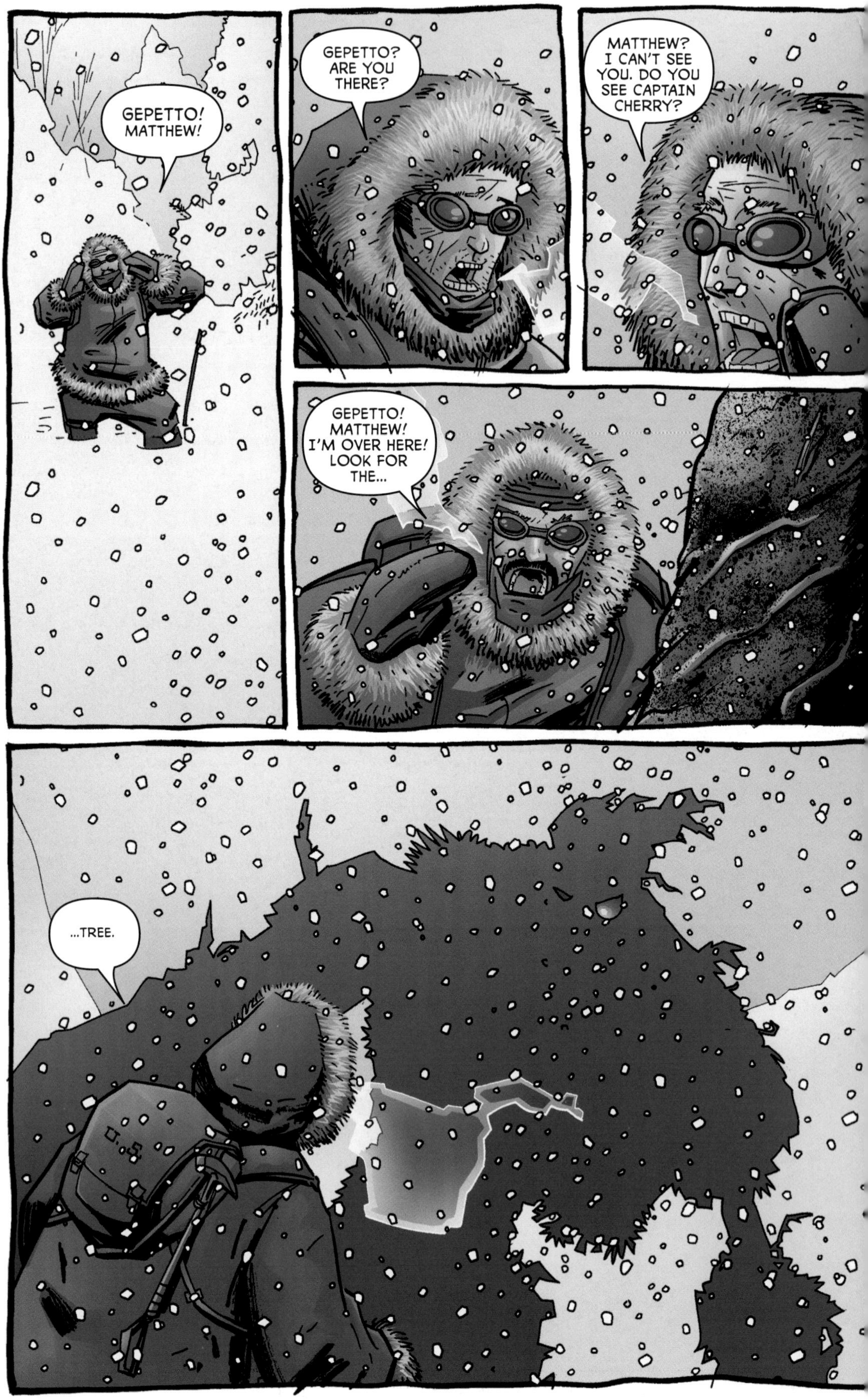
GEPETTO! MATTHEW!
GEPETTO? ARE YOU THERE?
MATTHEW? I CAN'T SEE YOU. DO YOU SEE CAPTAIN CHERRY?
GEPETTO! MATTHEW! I'M OVER HERE! LOOK FOR THE...
...TREE.

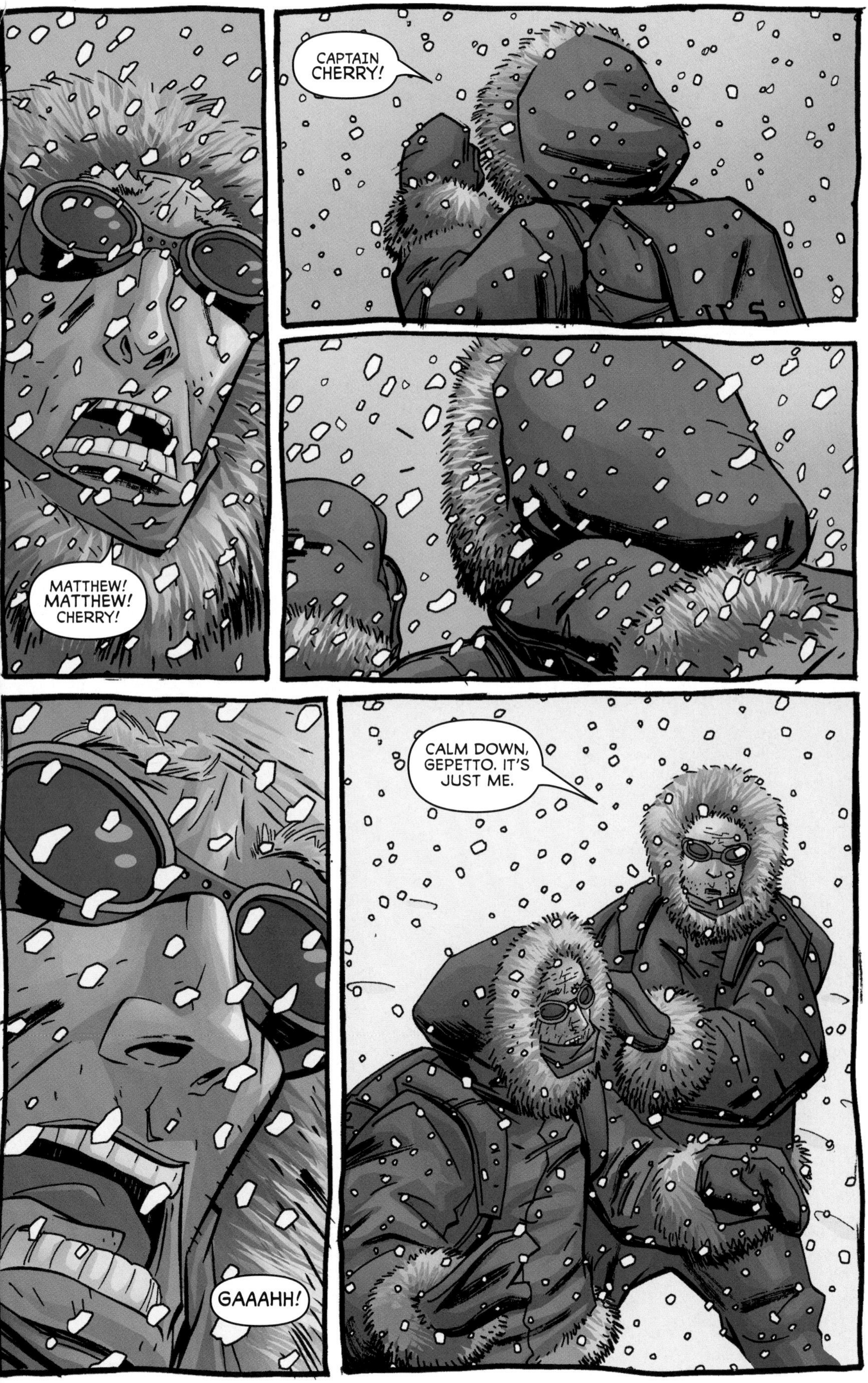
MATTHEW! MATTHEW! CHERRY!
CAPTAIN CHERRY!
GAAAHH!
CALM DOWN, GEPETTO. IT'S JUST ME.

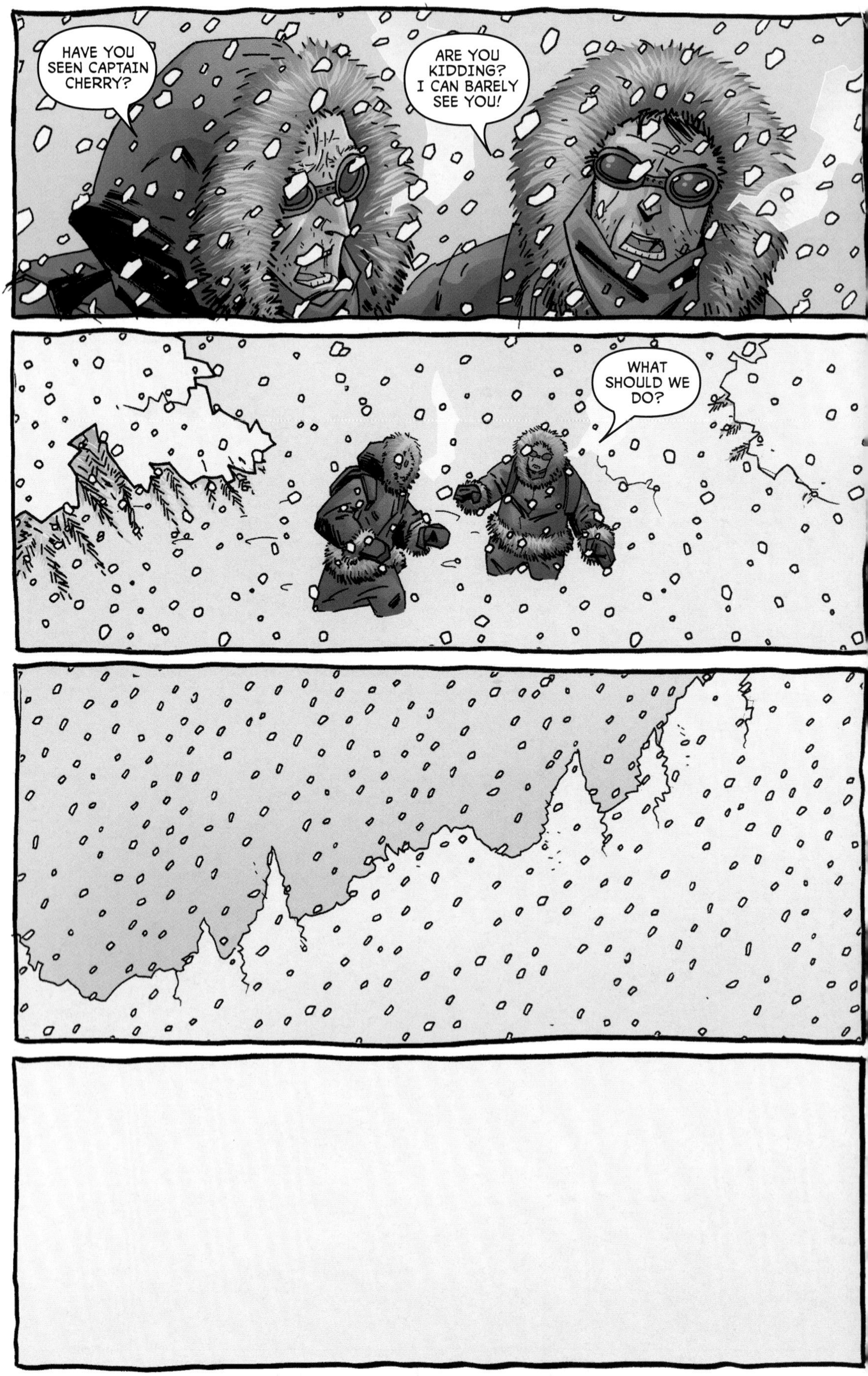
HAVE YOU SEEN CAPTAIN CHERRY?
ARE YOU KIDDING? I CAN BARELY SEE YOU!
WHAT SHOULD WE DO?

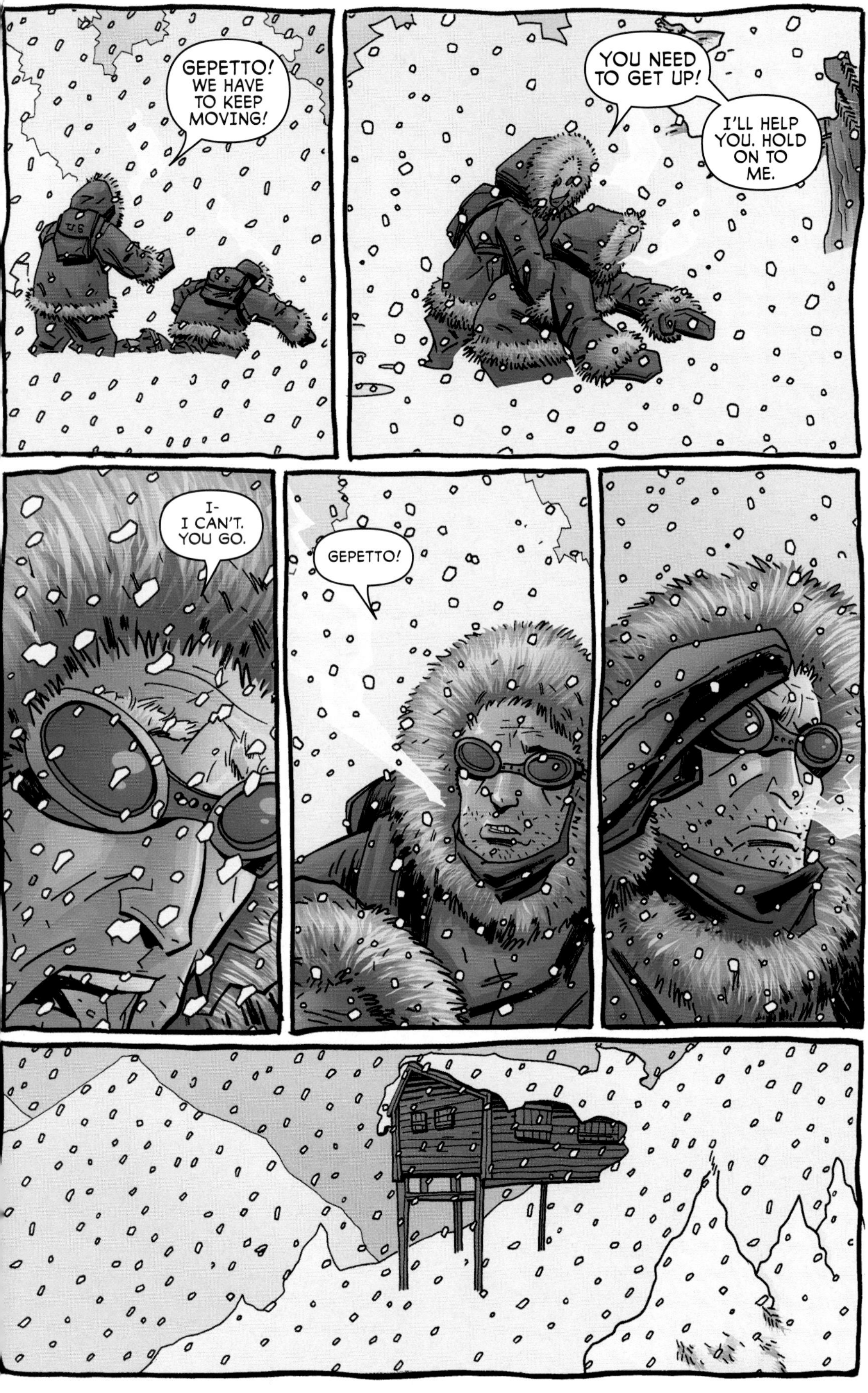
GEPETTO! WE HAVE TO KEEP MOVING!
YOU NEED TO GET UP!
I'LL HELP YOU. HOLD ON TO ME.
I- I CAN'T. YOU GO.
GEPETTO!

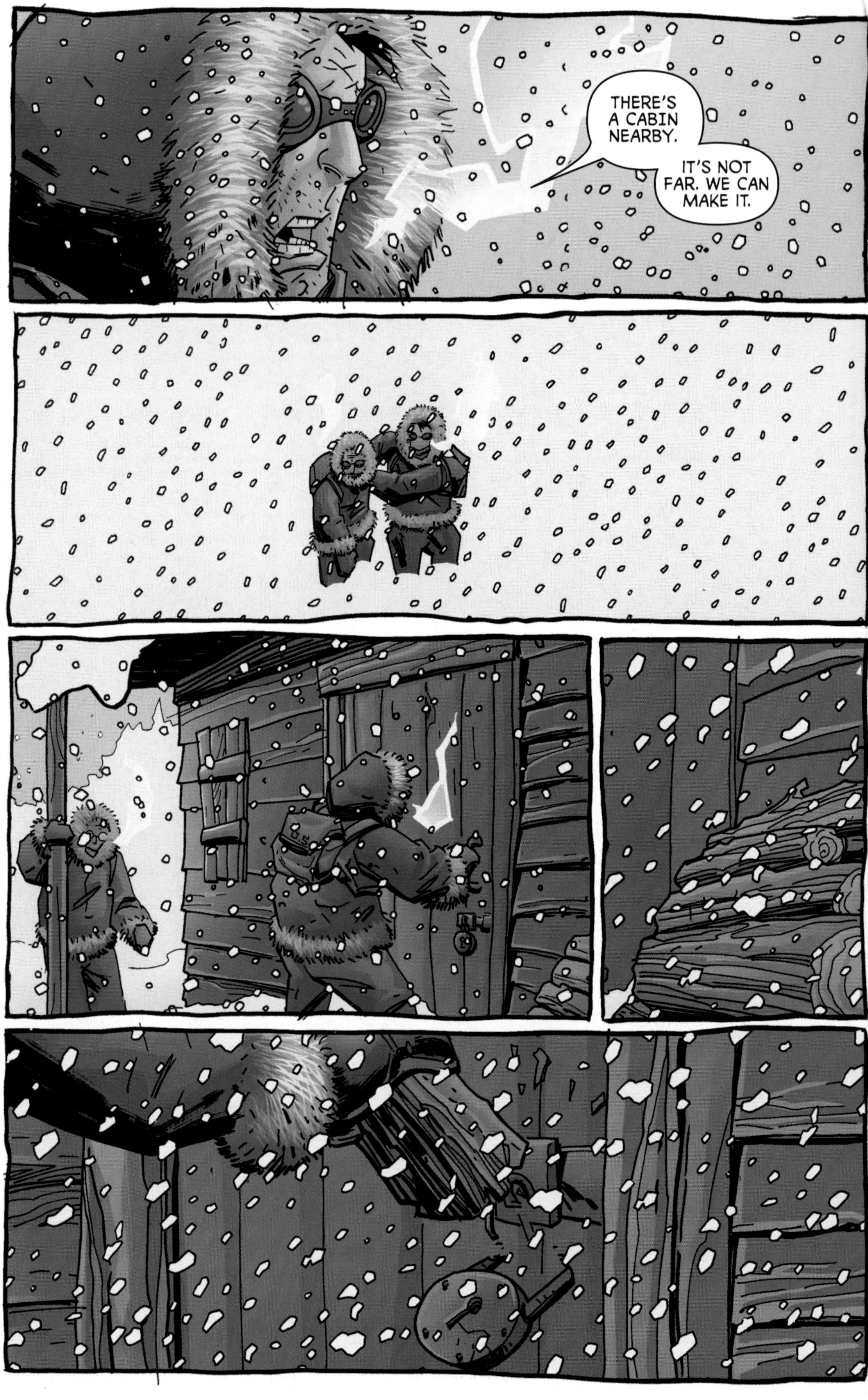
THERE'S A CABIN NEARBY.
IT'S NOT FAR. WE CAN MAKE IT.

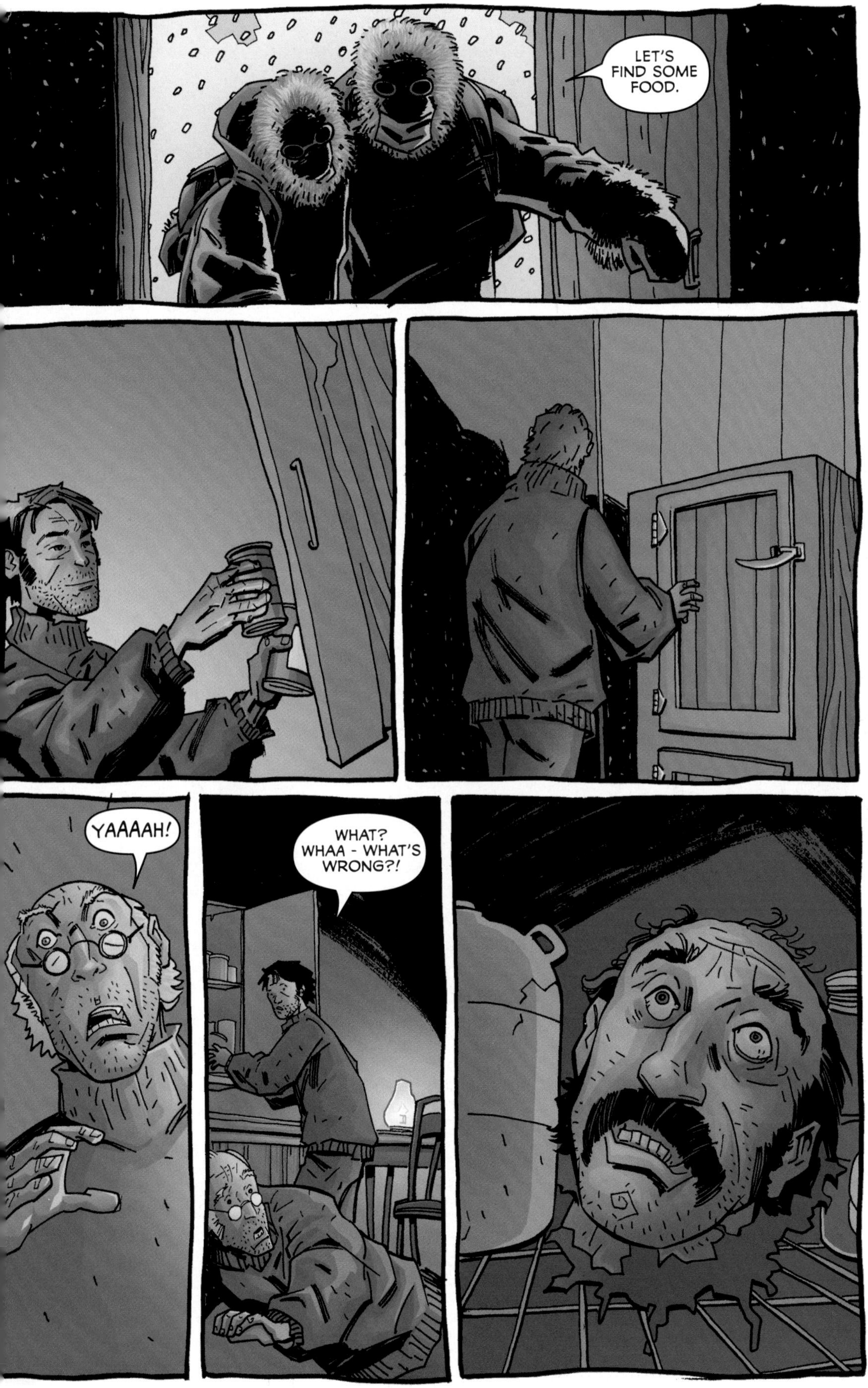
LET'S FIND SOME FOOD.
YAAAAH!
WHAT? WHAA - WHAT'S WRONG?!

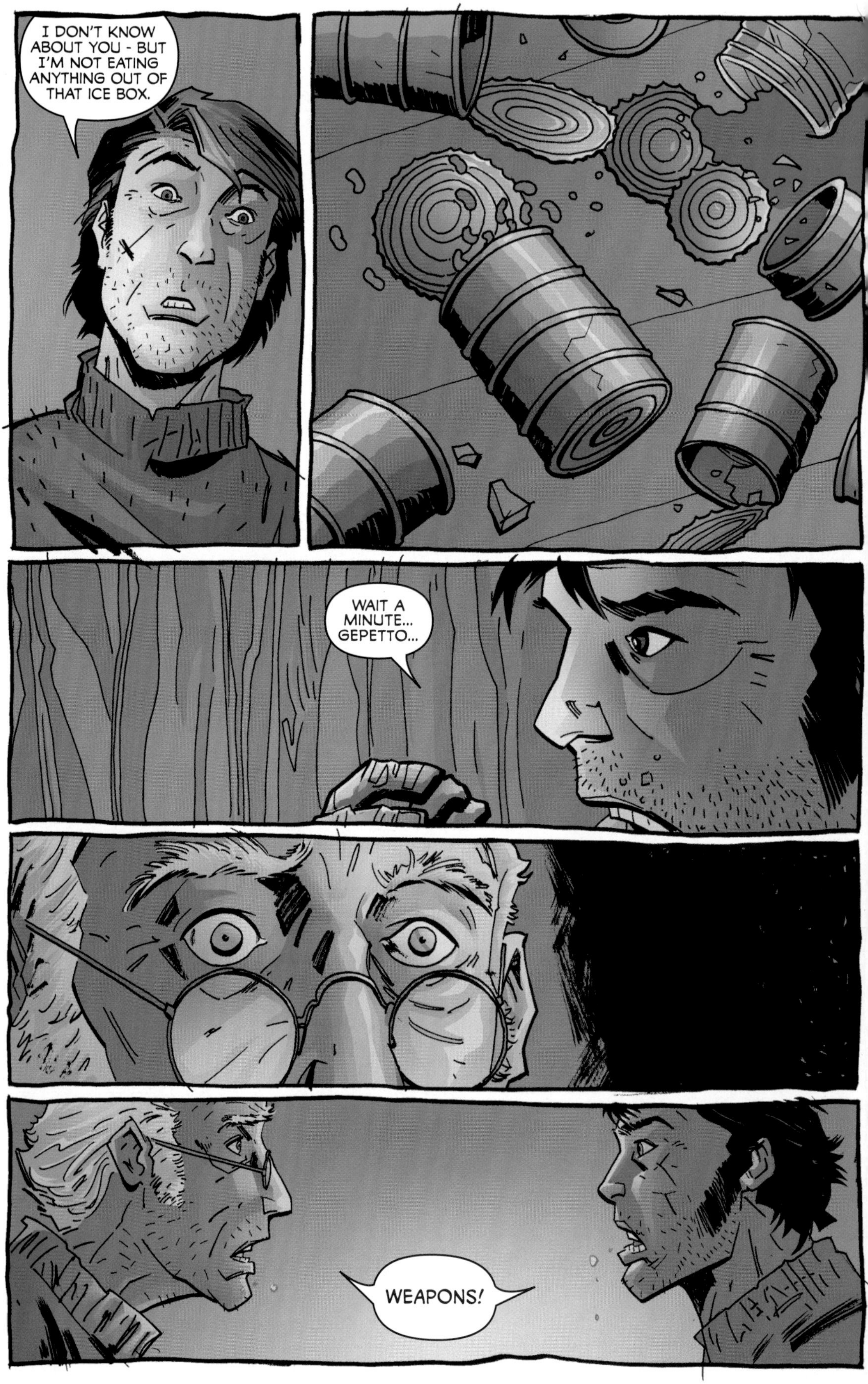
I DON'T KNOW ABOUT YOU - BUT I'M NOT EATING ANYTHING OUT OF THAT ICE BOX.
WAIT A MINUTE... GEPETTO...
WEAPONS!

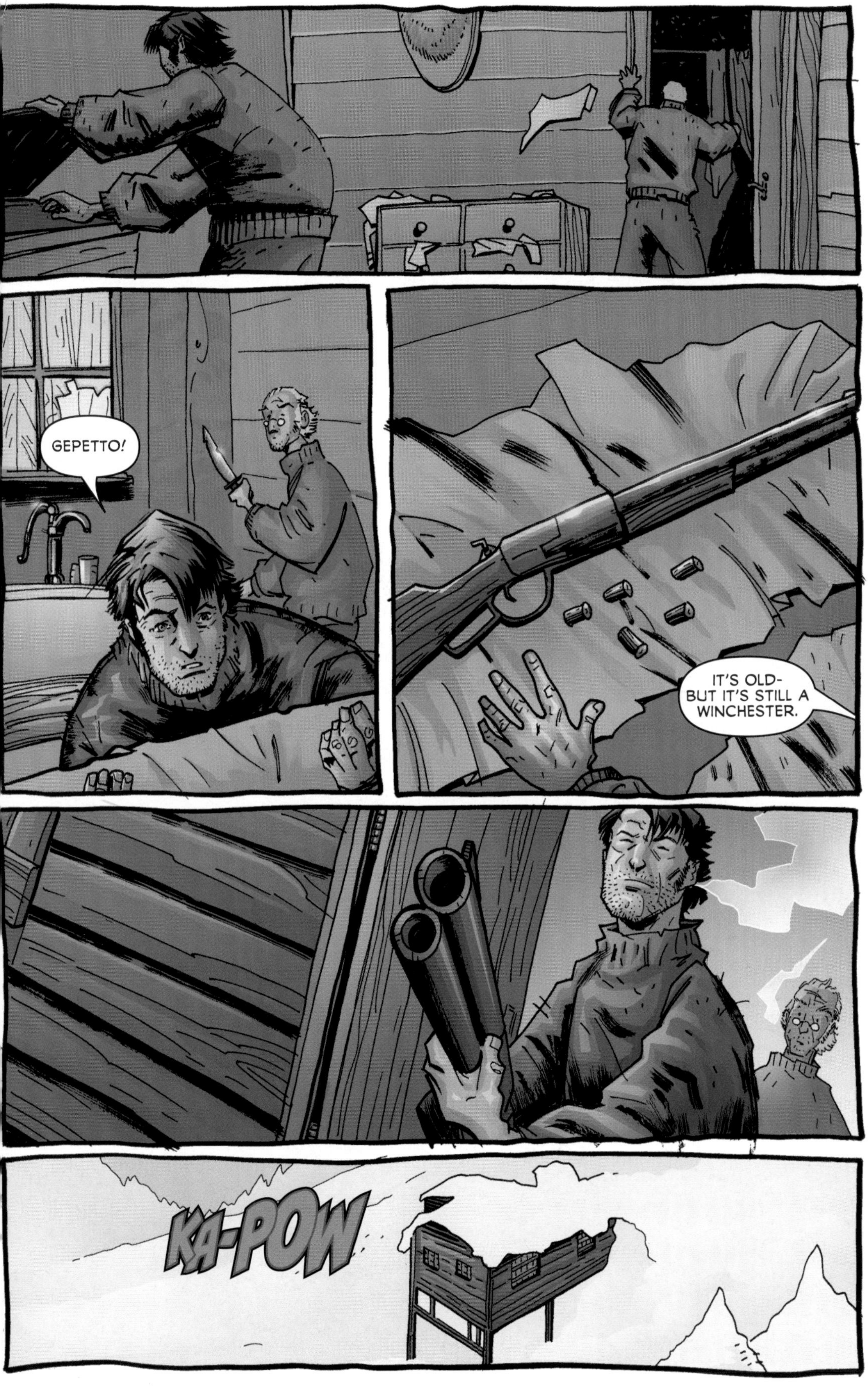
GEPETTO!
IT'S OLD- BUT IT'S STILL A WINCHESTER.
KA-POW

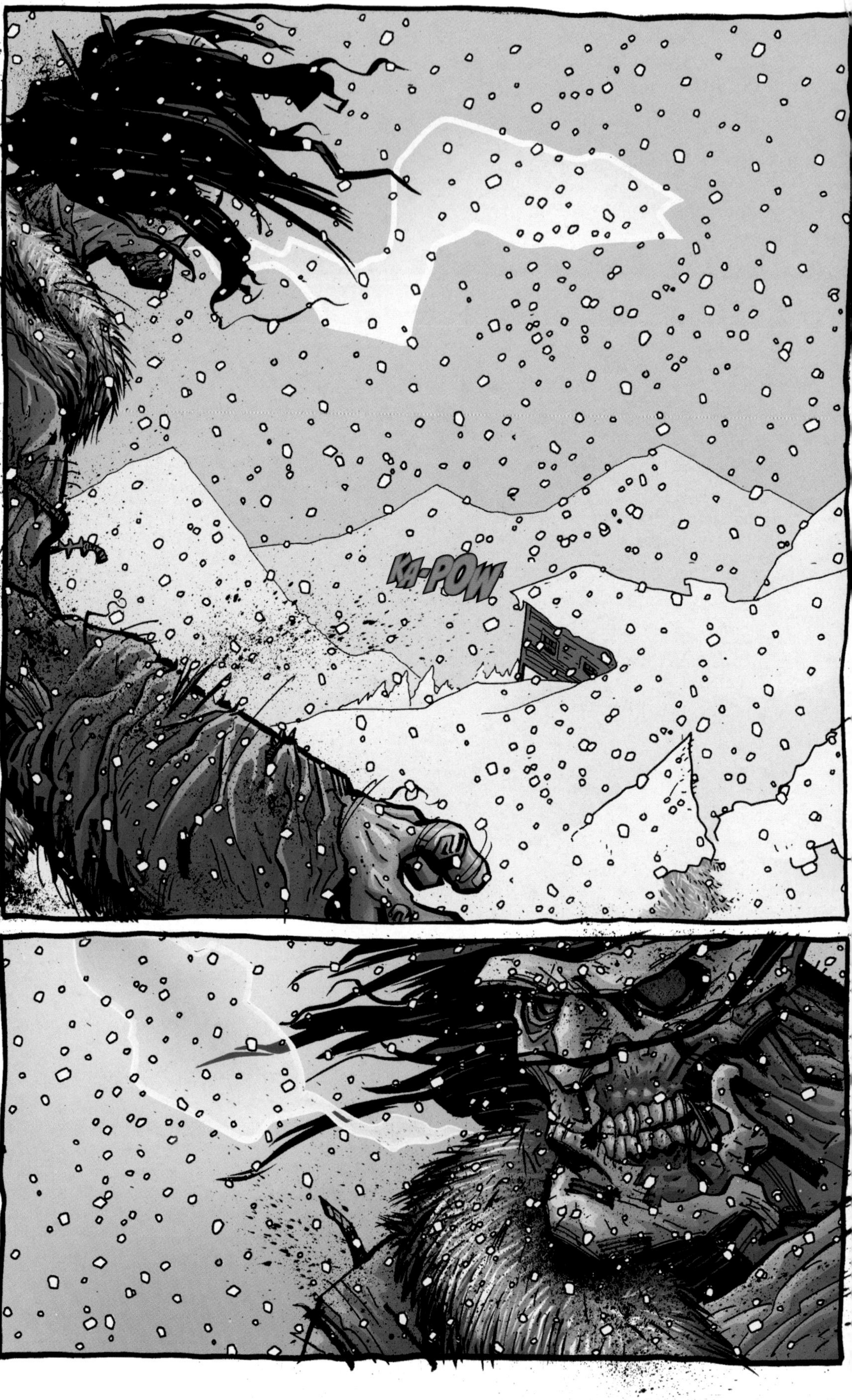
KA-POW

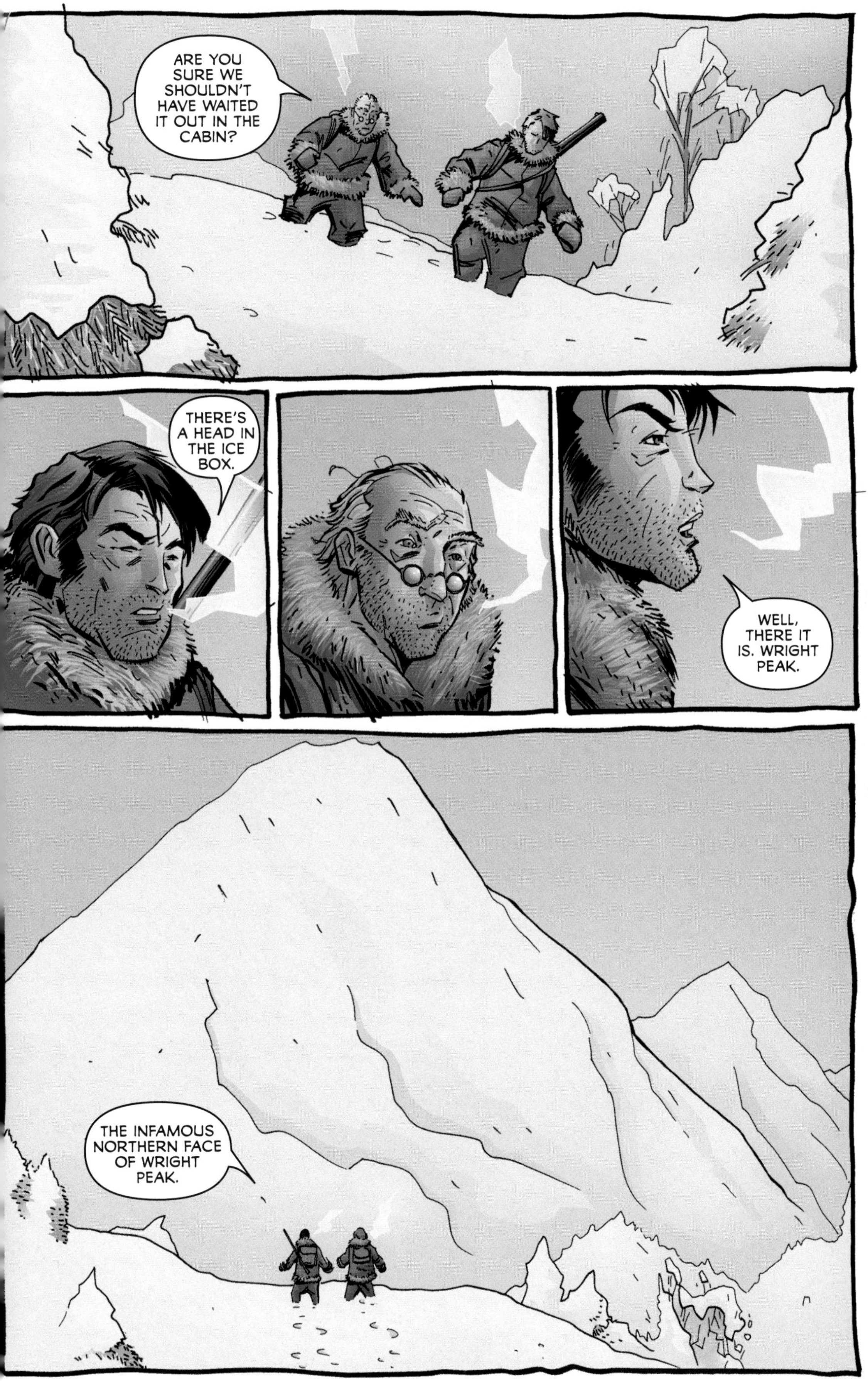
ARE YOU SURE WE SHOULDN'T HAVE WAITED IT OUT IN THE CABIN?
THERE'S A HEAD IN THE ICE BOX.
WELL, THERE IT IS. WRIGHT PEAK.
THE INFAMOUS NORTHERN FACE OF WRIGHT PEAK.

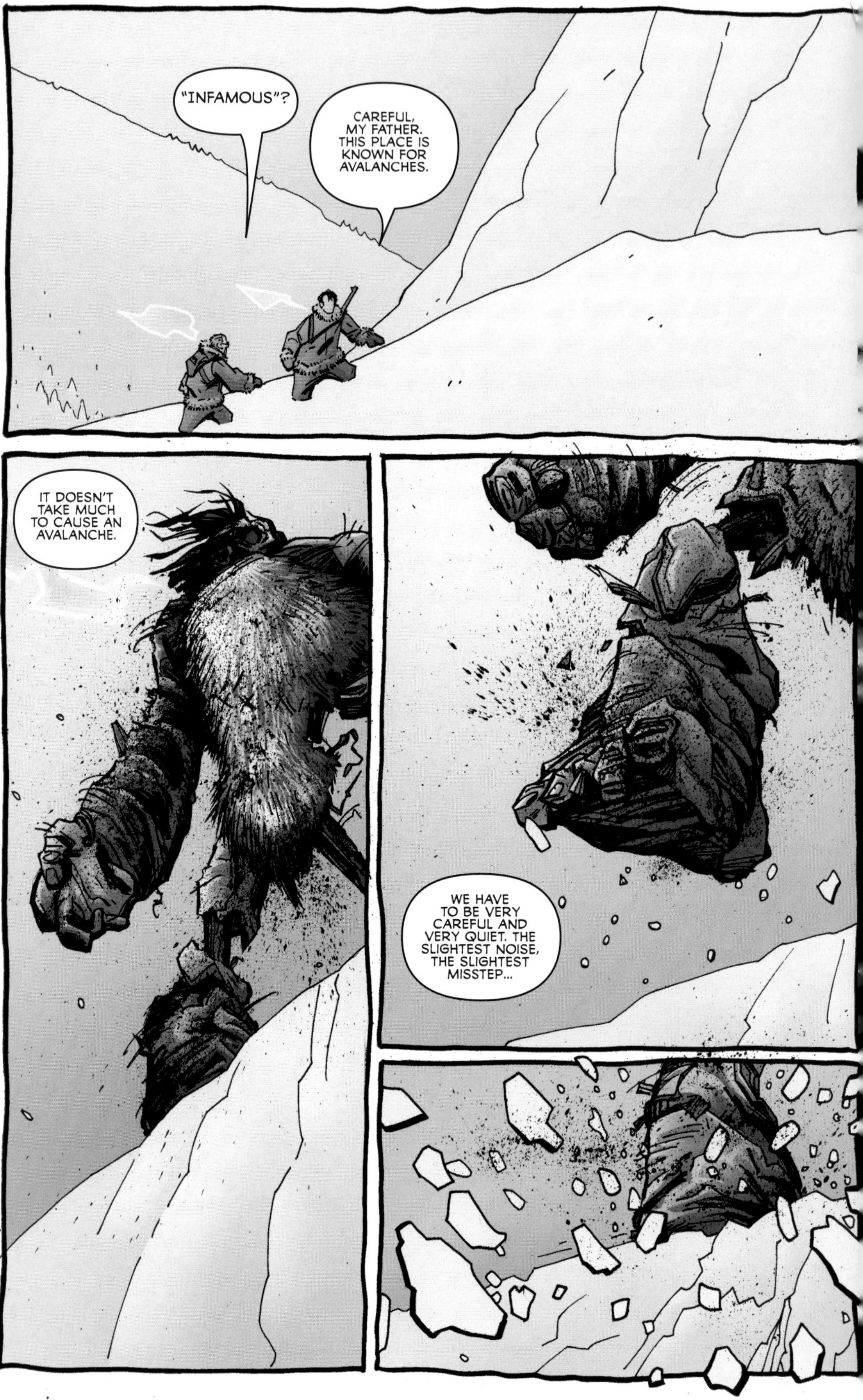

"INFAMOUS"?
CAREFUL, MY FATHER. THIS PLACE IS KNOWN FOR AVALANCHES.
IT DOESN'T TAKE MUCH TO CAUSE AN AVALANCHE.
WE HAVE TO BE VERY CAREFUL AND VERY QUIET. THE SLIGHTEST NOISE, THE SLIGHTEST MISSTEP...

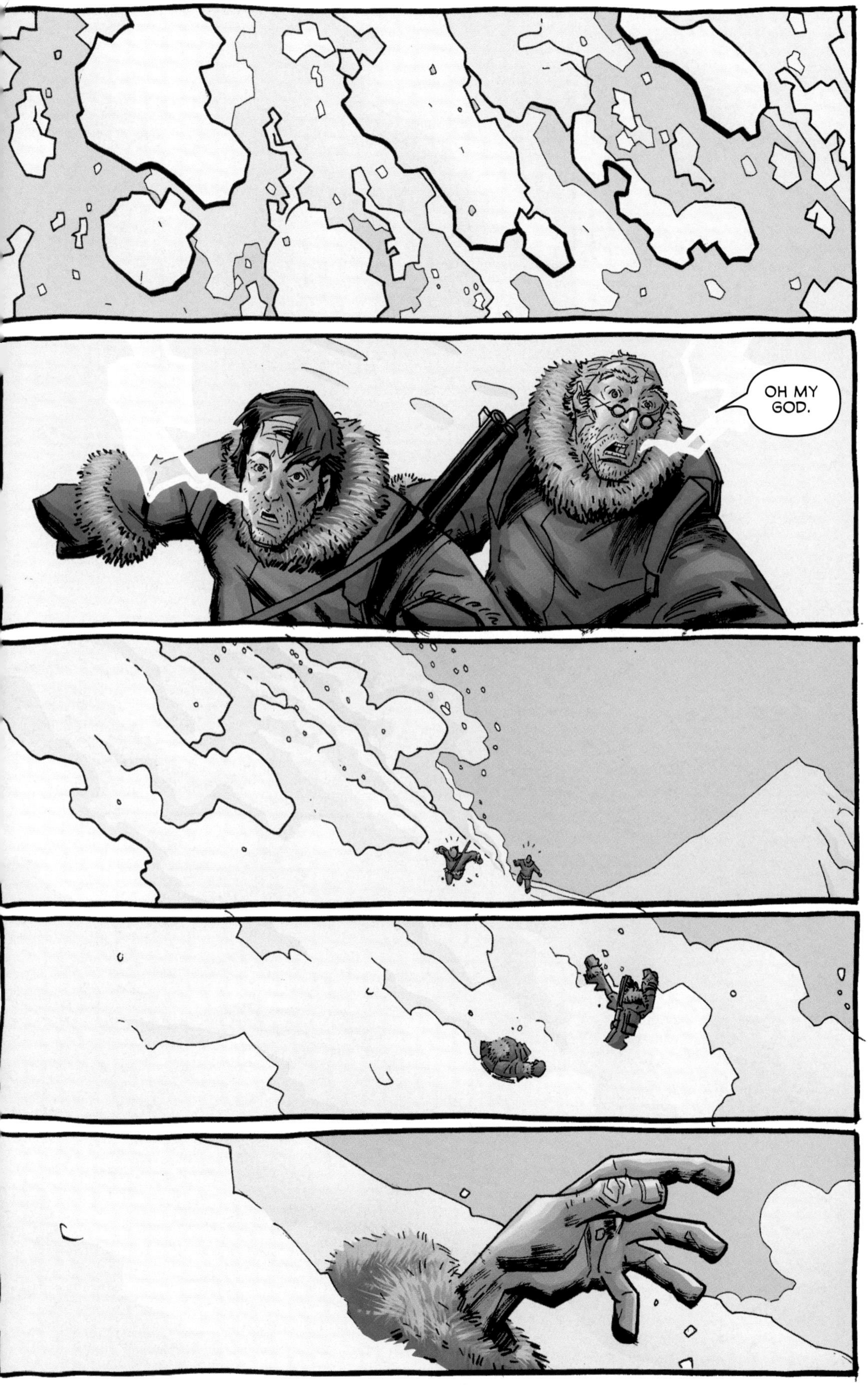
OH MY GOD.

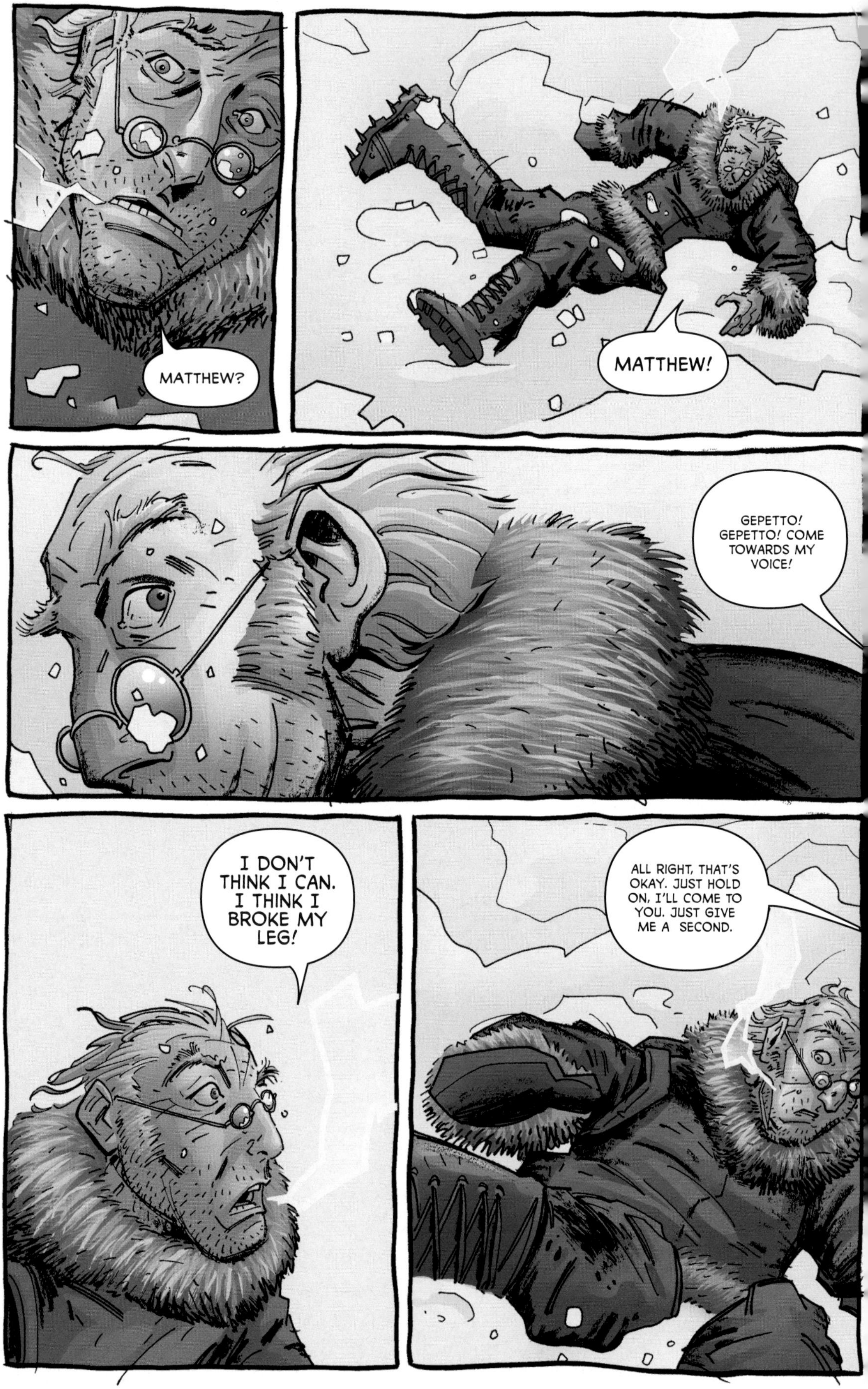
MATTHEW?
MATTHEW!
GEPETTO! GEPETTO! COME TOWARDS MY VOICE!
I DON'T THINK I CAN. I THINK I BROKE MY LEG!
ALL RIGHT, THAT'S OKAY. JUST HOLD ON, I'LL COME TO YOU. JUST GIVE ME A SECOND.

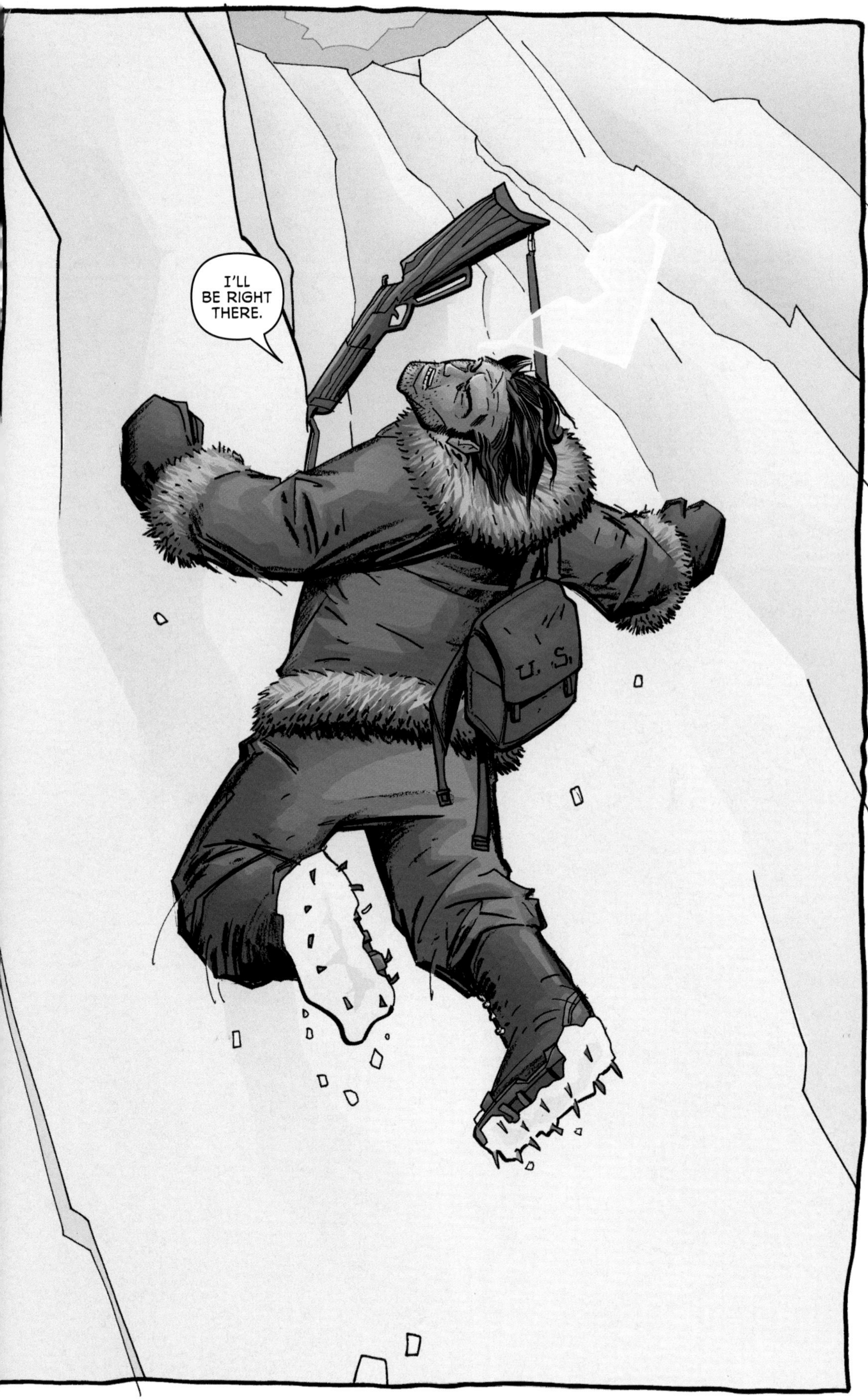
I'LL BE RIGHT THERE.
U.S.

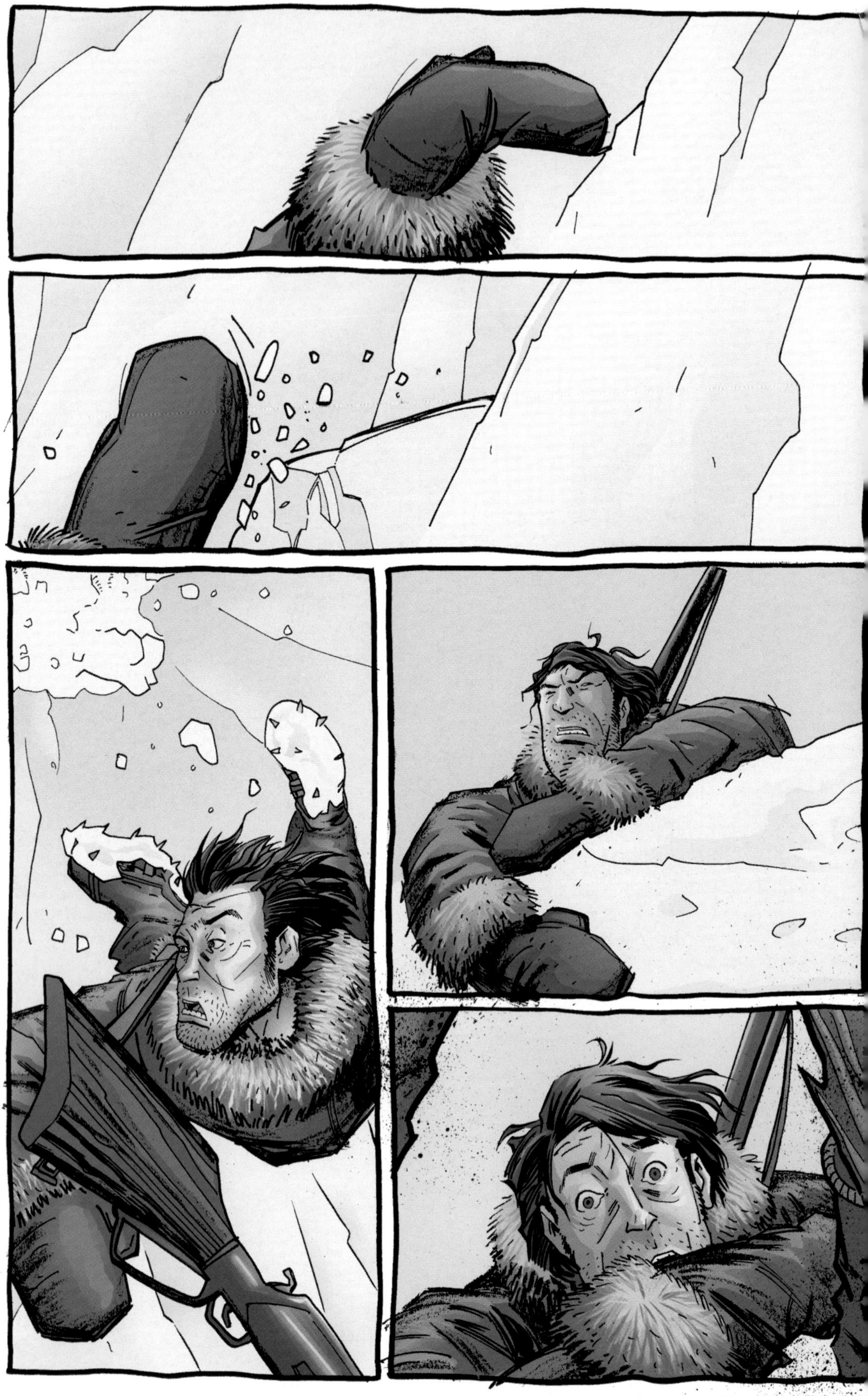

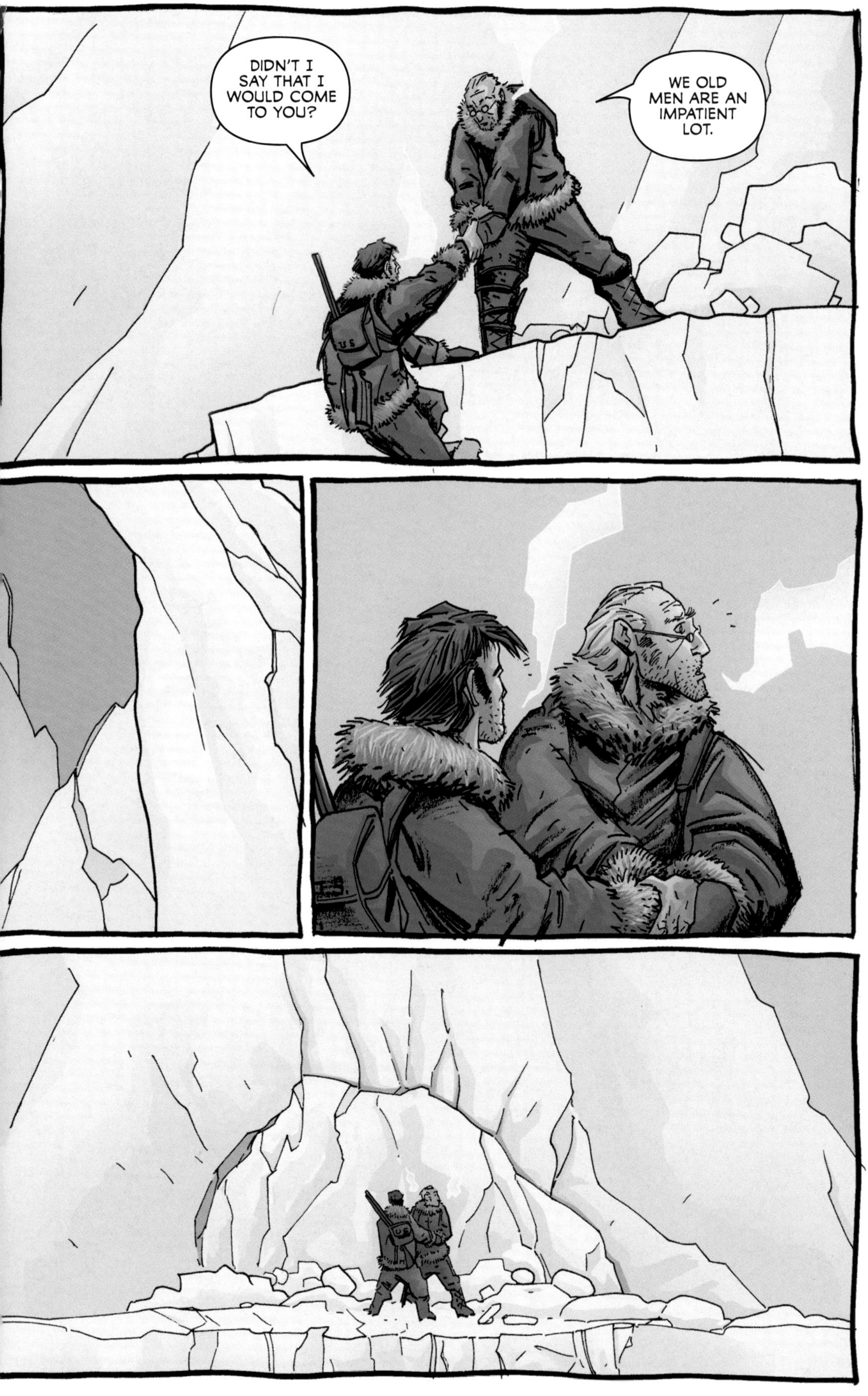
DIDN'T I SAY THAT I WOULD COME TO YOU?
WE OLD MEN ARE AN IMPATIENT LOT.

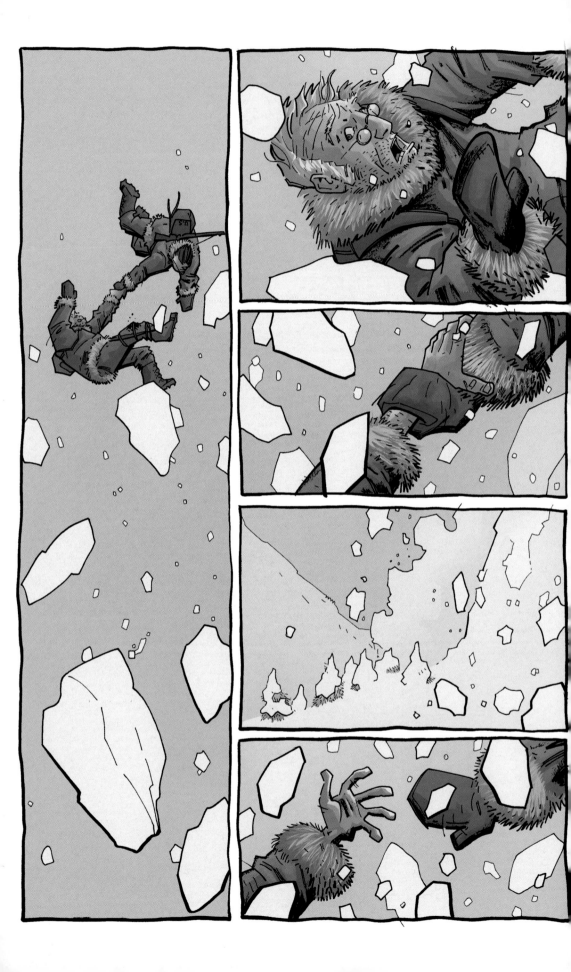

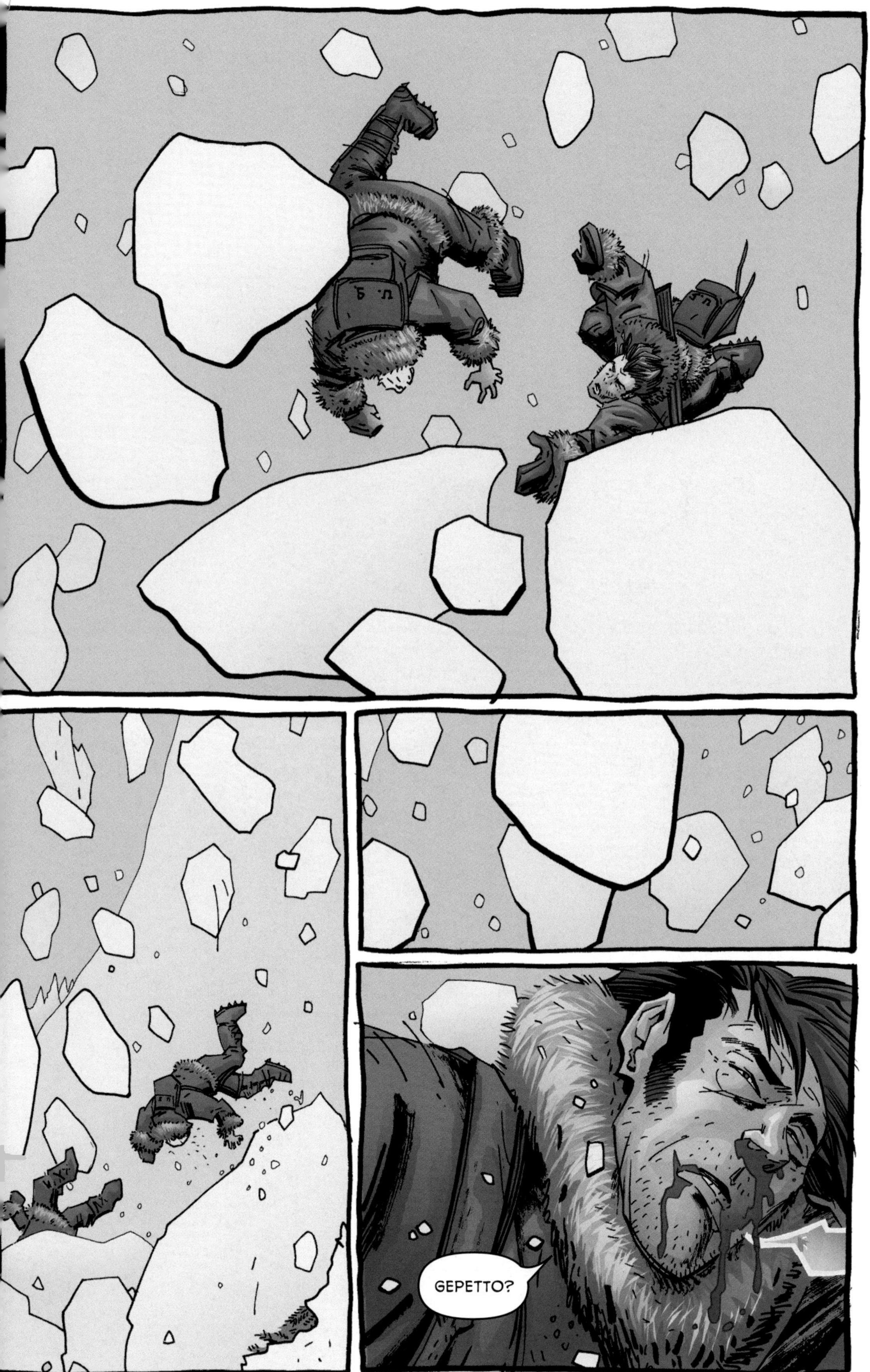
GEPETTO?

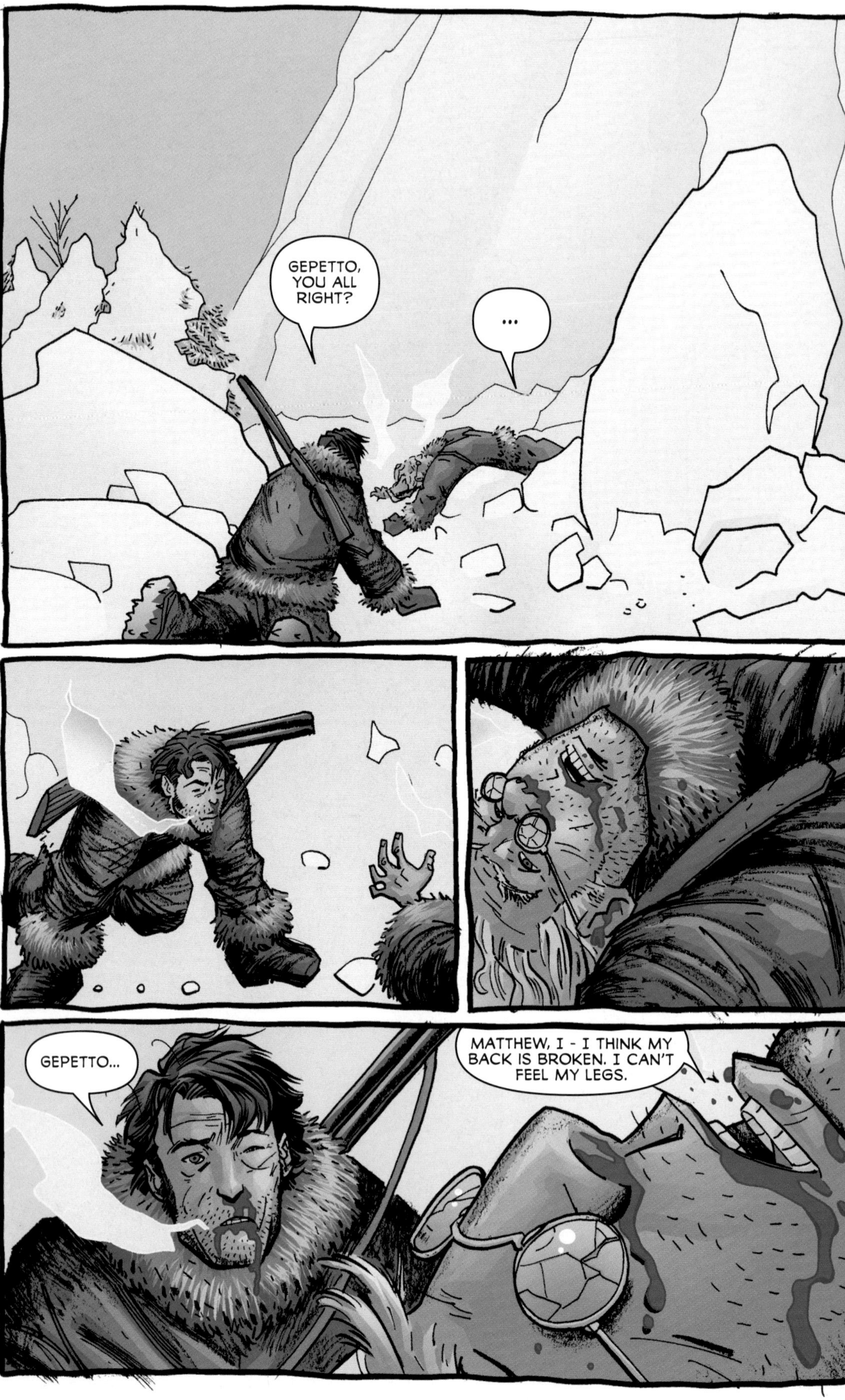
GEPETTO, YOU ALL RIGHT?
...
GEPETTO...
MATTHEW, I - I THINK MY BACK IS BROKEN. I CAN'T FEEL MY LEGS.

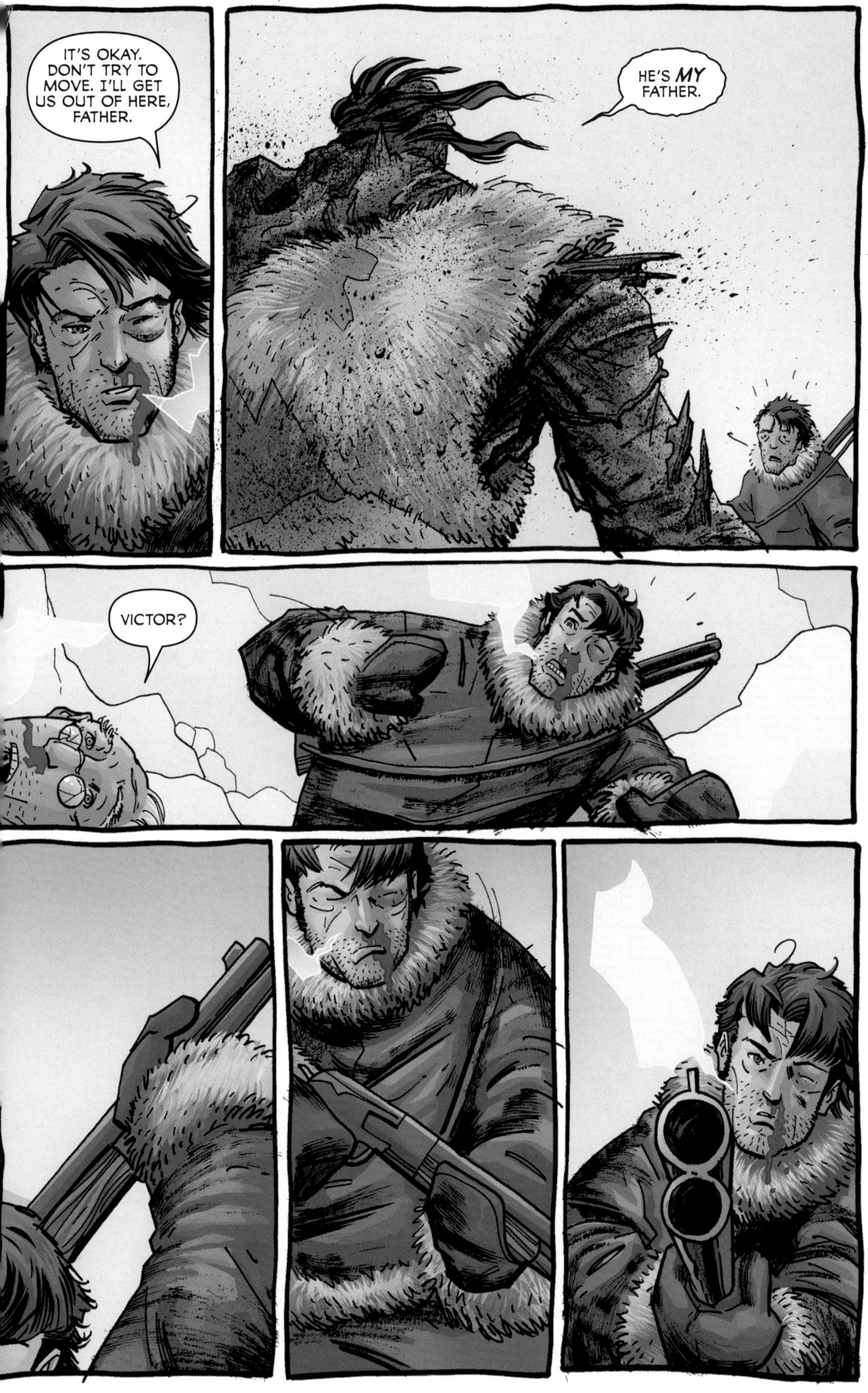
IT'S OKAY. DON'T TRY TO MOVE. I'LL GET US OUT OF HERE, FATHER.
HE'S *MY* FATHER.
VICTOR?

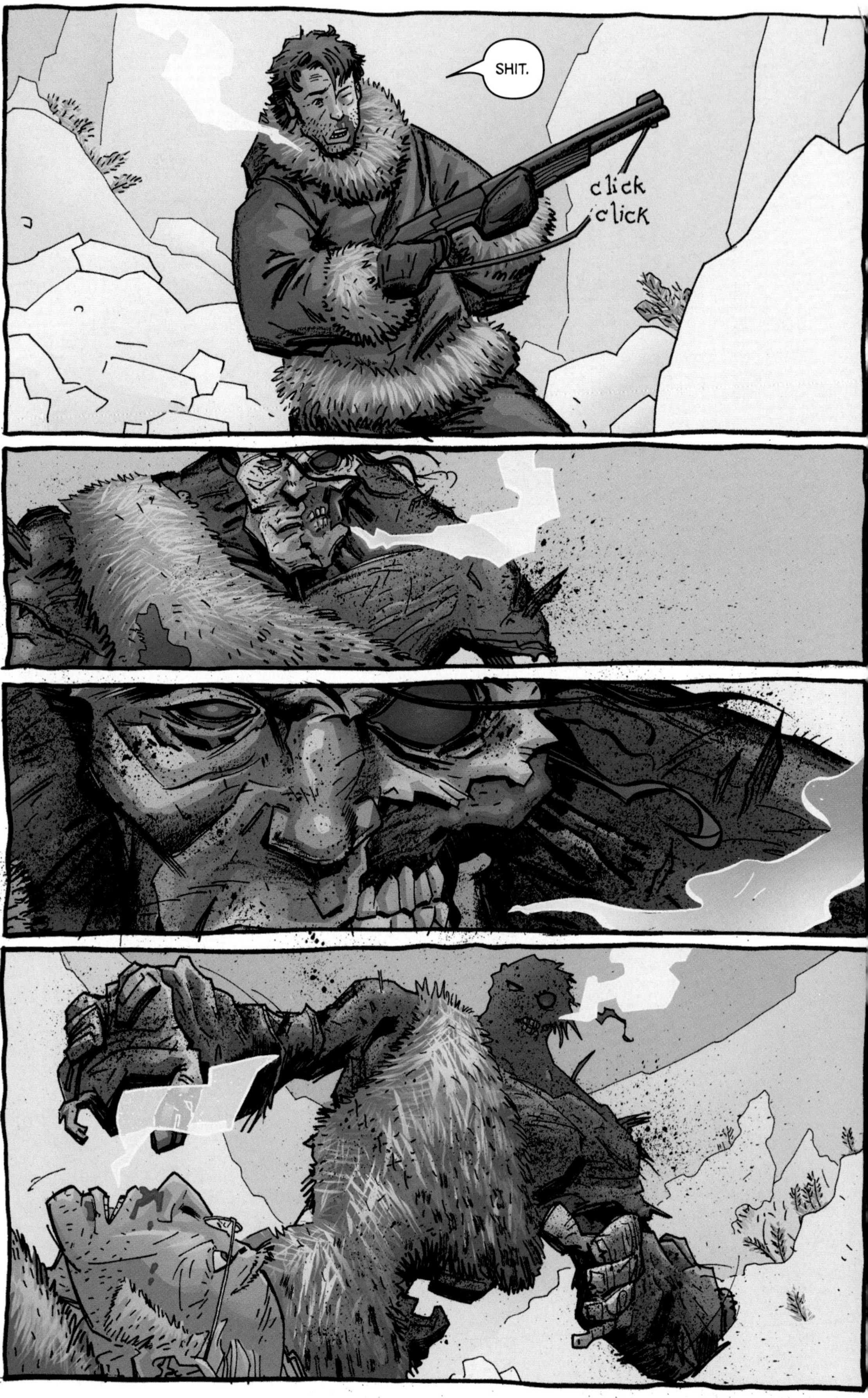
SHIT.
click
click

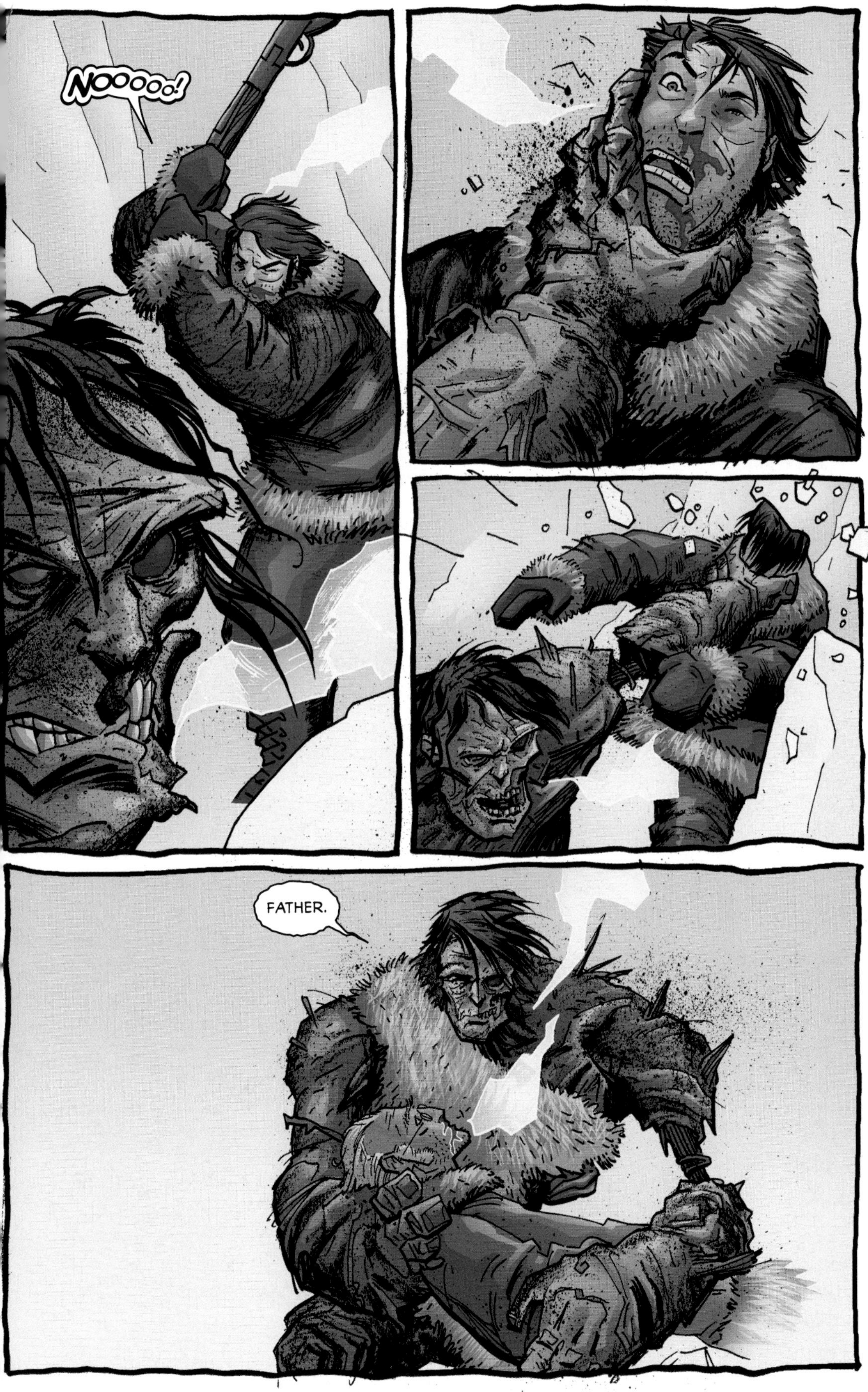
NOOOOO!
FATHER.

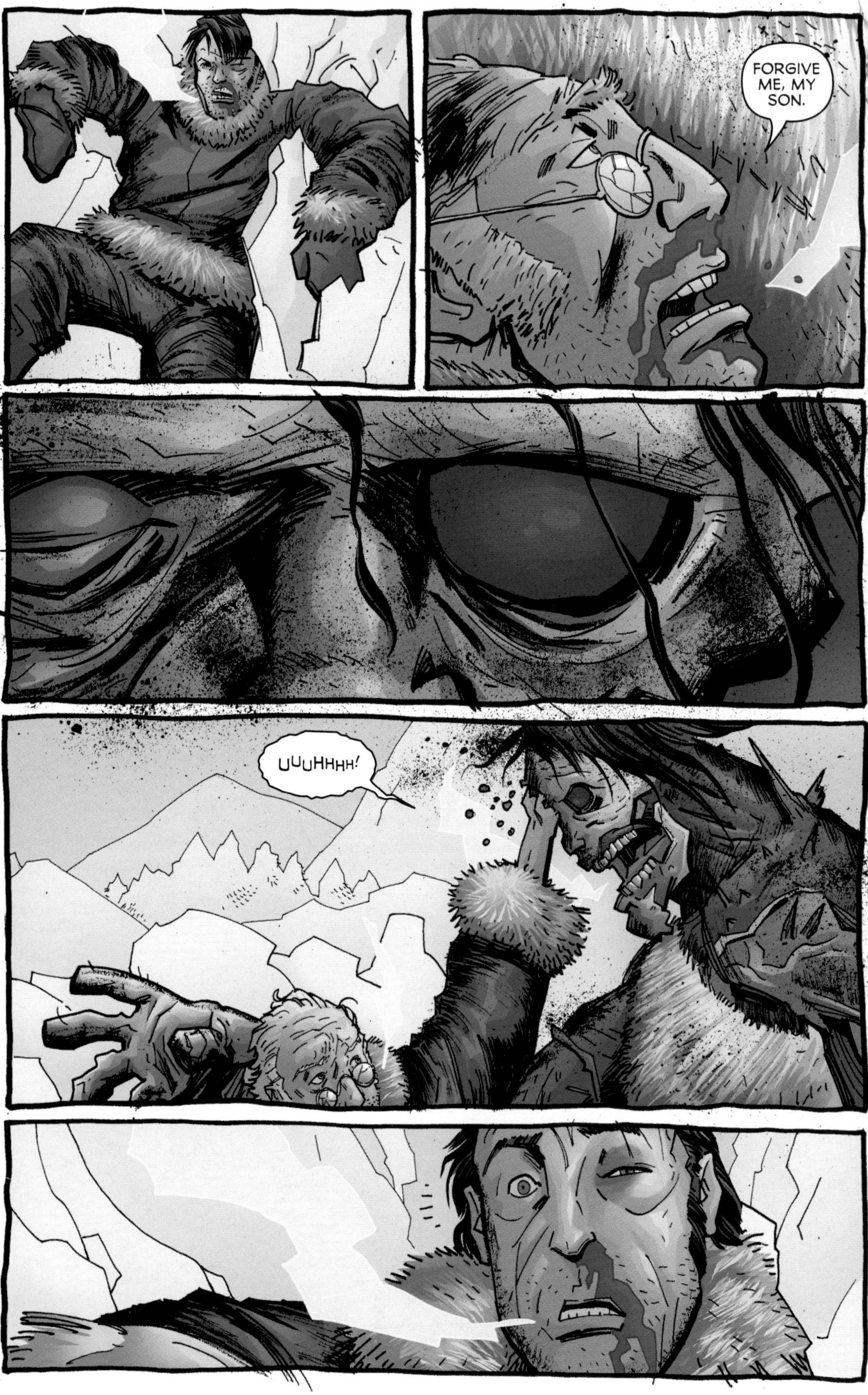
FORGIVE ME, MY SON.
UUUHHHH!

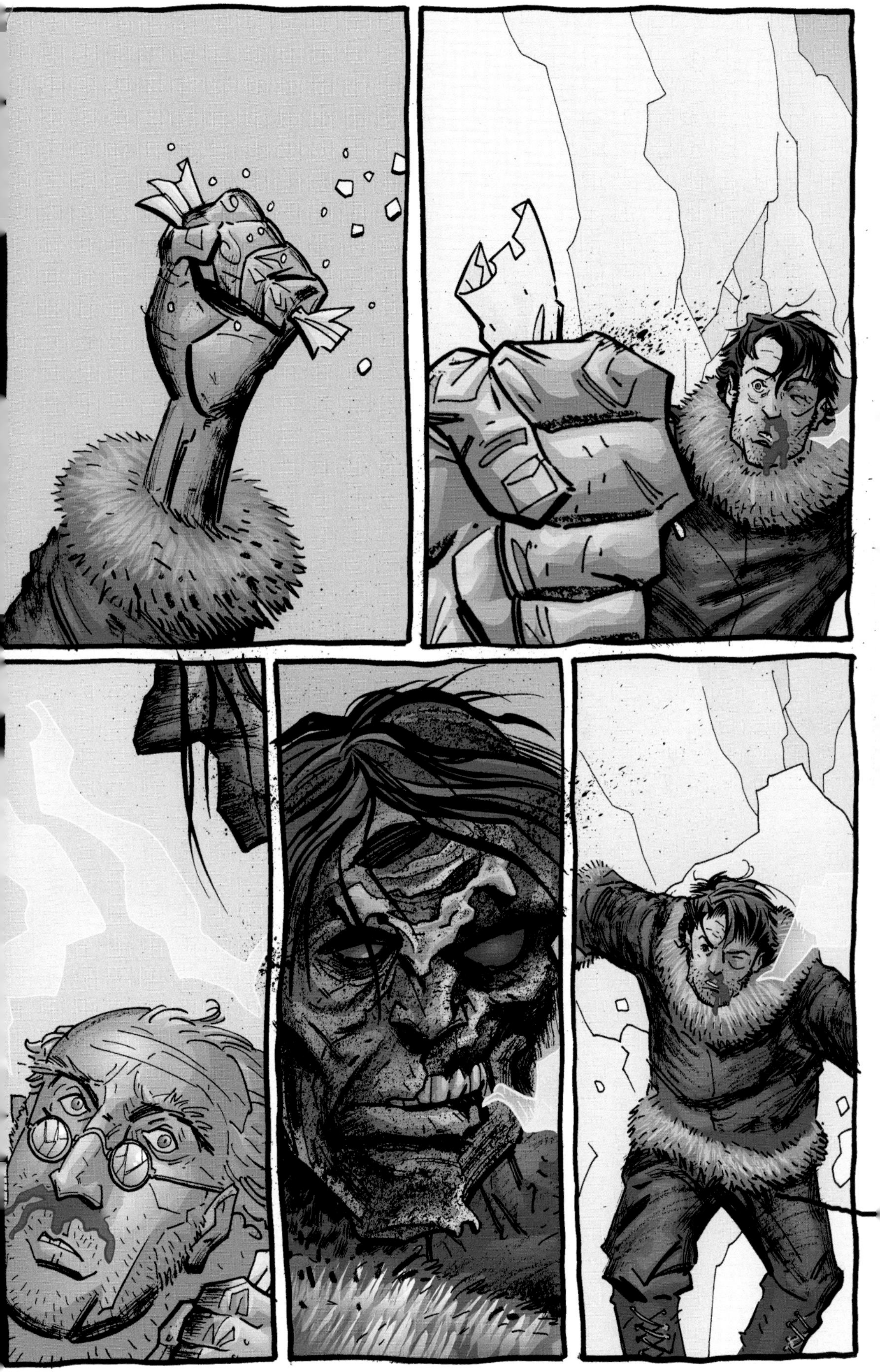

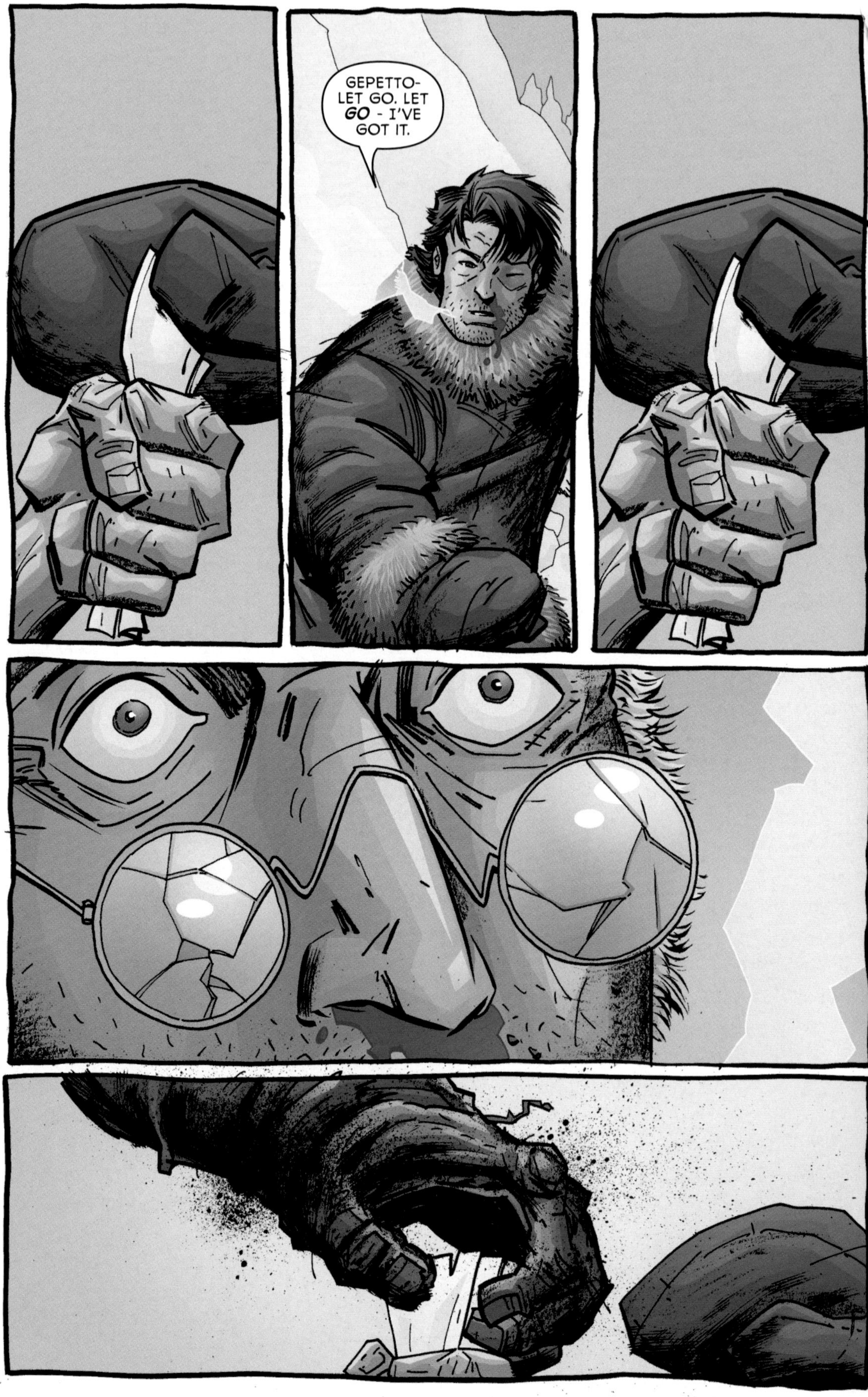
GEPETTO- LET GO. LET GO - I'VE GOT IT.

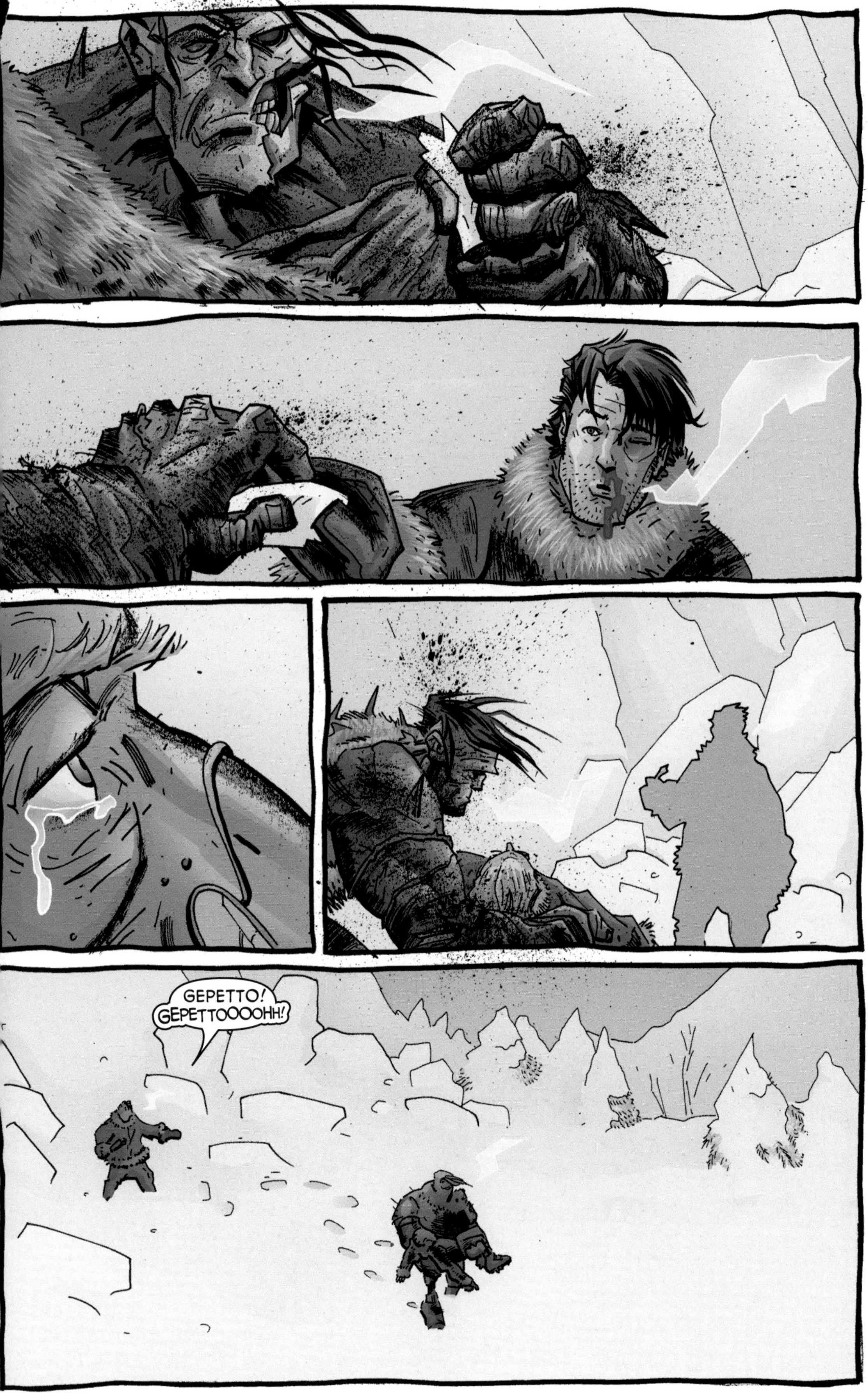
GEPETTO! GEPETTOOOOHH!

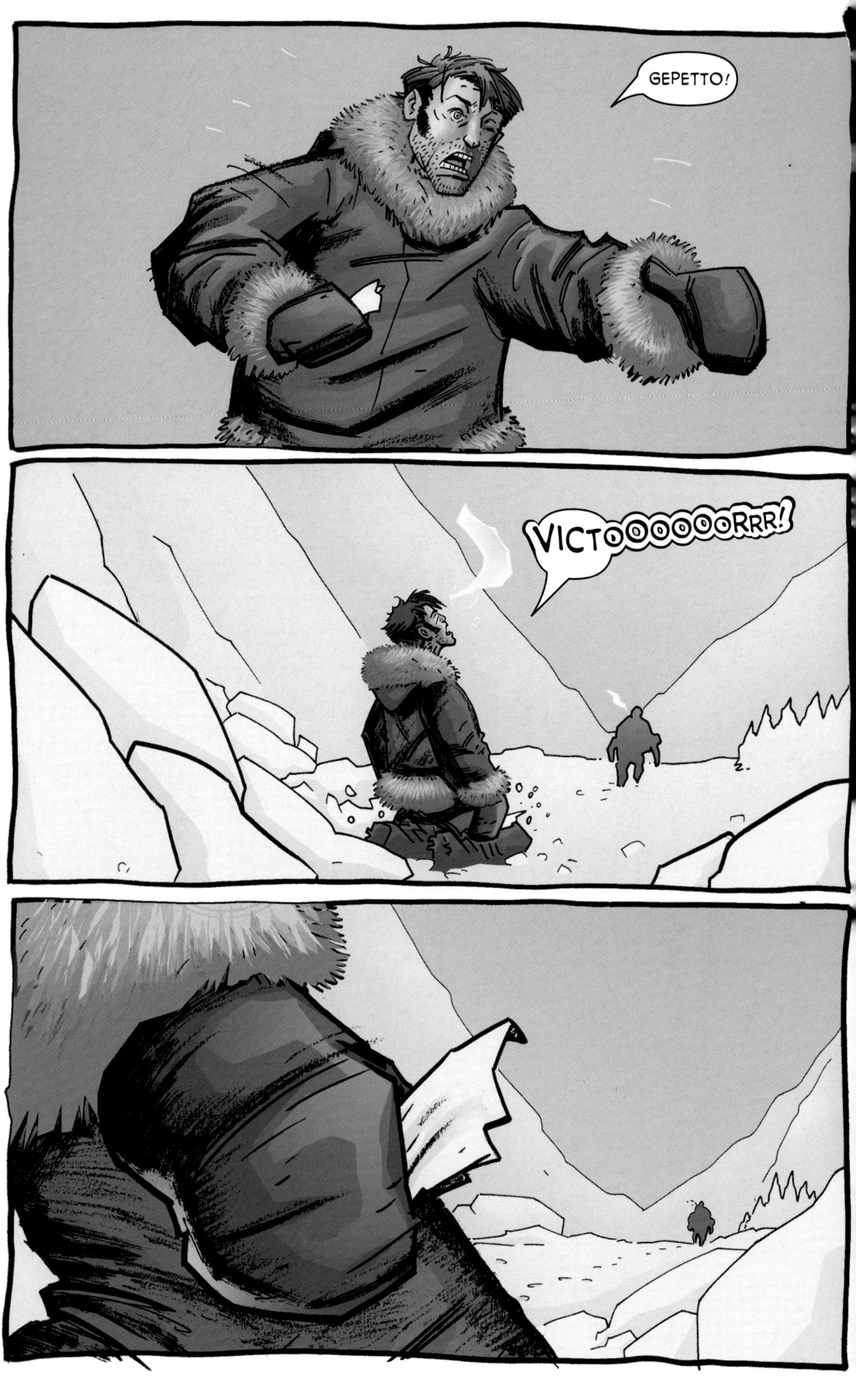
GEPETTO!
VICTOOOOOOORRR!

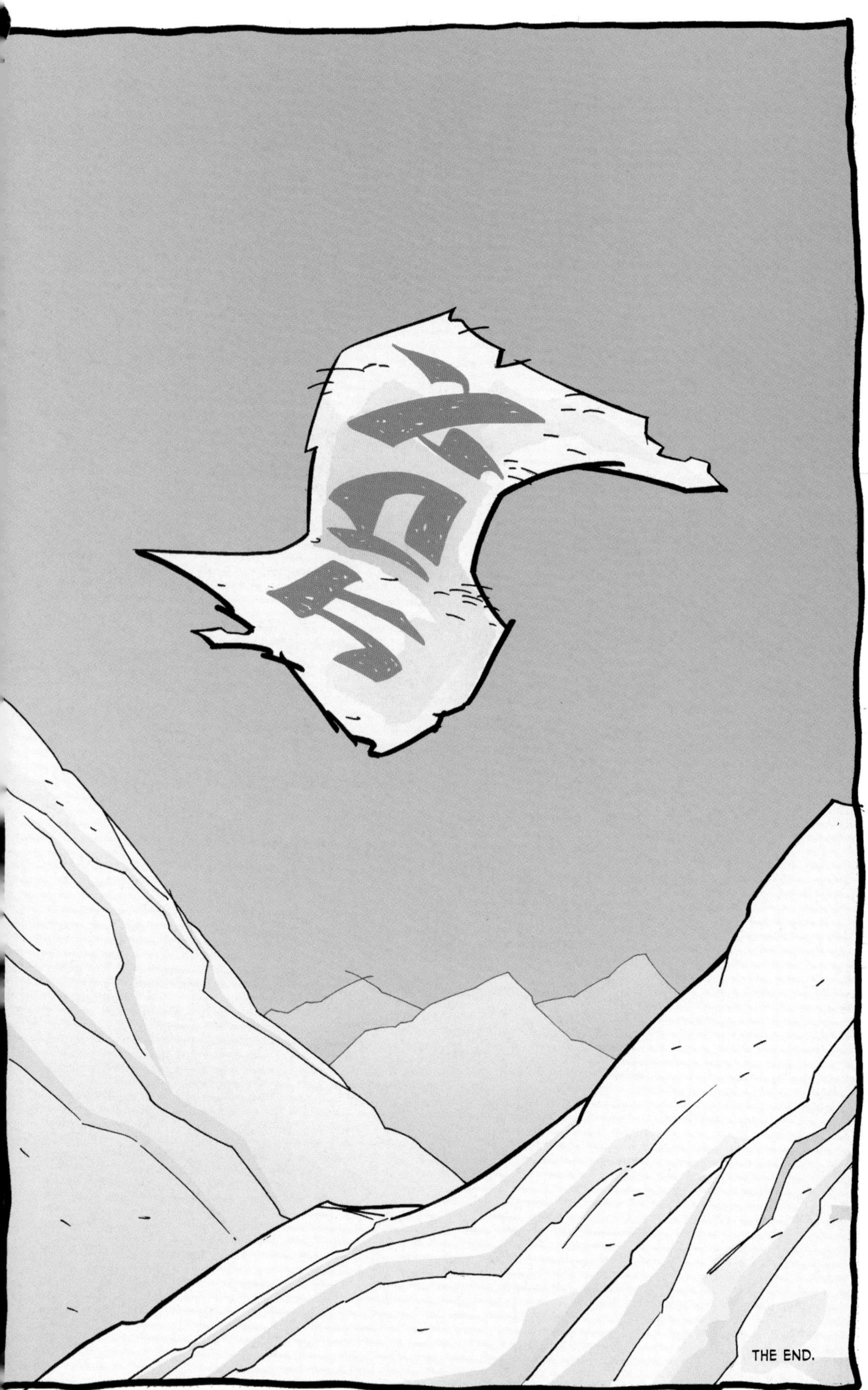
THE END.

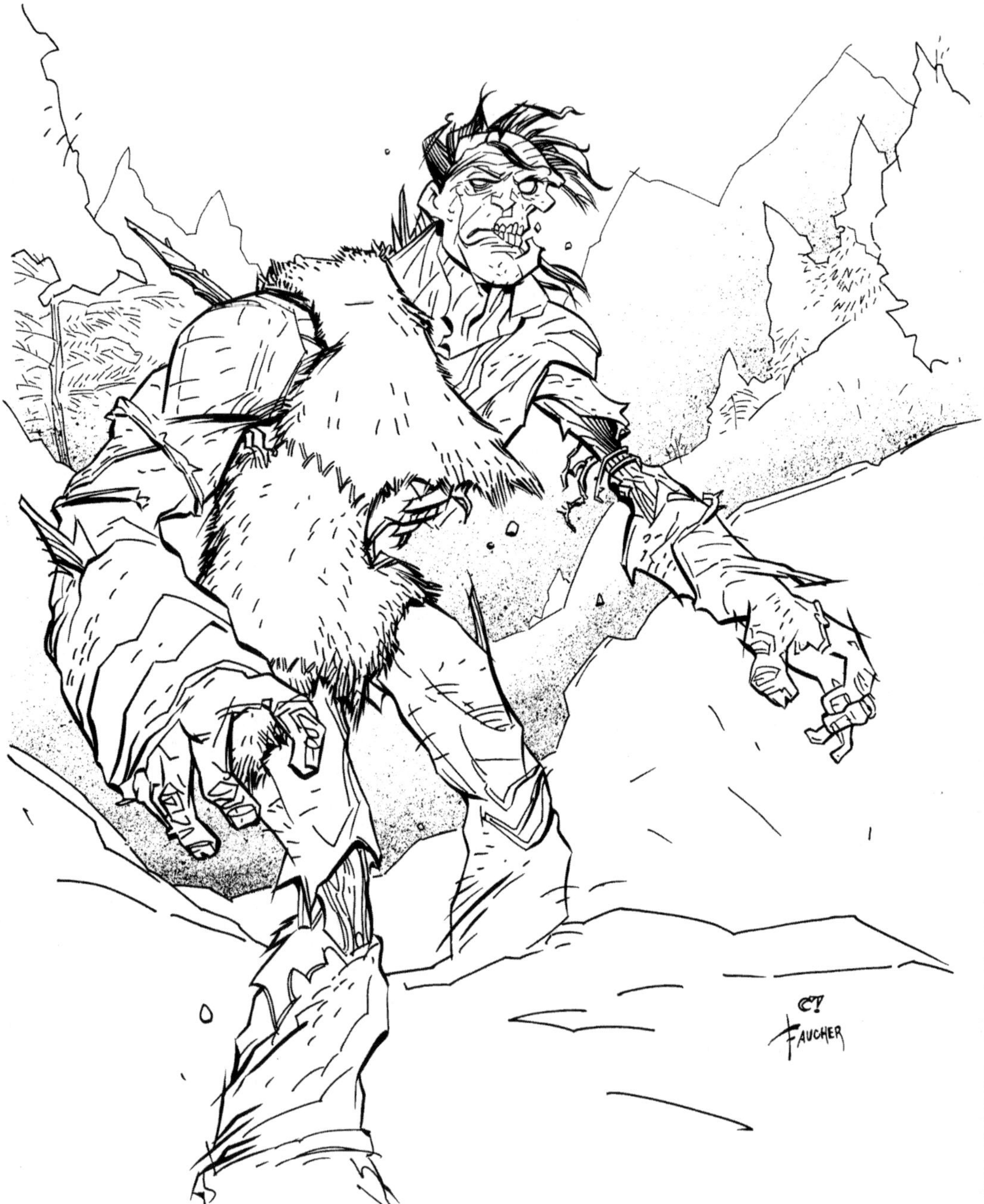
FAUCHER

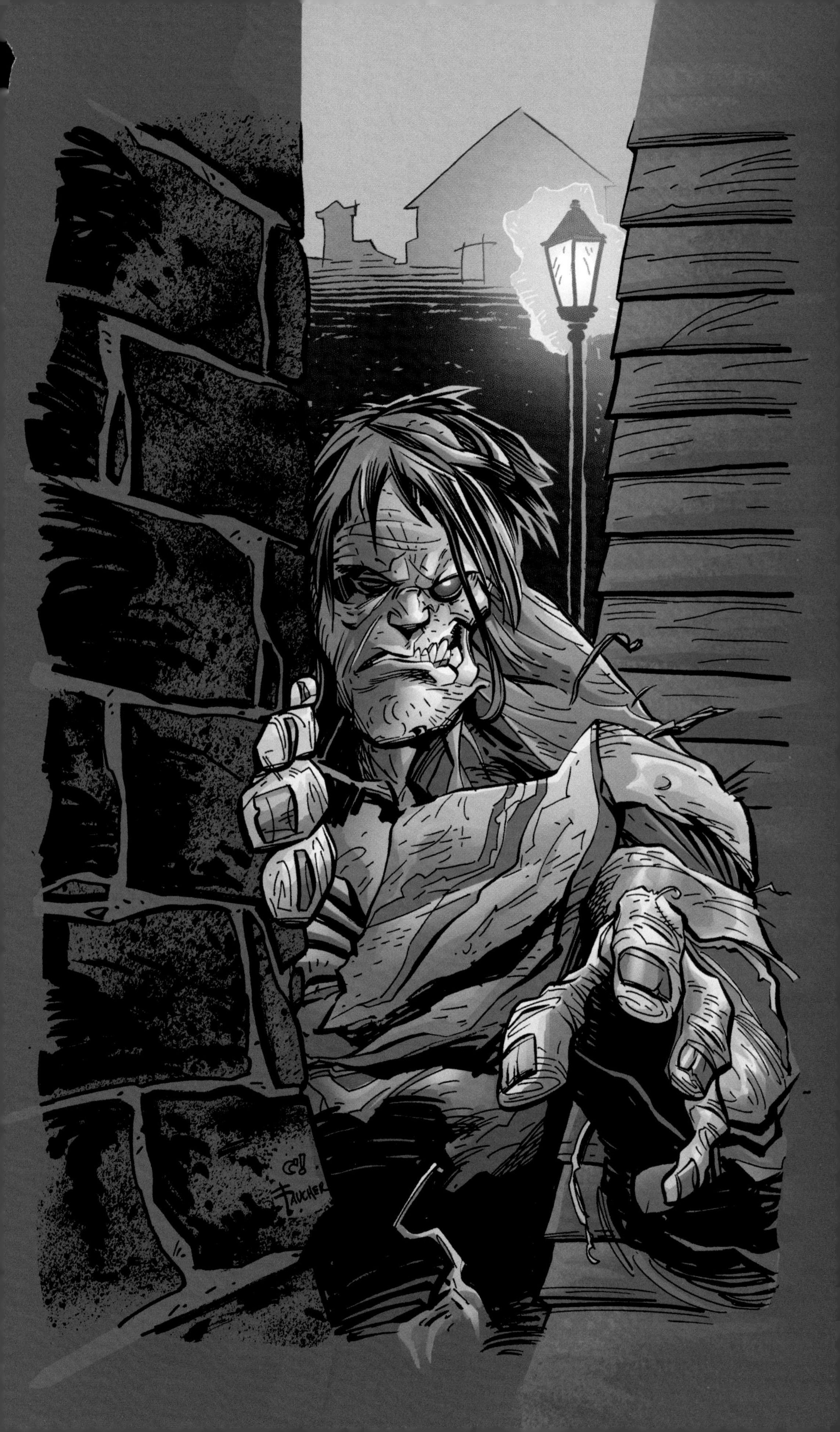

RED WARRIOR™

Assassin for the Thieves World

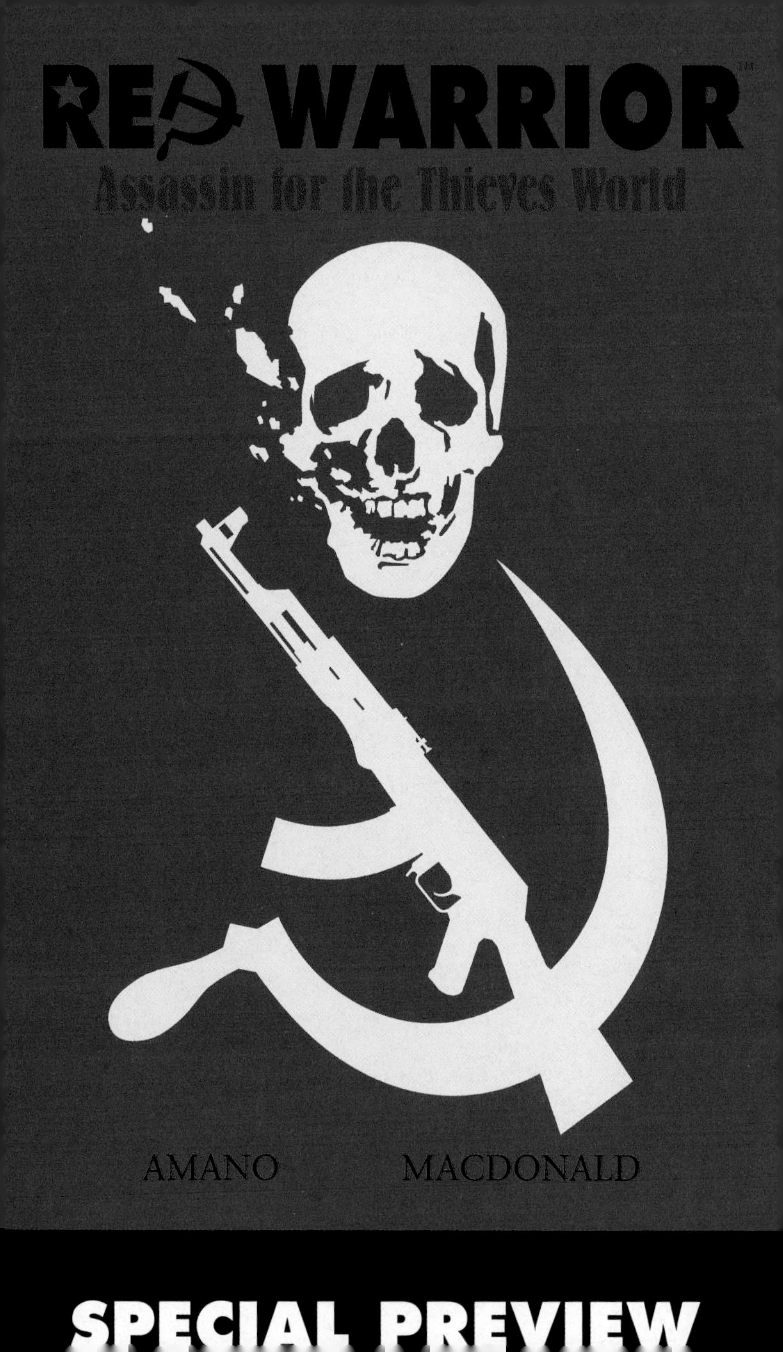

AMANO MACDONALD

SPECIAL PREVIEW

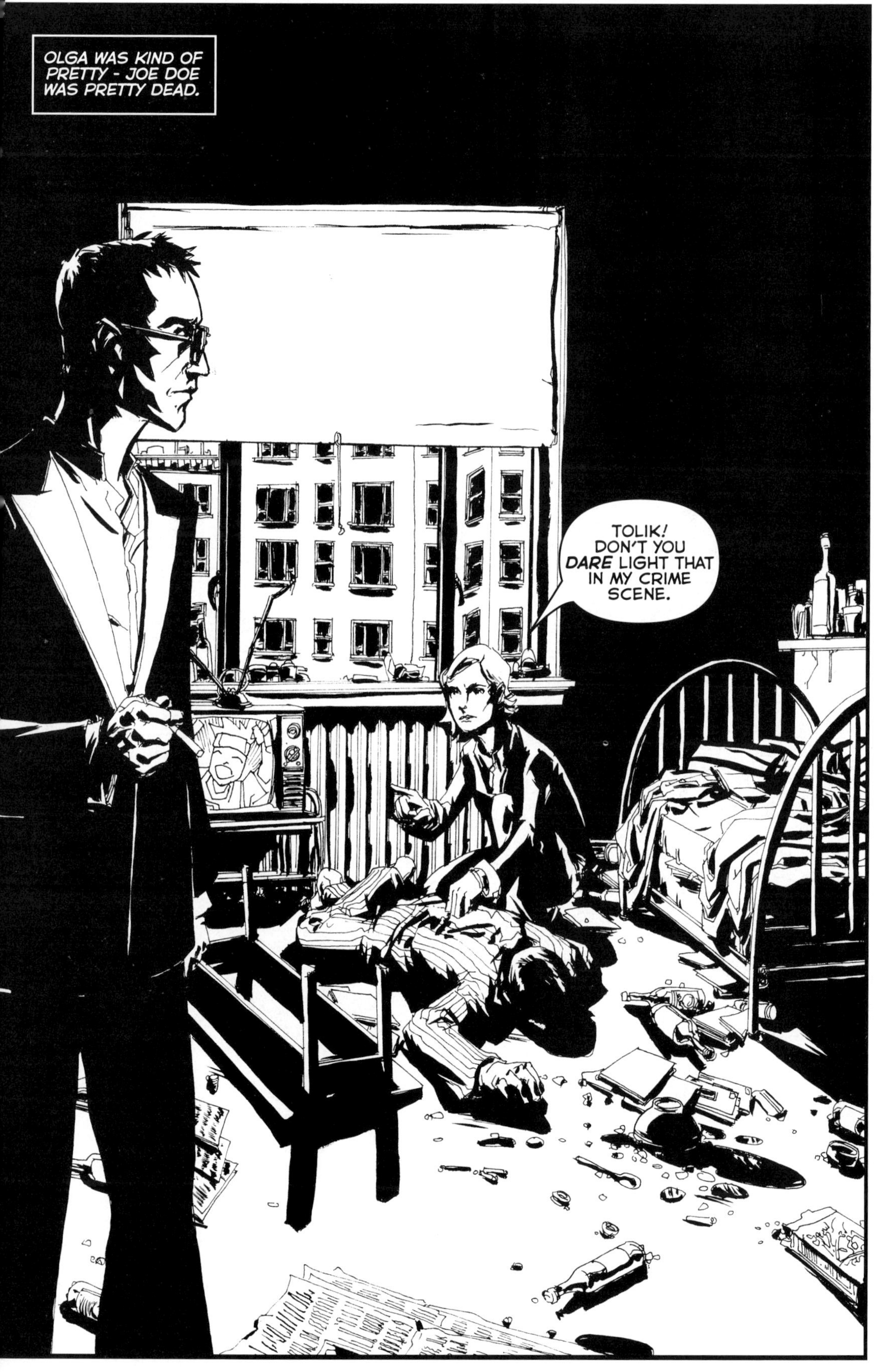
OLGA WAS KIND OF PRETTY - JOE DOE WAS PRETTY DEAD.
TOLIK! DON'T YOU DARE LIGHT THAT IN MY CRIME SCENE.

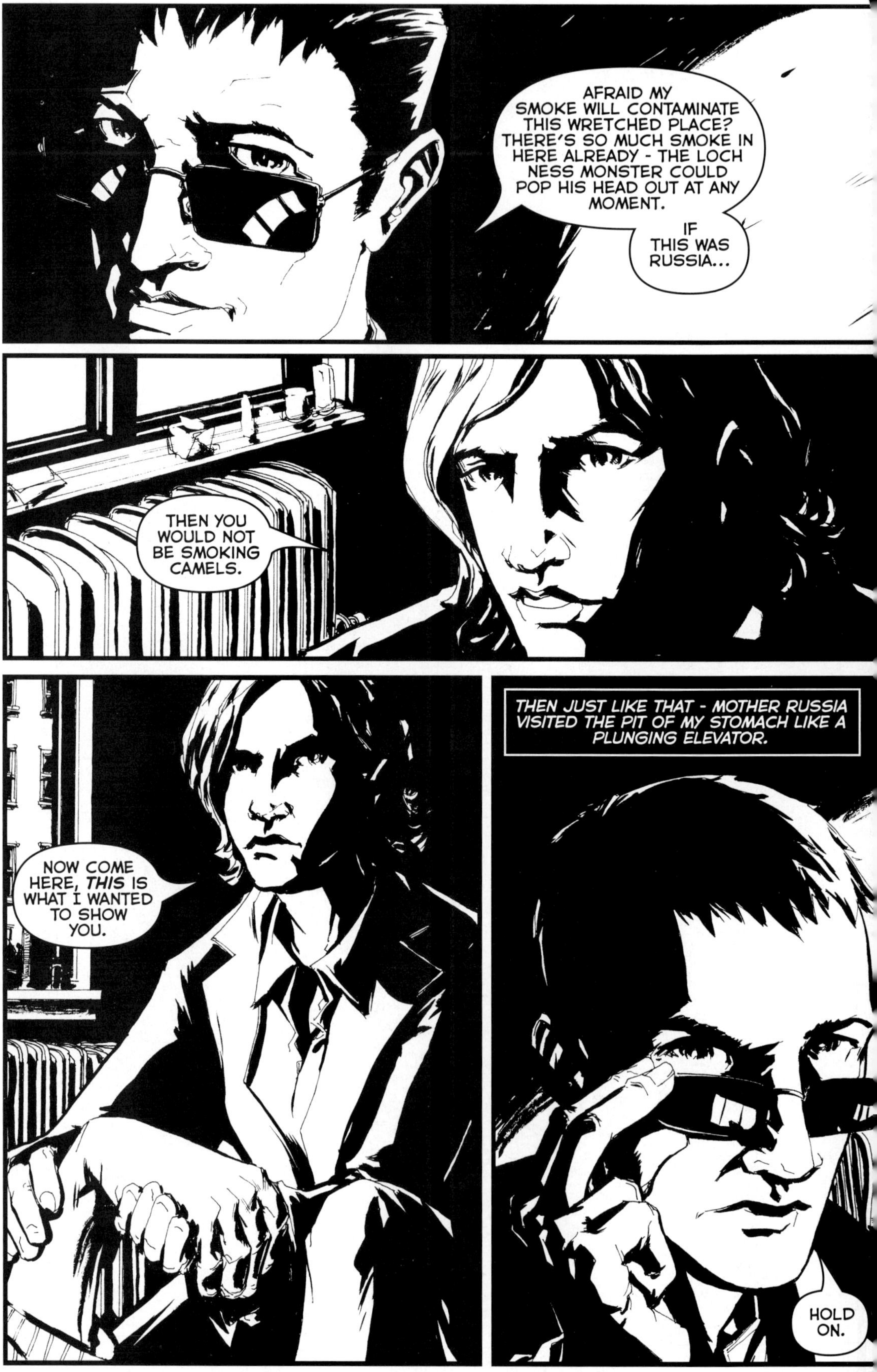
AFRAID MY SMOKE WILL CONTAMINATE THIS WRETCHED PLACE? THERE'S SO MUCH SMOKE IN HERE ALREADY - THE LOCH NESS MONSTER COULD POP HIS HEAD OUT AT ANY MOMENT.
IF THIS WAS RUSSIA...
THEN YOU WOULD NOT BE SMOKING CAMELS.
NOW COME HERE, *THIS* IS WHAT I WANTED TO SHOW YOU.
THEN JUST LIKE THAT - MOTHER RUSSIA VISITED THE PIT OF MY STOMACH LIKE A PLUNGING ELEVATOR.
HOLD ON.

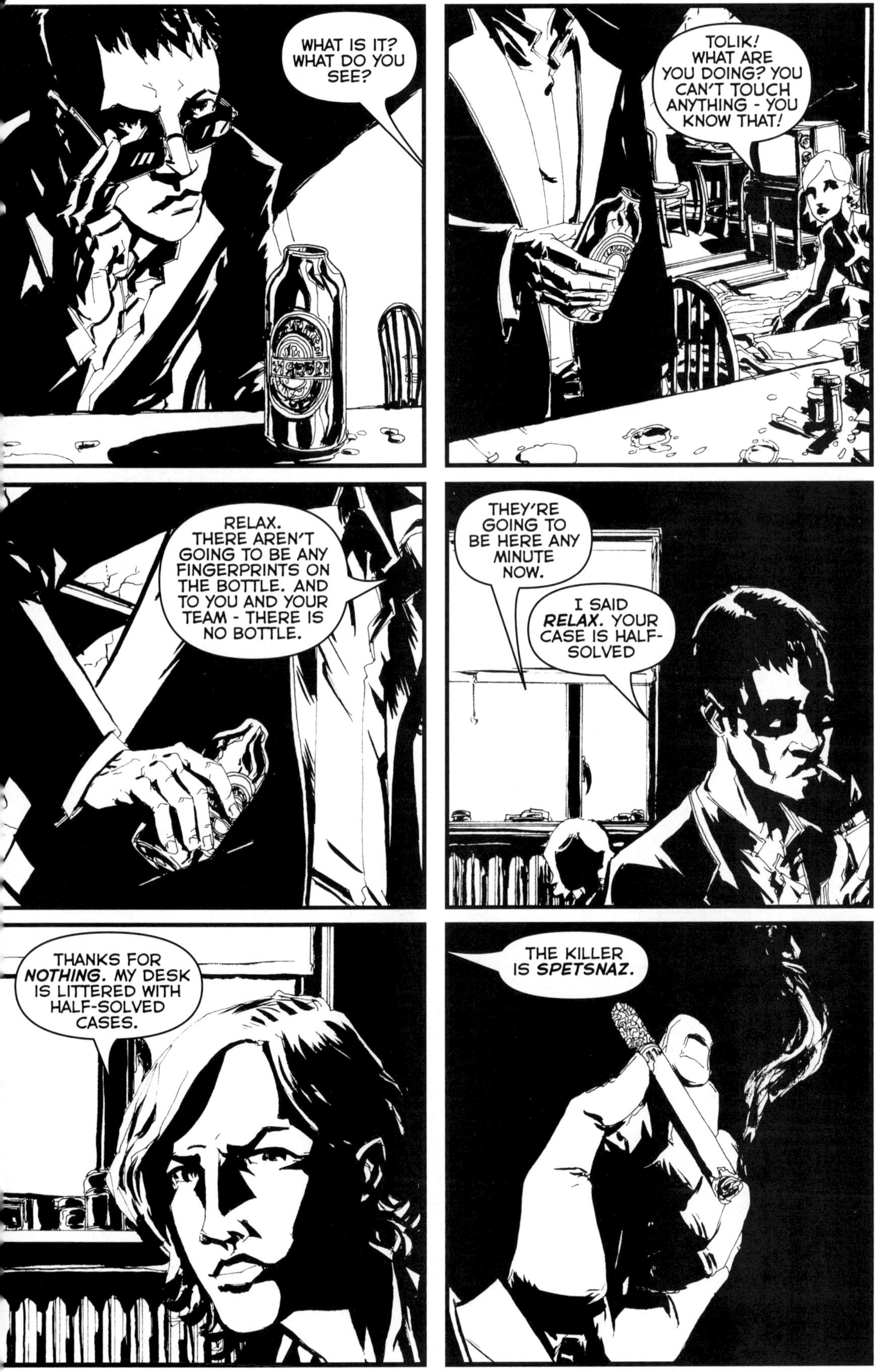
WHAT IS IT? WHAT DO YOU SEE?
TOLIK! WHAT ARE YOU DOING? YOU CAN'T TOUCH ANYTHING - YOU KNOW THAT!
RELAX. THERE AREN'T GOING TO BE ANY FINGERPRINTS ON THE BOTTLE. AND TO YOU AND YOUR TEAM - THERE IS NO BOTTLE.
THEY'RE GOING TO BE HERE ANY MINUTE NOW.
I SAID RELAX. YOUR CASE IS HALF-SOLVED
THANKS FOR NOTHING. MY DESK IS LITTERED WITH HALF-SOLVED CASES.
THE KILLER IS SPETSNAZ.

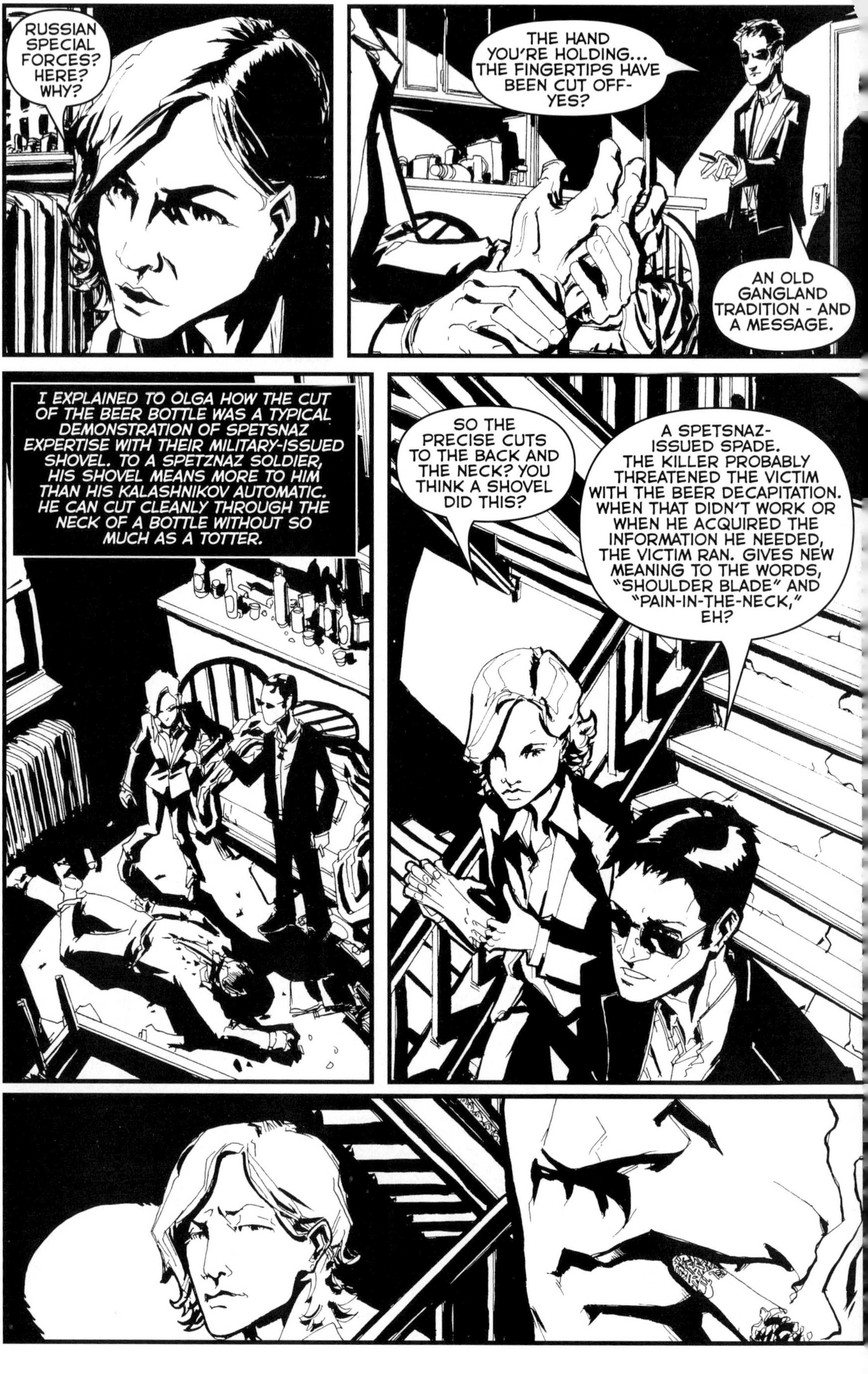
RUSSIAN SPECIAL FORCES? HERE? WHY?
THE HAND YOU'RE HOLDING... THE FINGERTIPS HAVE BEEN CUT OFF- YES?
AN OLD GANGLAND TRADITION - AND A MESSAGE.
I EXPLAINED TO OLGA HOW THE CUT OF THE BEER BOTTLE WAS A TYPICAL DEMONSTRATION OF SPETSNAZ EXPERTISE WITH THEIR MILITARY-ISSUED SHOVEL. TO A SPETZNAZ SOLDIER, HIS SHOVEL MEANS MORE TO HIM THAN HIS KALASHNIKOV AUTOMATIC. HE CAN CUT CLEANLY THROUGH THE NECK OF A BOTTLE WITHOUT SO MUCH AS A TOTTER.
SO THE PRECISE CUTS TO THE BACK AND THE NECK? YOU THINK A SHOVEL DID THIS?
A SPETSNAZ-ISSUED SPADE. THE KILLER PROBABLY THREATENED THE VICTIM WITH THE BEER DECAPITATION. WHEN THAT DIDN'T WORK OR WHEN HE ACQUIRED THE INFORMATION HE NEEDED, THE VICTIM RAN. GIVES NEW MEANING TO THE WORDS, "SHOULDER BLADE" AND "PAIN-IN-THE-NECK," EH?

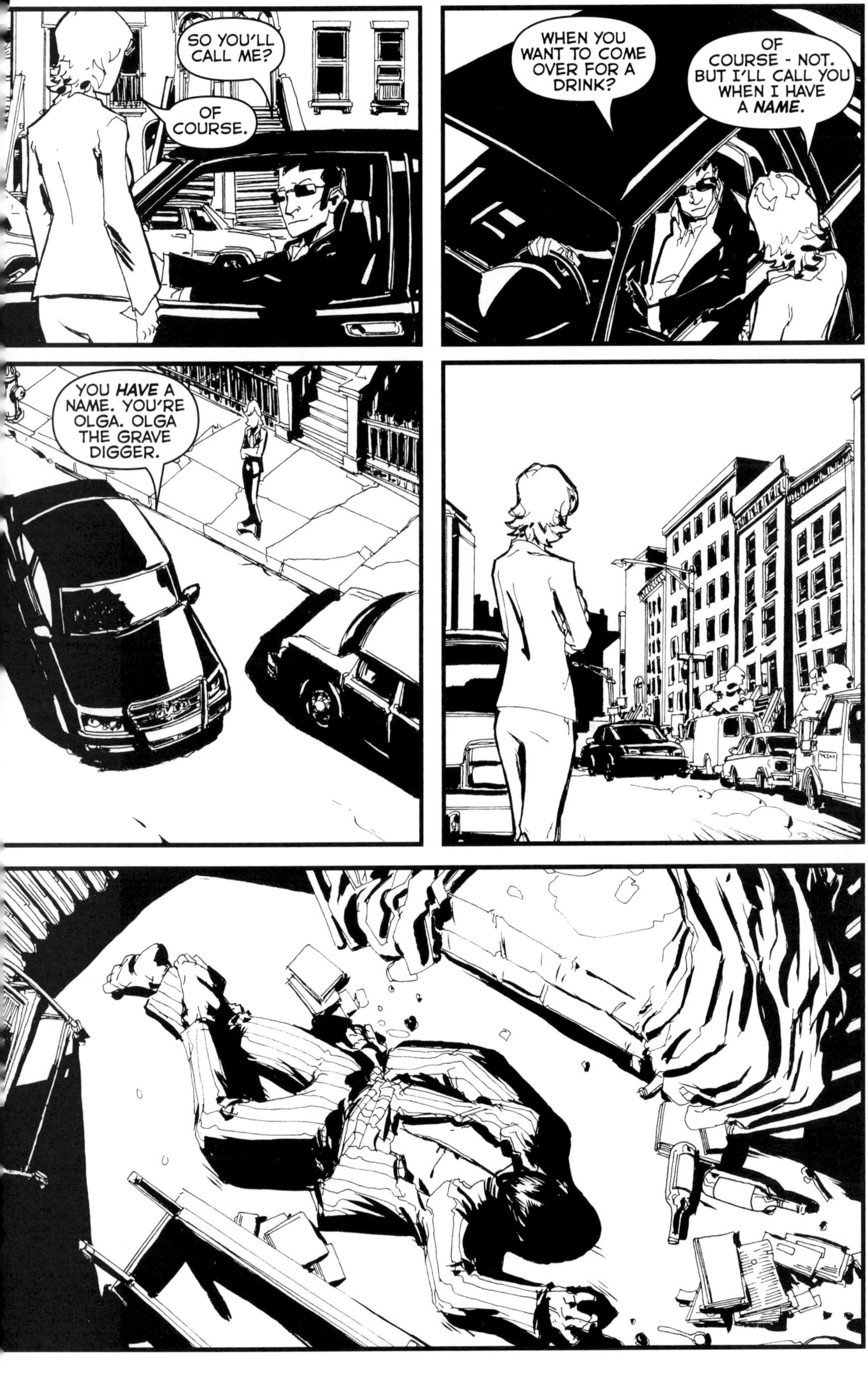
SO YOU'LL CALL ME?
OF COURSE.
WHEN YOU WANT TO COME OVER FOR A DRINK?
OF COURSE - NOT. BUT I'LL CALL YOU WHEN I HAVE A *NAME.*
YOU *HAVE* A NAME. YOU'RE OLGA. OLGA THE GRAVE DIGGER.

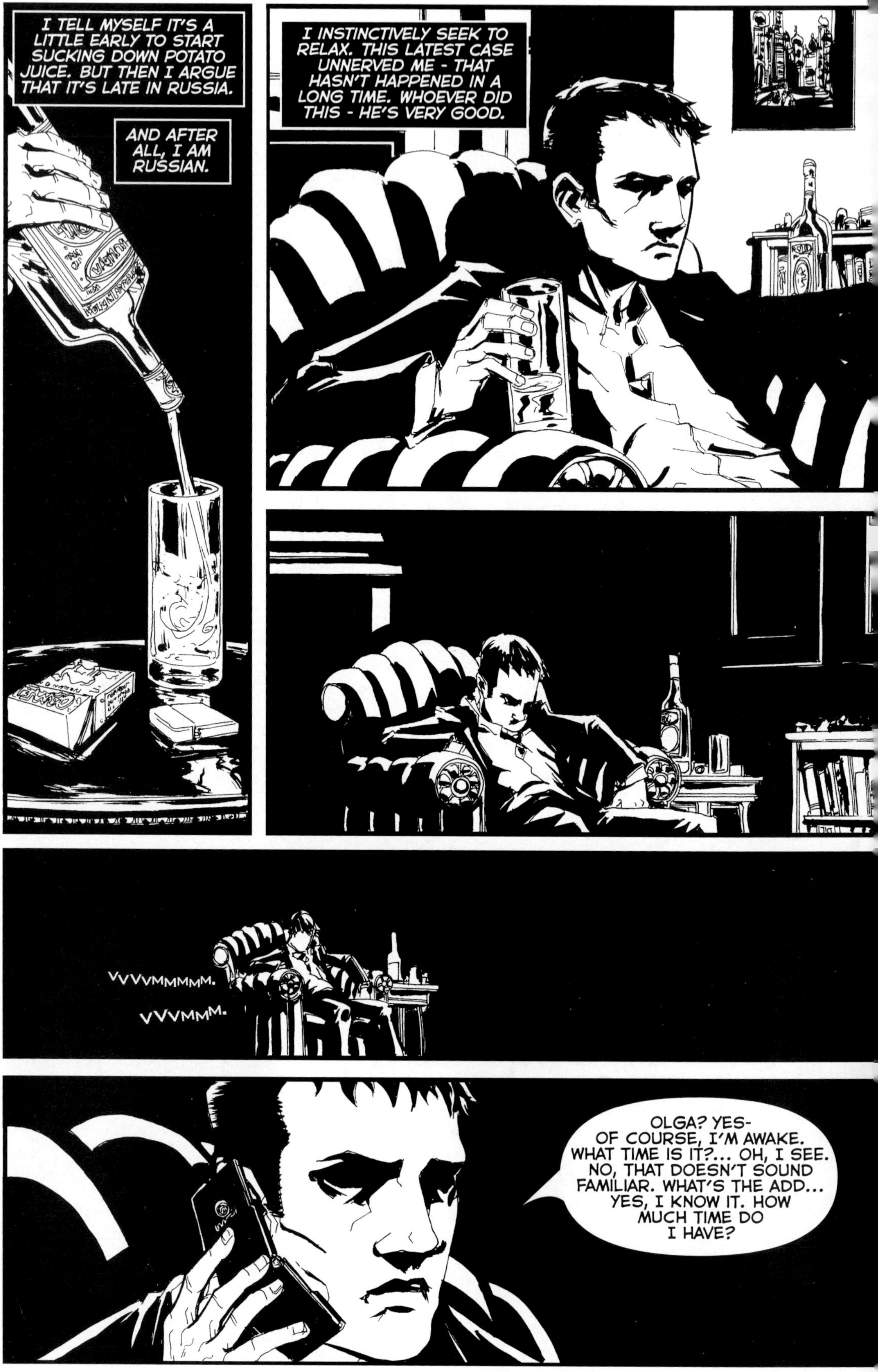
I TELL MYSELF IT'S A LITTLE EARLY TO START SUCKING DOWN POTATO JUICE. BUT THEN I ARGUE THAT IT'S LATE IN RUSSIA.
AND AFTER ALL, I AM RUSSIAN.
I INSTINCTIVELY SEEK TO RELAX. THIS LATEST CASE UNNERVED ME - THAT HASN'T HAPPENED IN A LONG TIME. WHOEVER DID THIS - HE'S VERY GOOD.
VVVVMMMMM.
VVVMMM.
OLGA? YES- OF COURSE, I'M AWAKE. WHAT TIME IS IT?... OH, I SEE. NO, THAT DOESN'T SOUND FAMILIAR. WHAT'S THE ADD... YES, I KNOW IT. HOW MUCH TIME DO I HAVE?

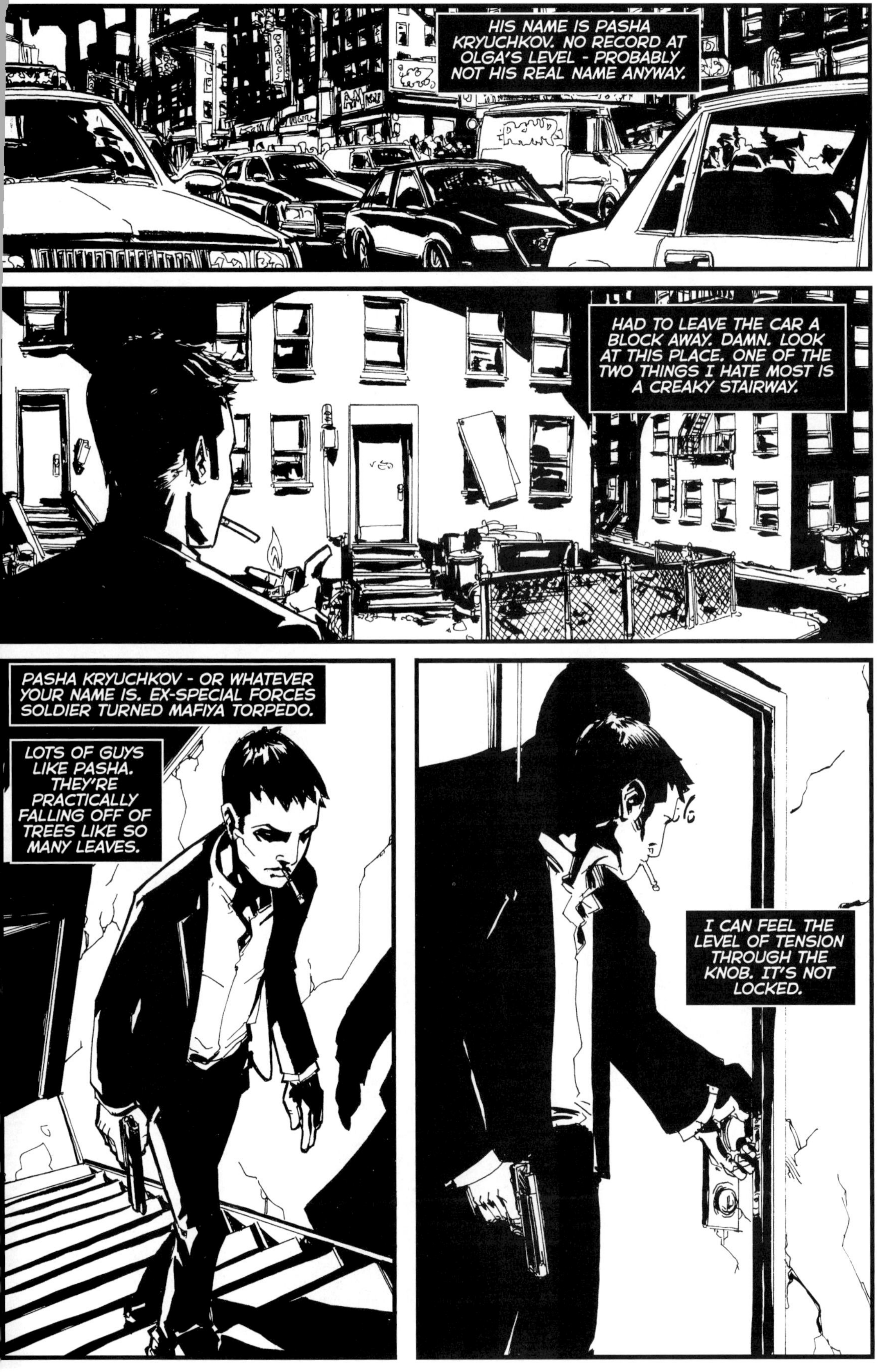
HIS NAME IS PASHA KRYUCHKOV. NO RECORD AT OLGA'S LEVEL - PROBABLY NOT HIS REAL NAME ANYWAY.
HAD TO LEAVE THE CAR A BLOCK AWAY. DAMN. LOOK AT THIS PLACE. ONE OF THE TWO THINGS I HATE MOST IS A CREAKY STAIRWAY.
PASHA KRYUCHKOV - OR WHATEVER YOUR NAME IS. EX-SPECIAL FORCES SOLDIER TURNED MAFIYA TORPEDO.
LOTS OF GUYS LIKE PASHA. THEY'RE PRACTICALLY FALLING OFF OF TREES LIKE SO MANY LEAVES.
I CAN FEEL THE LEVEL OF TENSION THROUGH THE KNOB. IT'S NOT LOCKED.

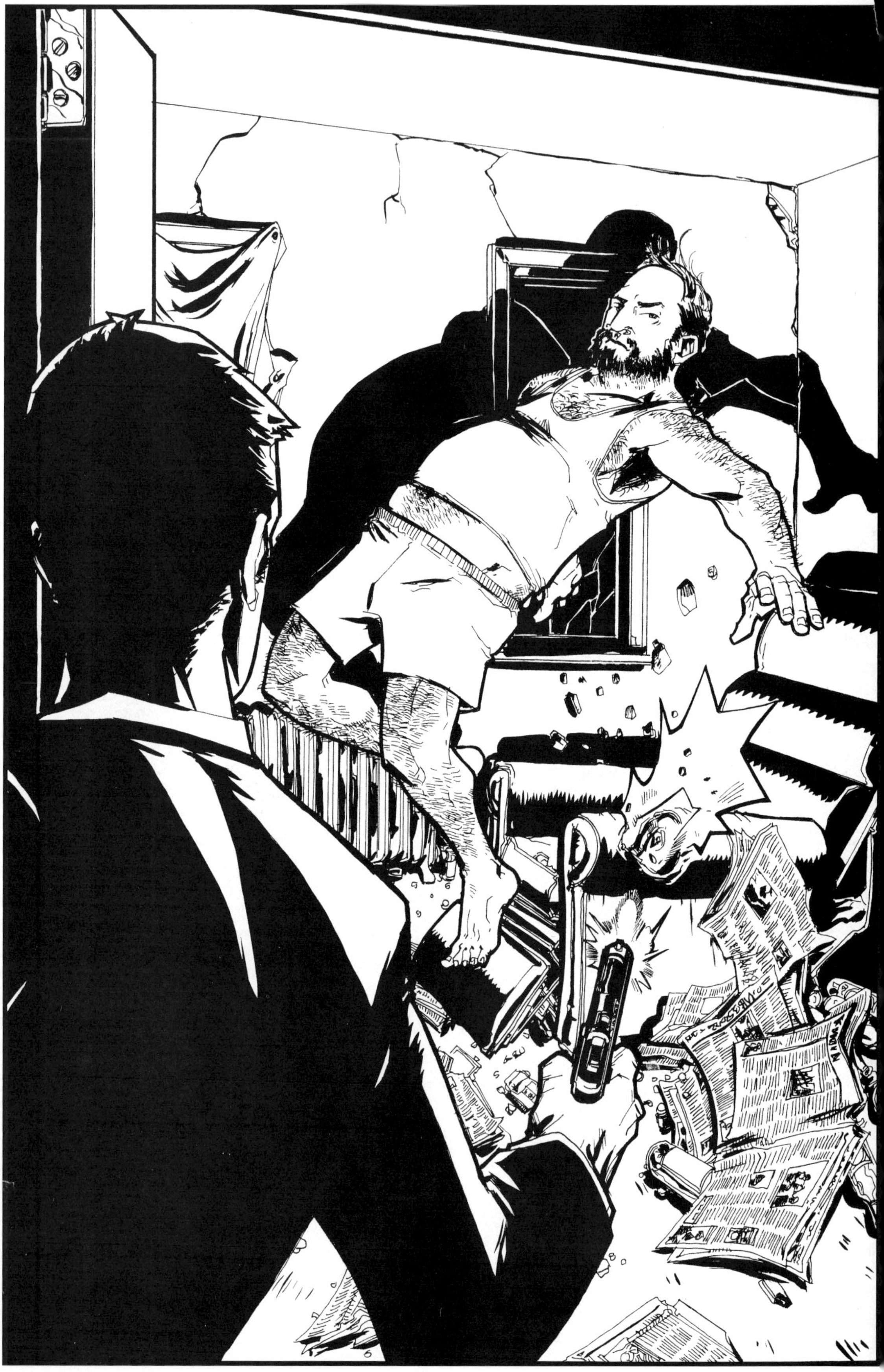

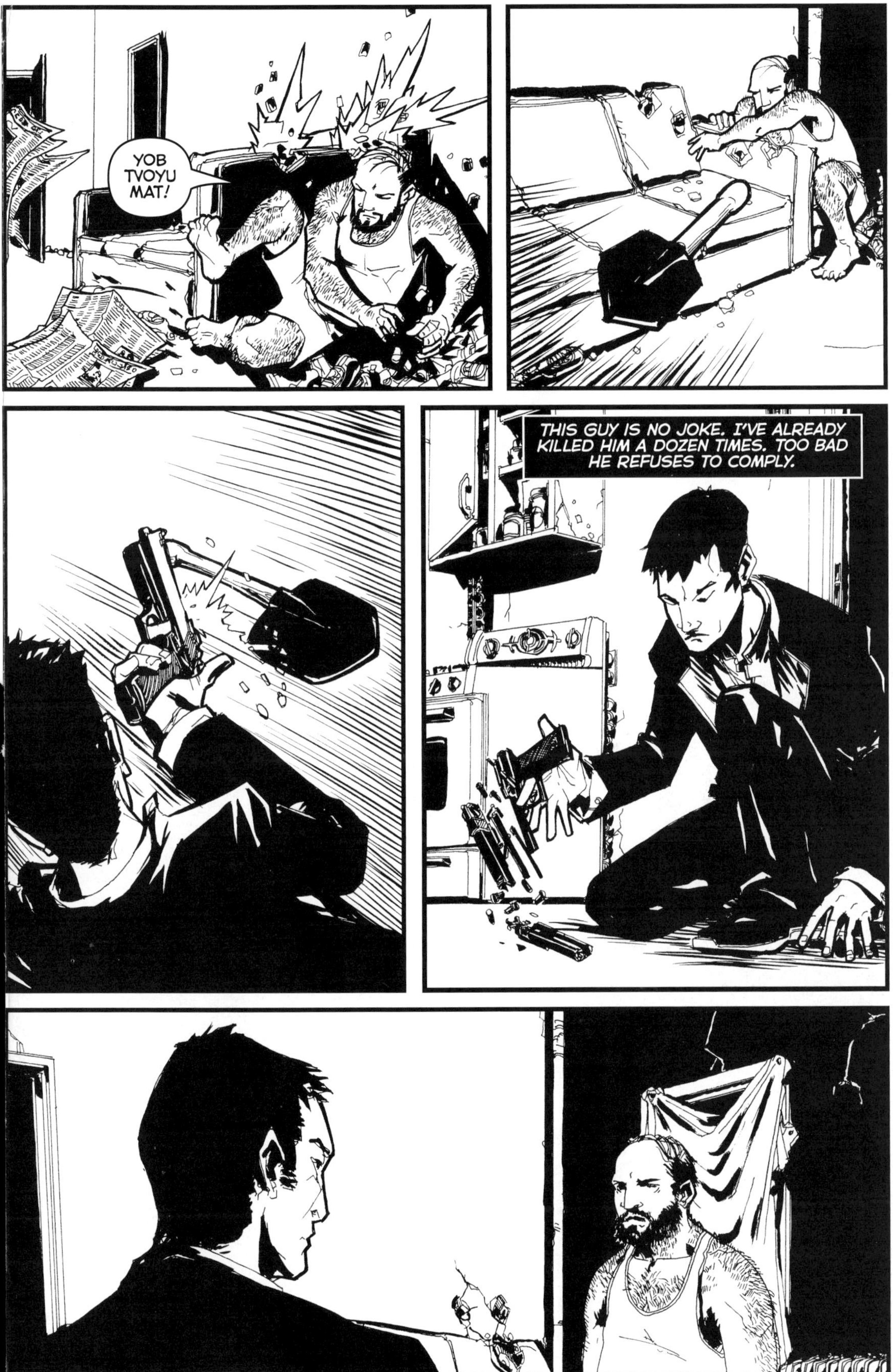
YOB TVOYU MAT!
THIS GUY IS NO JOKE. I'VE ALREADY KILLED HIM A DOZEN TIMES. TOO BAD HE REFUSES TO COMPLY.

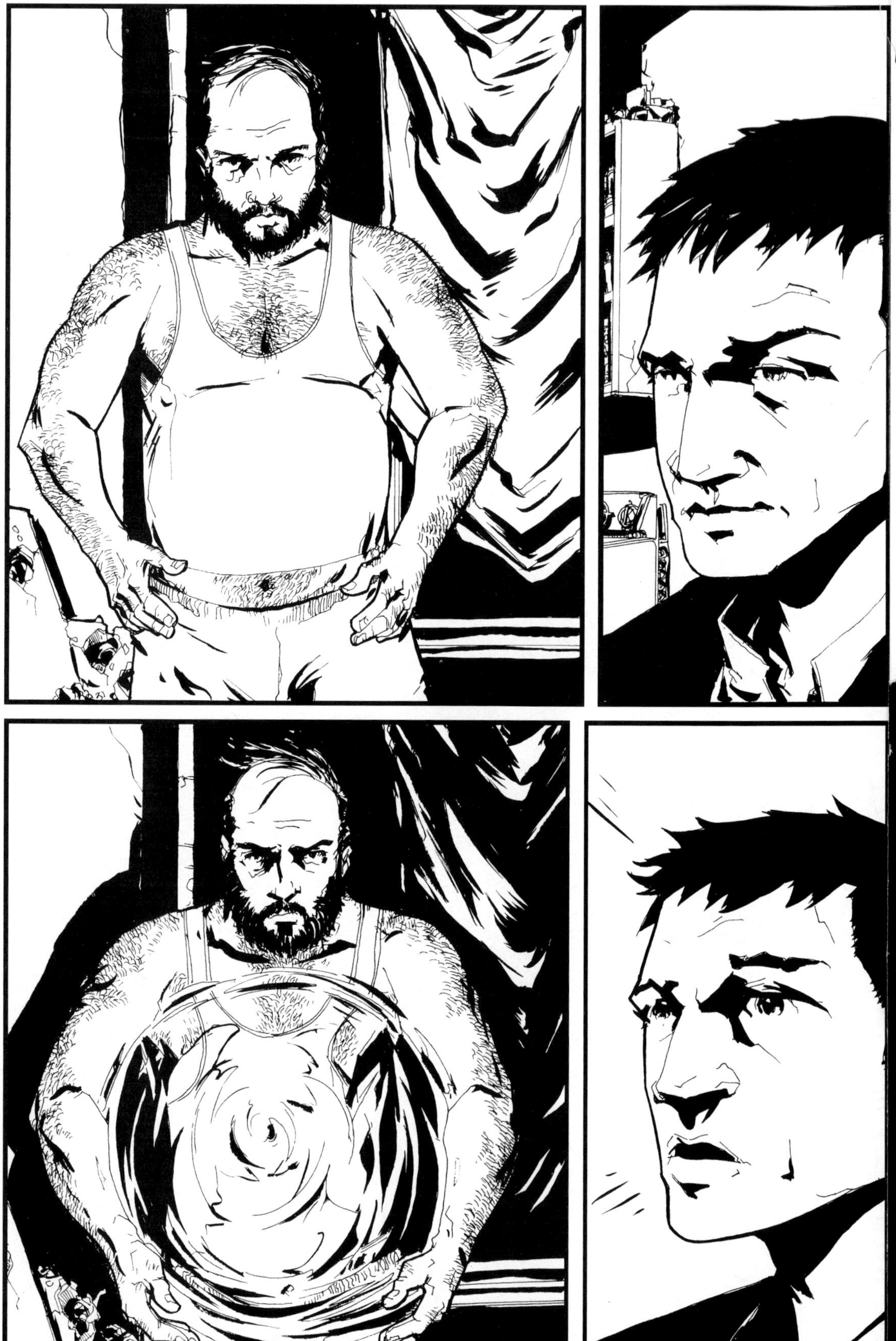

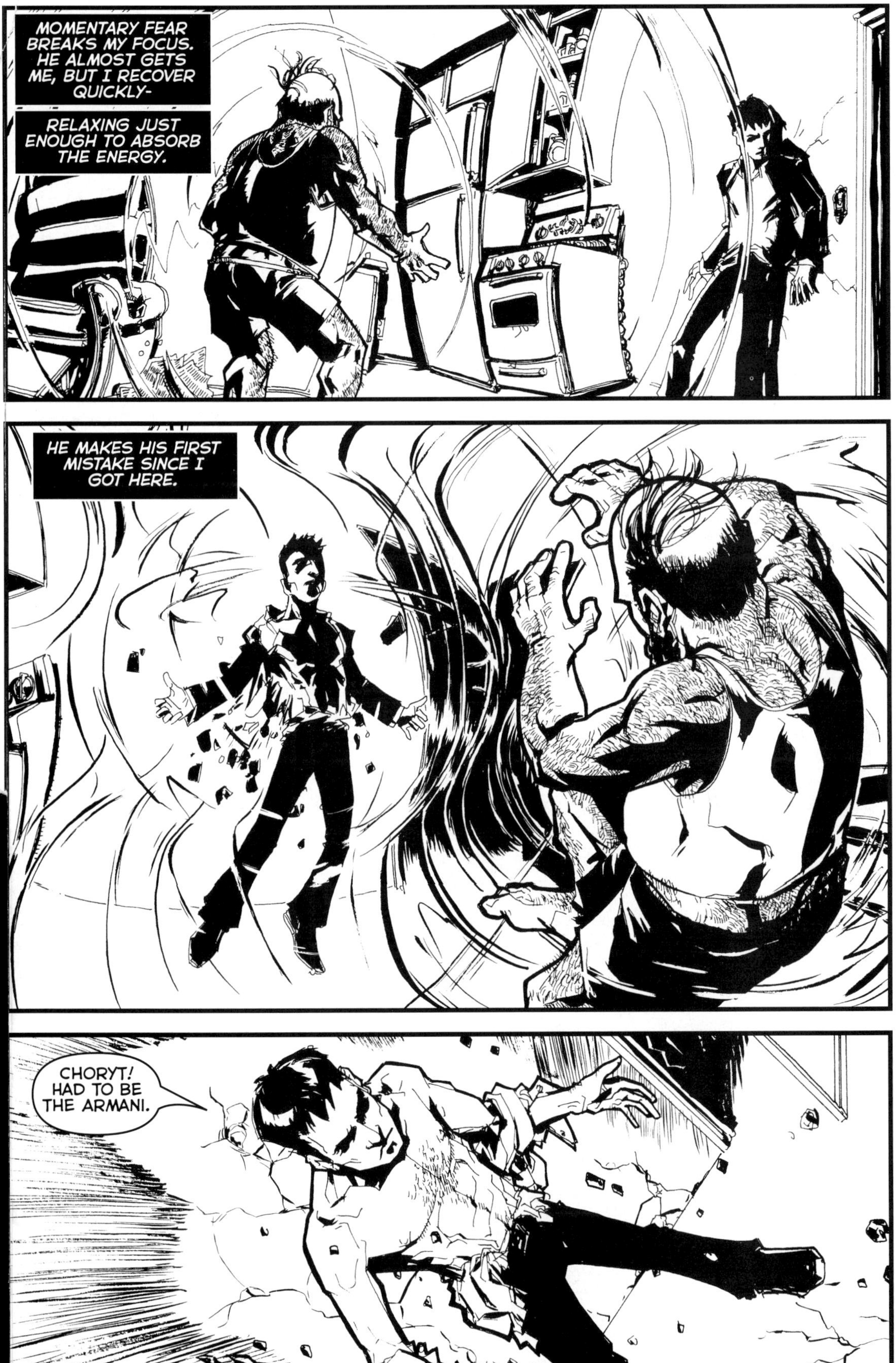
MOMENTARY FEAR BREAKS MY FOCUS. HE ALMOST GETS ME, BUT I RECOVER QUICKLY-
RELAXING JUST ENOUGH TO ABSORB THE ENERGY.
HE MAKES HIS FIRST MISTAKE SINCE I GOT HERE.
CHORYT! HAD TO BE THE ARMANI.

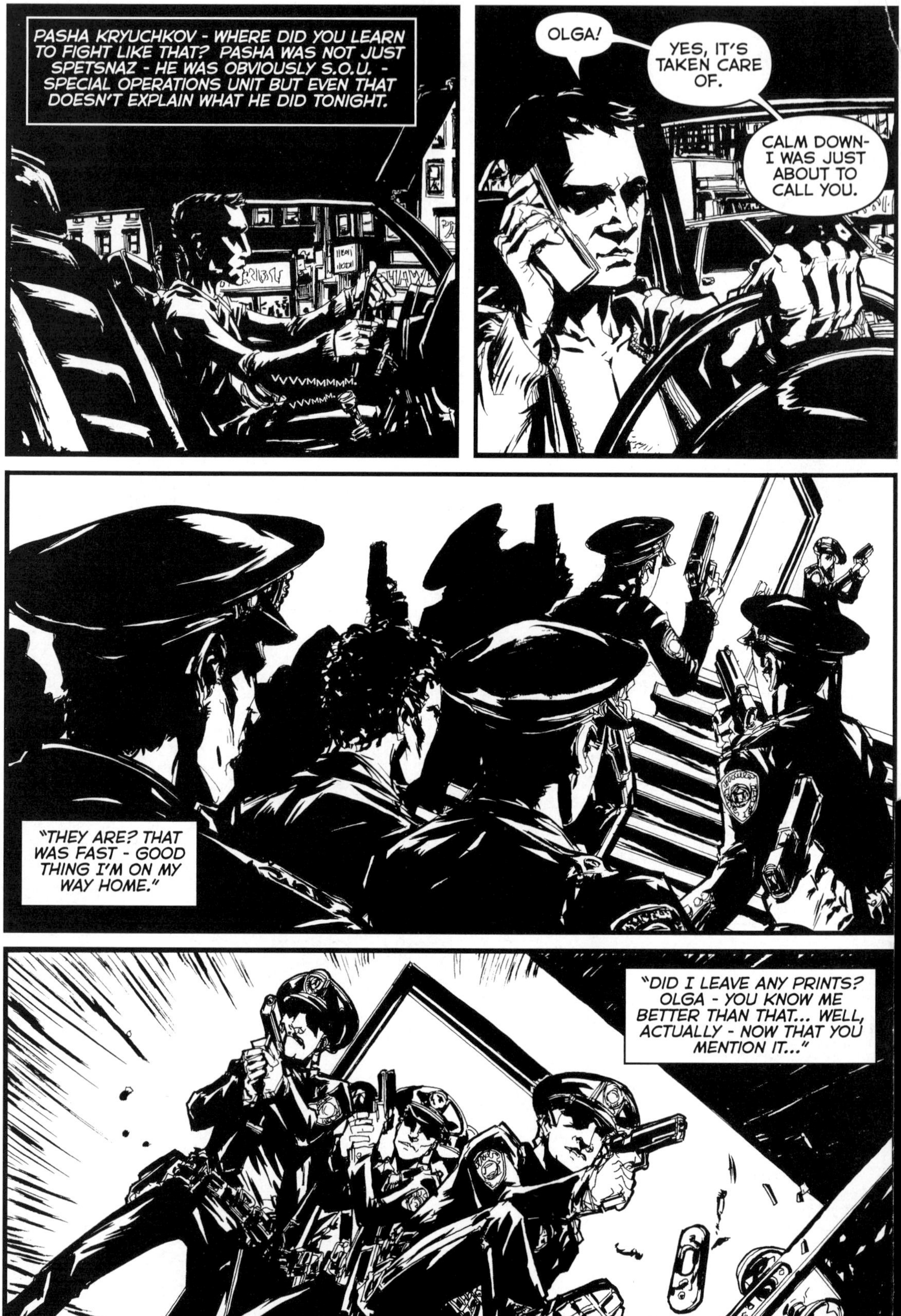
PASHA KRYUCHKOV - WHERE DID YOU LEARN TO FIGHT LIKE THAT? PASHA WAS NOT JUST SPETSNAZ - HE WAS OBVIOUSLY S.O.U. - SPECIAL OPERATIONS UNIT BUT EVEN THAT DOESN'T EXPLAIN WHAT HE DID TONIGHT.
VVVVMMMMMM.
VVVMMM.
OLGA!
YES, IT'S TAKEN CARE OF.
CALM DOWN- I WAS JUST ABOUT TO CALL YOU.
"THEY ARE? THAT WAS FAST - GOOD THING I'M ON MY WAY HOME."
"DID I LEAVE ANY PRINTS? OLGA - YOU KNOW ME BETTER THAN THAT... WELL, ACTUALLY - NOW THAT YOU MENTION IT..."

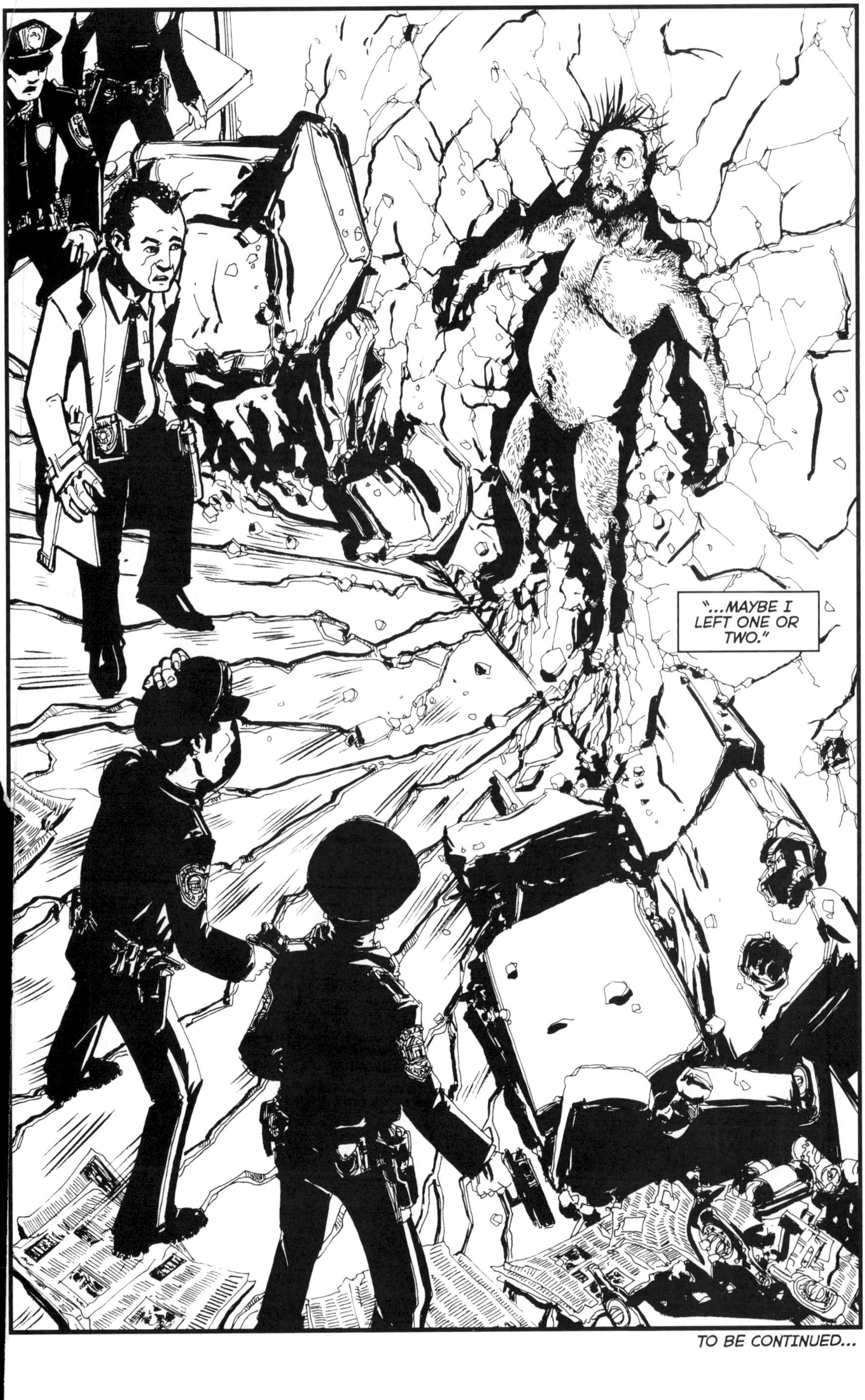
"...MAYBE I LEFT ONE OR TWO."

TO BE CONTINUED...

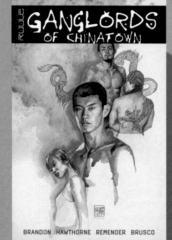